THE LAST JOB

THE
LAST
JOB

The "Bad Grandpas" and the Hatton Garden Heist

Dan Bilefsky

W. W. Norton & Company

Independent Publishers Since 1923

New York London

For information about permission to reproduce selections from this book, write to
Permissions, W. W. Norton & Company, Inc., 500 Fifth Avenue, New York, NY 10110

For information about special discounts for bulk purchases, please contact
W. W. Norton Special Sales at specialsales@wwnorton.com or 800-233-4830

Manufacturing by Sheridan
Book design by Lovedog Studio
Production manager: Lauren Abbate

Library of Congress Cataloging-in-Publication Data

Names: Bilefsky, Dan, author.
Title: The last job : the "bad grandpas" and the Hatton Garden heist / Dan Bilefsky.
Description: First edition. | New York : W. W. Norton & Company, [2019] | Includes
    bibliographical references and index.
Identifiers: LCCN 2018046576 | ISBN 9780393609516 (hardcover)
Subjects: LCSH: Hatton Garden Safe Deposit Company. | Burglary—England—
    London—Case studies. | Jewelry theft—England—London—Case studies. | Older
    offenders—England—London—Case studies. | Burglars—England—London—
    Case studies. | Safe deposit companies—England—London—Case studies.
Classification: LCC HV6665.G72 B55 2019 | DDC 364.16/2873927—dc23
LC record available at https://lccn.loc.gov/2018046576

W. W. Norton & Company, Inc., 500 Fifth Avenue, New York, N.Y. 10110
www.wwnorton.com

W. W. Norton & Company Ltd., 15 Carlisle Street, London W1D 3BS

1 2 3 4 5 6 7 8 9 0

For my parents,
Judy and Ralph Bilefsky.

We done the best bit of work of the whole century.
The whole fucking century.

—*Terry Perkins*

Contents

Just Another Retiree on a Bus

THE LARGEST BURGLARY IN THE HISTORY OF ENGLAND began on a bus.

On the Thursday evening before Easter and Passover, April 2, 2015, as the sun began to set, Brian Reader, a baggy-eyed seventy-six-year-old pensioner, boarded the No. 96 bus near his grand redbrick home in Dartford, Kent. His house was about twenty miles away from central London and more than an hour by public transportation. No matter. Reader decided to take the bus. A career thief with a ruddy face, a quick temper, and plenty of cunning, taking the bus would give him a chance to catch up on the papers and the time to think. Time was something that was not in short supply these days since he was semiretired. He had likely calculated that driving his own car to a jewel heist was probably not a good idea. And if London's ubiquitous black taxi drivers were able to memorize twenty-five thousand streets and twenty thousand landmarks, they could surely remember his world-weary face. Besides, he hated to waste money, and taxis were expensive.

For those harried fellow commuters who saw Reader on that double-decker bus, he must've looked like just another ordinary pensioner with a sullen permanent scowl. If only they knew that what he was about to attempt was anything but ordinary.

Just hours before Reader had stepped on that bus, the jewelers of Hatton Garden had been arriving in droves at the Hatton Garden Safe Deposit Ltd., at 88–90 Hatton Garden, to store their goods over the long Passover and Easter holiday weekend. Many were immigrants, including Jewish Holocaust survivors. Many trusted the safe deposit with their life savings and kept their inventory there, without insurance, believing the boxes and the Chubb vault that protected them to be impenetrable. The neighborhood, London's jewelry district since medieval times, has more than three hundred jewelry stores, including De Beers. The safe deposit company, which marketed itself as a reliable fortress, was the favored place to store valuable gems.

The handsome seven-story building itself hosted some sixty tenants, a majority of whom were in the jewelry trade and stored their precious valuables in the basement safe deposit. The safe deposit had been a fixture in the neighborhood stretching back decades—and its current owners were a Sudanese family of Indian heritage called the Bavishis. Mahendra Bavishi, the sixty-nine-year-old, pot-bellied family patriarch and director of the business, lived in Khartoum and had ceded the daily running of the company to his two sons, thirty-eight-year-old Manish and twenty-nine-year-old Alok. All three men had a 25 percent stake in the firm, along with Mahendra's wife, Aruna.

Manish was on a one-month vacation in Sudan with his wife during that long weekend, and so Alok was looking after the business. As it was, Manish had a number of businesses, helping his father import electrical goods to Sudan and exporting the hibiscus flower from Sudan to Europe and South America. He typically only dropped by the safe deposit once a week.

The company had been losing money for years. To try to attract new customers, Manish had recently upgraded the monitoring system for the alarm and CCTV cameras, advertised the safe deposit in the

Indian press, and created a new website, replete with spelling mistakes. But the seven-decades-old vault remained largely the same and the explosion in customers he and his father had dreamed of never came. As a result, on that long holiday weekend, only 562 of the 999 safe deposit boxes were in use. Some customers, who had defaulted on their payment for their boxes, hadn't checked their boxes in fifteen years and white stickers with the words "RENT OVERDUE" were sporadically taped to boxes in the cavernous basement space.

These being hard times, the number of security guards at the safe deposit had shrunk from five to two, while the building had done away with a full-time night watchman. Nevertheless, Alok was confident that his longtime security guards, Kelvin Stockwell, a slow-moving and white-haired sixty-year-old who had worked for the company for twenty years, and Keefa Raymond Kamara, who had worked there more than a decade, had things under control.

As the two security guards were preparing to leave for the night, Reader paid his bus fare with a special travel pass for senior citizens—registered to his longtime alias, Mr. T. McCarthy—and then began an eighty-minute journey to Hatton Garden. As the 96 bus edged its way through the city, the tree-lined streets of Kent soon gave way to the capital's urban sprawl. If Reader and the gang could pull off the caper, his children and grandchildren would never have to work again. And he would go down among the London criminal fraternity as "the Master" his contemporaries grudgingly revered.

The enormity of what he and the others were about to attempt must have been flashing through his mind as the streets of London rushed by the bus's windows. There had been three years of due diligence; things had already been set in motion. The others were counting on him and there was no turning back now.

After arriving at London's sprawling Waterloo East Station, Reader exited the station at 6:31 p.m. It being the evening before a long Easter weekend, the station would have been thronging with people, and it took another half hour until Reader was able to transfer to the No. 55 bus. He boarded at 7:02 p.m. For someone who had been accustomed to the solitary confines of a jail cell, it must have been a relief to escape the crowds. He got off at St. John Street, in the hip neighborhood of Clerkenwell in central London, an area peppered by architecture studios, designer lofts, tech start-ups, and gastropubs, many of them spilling over with *Guardian*-reading media types. As Reader walked briskly on St. John Street in the direction of Hatton Garden, he passed by converted warehouses inside of which dozens of twentysomethings would spend their days hunched over their sleek Macintosh computers. It was a fitting contrast for a villain about to commit the last great analog crime of the digital age.

Reader had long suffered from migraines, according to friends, the product of his fall from a roof on a burglary job decades earlier when he had fractured his skull. He also suffered from a host of ailments, including back pains and arthritis. But on that day he was surely feeling sprightly. He decided to walk the final few blocks to his destination.

This was going to be a big night.

THE LAST JOB

Chapter 1

The Inspiration of a Botched Crime

IN LATE AUGUST 2010 ON THE SUNDAY OF A BANK holiday weekend, four men wearing high-visibility jackets arrived via a white van to Chatila, a glittering jewelry boutique on Bond Street, in London's posh Mayfair district. It was 9 a.m. After lugging their equipment out from the van—including a diamond-tipped drill and rolling trash cans—the thieves, disguised as maintenance men, used scaffolding outside the store to climb to the roof. From there, they broke into the building and deactivated the alarm. Then, they climbed down a disused elevator shaft. Once inside the vault, they used a diamond-tipped drill to try to break into a safe containing about £40 million ($61 million)* worth of gems. To try to cover their traces they stole one of the company's CCTV hard drives.

Chatila was a daring and attractive target. The company, which has its headquarters in Geneva and has been owned by a Lebanese family for 150 years, also has offices in Riyadh and Doha; its tony London branch caters to Hollywood celebrities, Saudi sheiks, and Russian oligarchs. It famously created the 171-carat heart-shaped sap-

---

* Currency conversions are in 2015 U.S. dollars, unless the event specified takes place in a different year.

phire and diamond necklace inspired by the Coeur de la Mer neck-lace Kate Winslet wore in the blockbuster film *Titanic*. Its vaults have also housed some of the world's most priceless and rare gemstones, including a flawless 87-carat diamond dubbed the "Hapsburg," one of a mere fistful of the world's known red diamonds, and an oval-shaped 62-carat ruby called "The Burmese Excellence." More recently, the jeweler made the carefully crafted pearl and diamond earrings Amal Clooney, George Clooney's wife, wore to her wedding.

Leading the gang of jewel thieves on that day, according to Scotland Yard, was Danny Jones, a marathon runner, then in his midfifties, with a macho demeanor. Eccentric to the core, he obsessed about crime and sometimes slept in his mother-in-law's dressing gown and a fez, accompanied by his dog, Rocket, according to friends. He was also an avid fortune-teller. An experienced burglar, his lithe physique, as well as his agility and strength, made him ideal for slithering through a hole in the wall or wielding a heavy drill big enough to bore through concrete.

One of his criminal associates, Carl Wood, a sometime burglar who had known Jones for years, compared him to Walter Mitty, the James Thurber character, who daydreams on an epic scale and variously imagines himself as a fighter pilot battling the Germans during the war, as a globally celebrated surgeon saving lives, and as a wily killer. Jones was not a violent man, but he had a similarly active fantasy life. He talked to Rocket, believing he could communicate with canines. He liked to sleep on the floor of his room in a military sleeping bag, and urinate into a water bottle.[1]

Possessed of a sweet demeanor but the vanity of a wannabe celebrity, Jones's white hair was always impeccably combed. He liked to talk like a gangster, peppering his East End Cockney slang with enough "fucks" and "cunts" to make even the most hardened criminal blanch.

A fitness freak who never drank or smoked, he had a tendency to invent stories. Fellow thieves say he had a tendency to blab, and tell everything to his common-law wife, Val, which was considered a liability among the criminal fraternity—since a bust-up with the "missus" could lead to her loosening her tongue and then everyone would be in trouble. He could run twenty miles with a heavy army bag on his back. He liked to say to anyone who would listen that he was in the army, special forces, and offered survival training sessions to officers who wanted to learn how to survive in hostile territory. His physical fitness was such that he probably could.

While he was fibbing, he nevertheless had impressive skills that were handy in a burglary. He could contort his body with acrobatic virtuosity, hold his head under water long after it was advisable, walk with handstands down an entire city block, and run very, very fast.

But on that particular long weekend, Jones's contortionist skills proved obsolete as he tried to drill into the safe before realizing that the drill itself was too short. Unable to get into the safe, the gang abandoned their initial plan. Instead, they ransacked a showroom and stole about £1 million ($1.5 million) in jewelry and precious stones, lugging it away in white containers and bags. Somewhere between 9 and 10 p.m., they fled.

Recalling the crime, whose perpetrators had remained elusive for years, Philip Evans, who went on to prosecute the case, would later observe at the Chatila trial that there were only a handful of thieves in London with the audacity to try to pull off such a brazen feat. "There can be very few people who have the necessary skills, experience, and preparedness to carry out a crime with this level of high stakes, high reward, and high risk," he said. "Very few people who have the contacts to dispose of such huge amounts of high value property. Very few people who would even know how to begin the immensely difficult and complex task of burgling a highly secure jewelers such as this one."[2]

Members of Chatila's staff discovered the break-in on Tuesday after the holiday weekend, and Jones would later be connected to the crime via his DNA left on a glove at the scene of the crime. But as the men fled with less booty than they had hoped, the botched burglary had provided a cautionary tale. They had managed to spirit away about £1 million in jewels but it had been a fraction of what could have been possible. The burglary had provided several lessons including the virtue of breaking in on the Sunday of a long weekend when patches of central London were deserted. It also brought home the need to have the right-sized drill. But power tools aside, there was another big lesson: if you wanted to attempt a heist of this magnitude, a master thief was needed to help with the planning and execution.

Chapter 2

The Making of a Master Thief

A Restless Pensioner

It was around the autumn of 2012 and Brian Reader was feeling restless. Or, at least, it seems, ready for a change.

His wife, Lyn, a former accountant's assistant with wavy red hair and an easy sense of humor, had been the love of his life, the one person who centered him, even when he was living in a jail cell. A heavy smoker, she had died a few years earlier from lung cancer. Friends say her absence had left a heavy void.

Reader was a widower, living in his imposing £640,000 (about $1 million) house in Dartford, Kent, a county bordering London known for its apple orchards and tony middle-class contentment. After having orchestrated some of the most renowned crimes of the century, he had been reduced to selling used cars from the driveway. He had always had a taste for the good life. But he had been out of the crime game for a while, and, according to his friends, he complained that money was fast running out.

Handsome and rugged in his youth, Reader now had wisps of thinning white hair and had been recently diagnosed with prostate cancer. Even without the cancer, the effects of aging were already taking their toll. He was prone to sudden tantrums—at least in the company of his fellow senior citizens—and his patience seemed brittle at best. But he could also be courteous and kind to a fault—for example, when faced with police officers or defense attorneys, whom had been a fixture throughout his life.

A penchant for nighttime burglaries meant he had been a very present and devoted father and husband. His abiding love for Lyn, his two children, Paul and Joanne, and his grandchildren had been a crack in the tough emotional armor he had donned during years of operating in the ruthless and sometimes violent world of London crime. But Lyn was gone. Paul, who worked in his used car business, and Joanne, who worked for Goldman Sachs, were grown up. They had their own lives and families.

Asked what would motivate him to try one last job, a former criminal associate said he had been motivated by money and his children. "He was close to his kids. He would give all the proceeds to his boy and he'd have said to the boy, 'look after Joanne.' You know what I mean, I don't suppose he was really into it for himself."

Boredom also seemed to play a role. When not selling cars, he would meet old cronies to talk about the old times. But there was only so much time a man could spend reminiscing about the past with other aging villains at a Monday club. In any case, some of his so-called friends didn't actually seem to like him. While generous to his family, he never seemed to buy anyone a pint of beer.

"He sits in that cafe and talks about all their yesterdays," his friend Terry Perkins, a fellow burglar with his own long rap sheet, said about Reader, grousing about his arrogance, his misplaced nostalgia, and his apparent stinginess. "Never bought a drink at the pub and that's his intention there you know," he complained. "Never buys fuck all."

Danny Jones, a longtime acquaintance of Reader, was equally uncharitable about his old friend. "He's a fucking know-it-all, that's what he is and anything he knows he's got wrong," he said of Reader. "Every bit of fucking work we've been on, he's fucked up."[1] Yet for all of their complaints, Reader was an experienced thief and strategist and had contacts for laundering gear that the other two lacked.

As the "firm" began to take shape for one last, ambitious career-topping caper, Reader was perhaps also possessed by a fearlessness borne of age. What was there to lose?

* * * *

"Let's See How Sherlock Holmes Solves This One"

When Reader was thirty-two, law enforcement officials and former criminal associates say, he was the leader of a gang of expert thieves known as the "Millionaire Moles" who pulled off a now legendary robbery on the night of Saturday, September 11, in 1971. At that time, London, a burgeoning financial center, was rife with burglaries, and there was an armed robbery every five days. This heist took place at 188 Baker Street, the northwest London street where the fictional detective Sherlock Holmes lived. To begin with, the gang rented a leather goods shop called Le Sac a few stores away from the bank. Then, using cutting equipment, they burrowed a forty-foot tunnel underground, passing under a chicken take-out restaurant, until the tunnel reached underneath the vault. The men dug over the course of three long weekends to avoid being overheard. On the day of the heist, they crawled through the tunnel, only to discover that the vault's floor was protected by three feet of reinforced concrete. Undeterred, they used a thermic lance, and then explosives to blow a hole through it, barely large enough to wiggle through. All the while, one member of the group stood watch on a nearby rooftop, with a walkie-talkie, ready to alert the others if Scotland Yard showed up.

Once inside, the gang ransacked 268 safety deposit boxes, walking away with valuables estimated at more than £500,000 ($1.2 milion)—worth about £7 million ($9 million) today, at the time Britain's largest bank robbery. They left a mocking message scrawled in graffiti on the walls of the bank vault: "Let's see how Sherlock Holmes solves this one." (Reader, through his lawyer, has denied having anything to do with Baker Street and was never tried for the crime.)

During the heist, an amateur radio enthusiast accidentally overheard the gang's every word, spoken on their walkie-talkies. He called the police, who initially did not take him seriously, according to Tony Lundy, a former Scotland Yard detective who was on duty in London's West End during the robbery and was called to the scene.[2] When the police eventually responded, they descended on 750 banks in the area, including the targeted Lloyd's bank. But Lundy said the thieves initially remained undetected. "We visited every bank. But all were sound-proof and all the vaults were locked and on timers and couldn't be opened until Monday at 9 a.m. I was part of the team that went to Lloyds. But not one bank showed signs of breaking and entry." On Sunday, the thieves fled, and the heist was discovered the next day, unleashing a media frenzy.

To this day, unsubstantiated rumors swirl that Reader and his gang of outlaws were hired by MI5, the domestic intelligence service, to rob the vault because it contained in a safe deposit box compromising photographs of the late Princess Margaret, the sister of Queen Elizabeth II, in flagrante delicto. Perhaps even more insidious, a former member of the Baker Street gang said Reader and the others had discovered in a safe deposit box photographs of a Conservative politician sexually abusing children, and had purposely spread the photographs on the floor of the vault in the hopes that police would find them. If they did, they were never exposed.

The audacity of the Baker Street robbery arguably surpassed even the surprise attack on a post-office train during the legendary Great Train Robbery of 1963. The crime was later immortalized in the 2008 film *The Bank Job*, featuring a car dealer, like Reader, who commits the crime as part of an elaborate setup. In real life, four men were eventually arrested, but not Reader. Had he been involved, he had been too wily to get caught.

Reader's luck finally ran out in 1985, when he was sentenced to nine years in prison for his role in helping to launder stolen gold from another brazen caper, two years earlier, at the Brink's-Mat security depot at London's Heathrow Airport during which roughly £26 million, or about $36 million, worth of gold bars had been spirited away. Along the way, he was also implicated in a string of commercial burglaries and—in an episode that would irreparably mark him— accused of the murder of an undercover police officer. But after having been released from prison in 1994, he was living a quiet life. Or so it seemed.

Neighbors next to his home in Dartford, Kent, say they seldom saw him leave the house. The house is bordered by a brick wall, a fence, and dense row of bushes that seem calculated to defend against the twitching curtains of nosy neighbors, of which there were plenty. A sign on the house's incongruously small wooden front door says No Entry. It is a comical flourish for the home of a man notorious for his breaking-and-entry skills.

Occasionally, neighbors would see him playing with his grandchildren through a crack in the vast hedges that obscured part of the front of the building. But in his middle-class suburban neighborhood— whose one famous native son Mick Jagger had long since left— Reader was a low-key and enigmatic figure. No one seemed to know who he was, or about his past, or about what he now planned to do. He appeared to cultivate anonymity after decades of being known for the wrong reasons.

"Dartford is a place you came to raise children and a family out-side of London, and want a quiet suburban middle class life," said a neighbor. "I always thought it strange that they lived in one of the nicest houses in the neighborhood, but they never seemed to work. No one knew where he got the money," she said. "They never mixed with the other neighbors. I always felt like something was happening behind closed doors."

* * * *

The Making of the Guv'nor

Reader's storied criminal career began in 1950 at the age of eleven when he was arrested for stealing a can of fruit at a corner shop, according to police records. In the decades that followed, his name would crop up in some of the most headline-grabbing burglaries of the era. His specialty: breaking and entering and later laundering sto-len goods such as jewelry and gold.

Born on February 28, 1939, in London Docklands, in the south-east of the capital, Reader came of age in an impoverished industrial area that has long attracted the criminal fraternity.[3] The firstborn son of Doris, nineteen, and Harry Reader, twenty-four, Reader's person-ality was formed during an era of food rationing and Nazi bombs, which inspired his dogged self-preservation. The Docklands hosted one of the biggest ports in the world, and local villains and villains-in-training would sneak in at night, pry open shipping containers, and steal whatever they could find.[4]

When he was a teenager, Reader's father abandoned the family, forcing him to become the man of the house and to be independent from an early age, even if that meant stealing. As the eldest, he also took on the role of breadwinner, and was close to his two sisters and brother, for whom he became a father figure, according to a childhood friend. He left school at the age of fifteen, and did a number of menial jobs, including as a butcher and shoveling coal for the railway.

At the age of eighteen, he faced his first judge at London's storied Old Bailey Criminal Court on attempted burglary charges. Shortly after, in 1958, he was conscripted for military service and joined the Royal Engineers, where he went through basic training and learned how to handle a gun. His army salary was a pittance but a friend from that period recalled that he used part of the money to buy a motorcycle.

After leaving the military, he worked as a driver for a while and, hungering to be his own boss, bought his own truck and started to transport goods such as fruits and vegetables and industrial supplies across the country.[5] At the age of twenty-four, Reader, just a couple of years out of the army, met Lyn Kidd, four years his junior. She was pretty, a horse lover, with a quick wit and inner toughness he recognized in himself. The two married in 1963 and soon had two children. Desperate to earn some real money to support his young family, Reader came under the tutelage of Bill Barrett, an experienced thief, who was about a decade older, and tutored him on the finer points of breaking and entering, how to choose a target, how to break open a safe, and how to disappear into the shadows. Soon, Reader joined a gang of canny cohorts, among them Micky "Skinny" Gervaise, a burglar alarm expert who in 1980 disguised himself as a policeman and robbed a security van carrying £3.4 million (about $7.7 million) in silver bullion; John "The Face" Goodwin, an expert safe breaker,[6] and "Little Legs" Larkins, an expert locksmith known for his diminutive stature.

Paul Lashmar, a veteran crime reporter and investigative journalist who worked for the *Observer*, recalled Reader from those heady days as being part of a band of East End burglars hitting banks and security companies in the city. "Their big thing was doing warehouses, and jewelry production places," he said. "They liked to hit places around Hatton Garden."[7] This was an era before surveillance cameras when factories or commercial properties or security vans were easy targets.

Reader was also part of a now nearly extinct generation of old-school professional thieves in London, who operated with a well-defined code of honor: they abhorred violence, valued their breaking-and-entering skills as if a lost art, loved their wives and families, did prison time without complaint, and looked down on gangsters of that era like the Kray twins or the Richardsons as little more than professional thugs, whom they ridiculed as "poncy"—overpriced, over styled, overrated.[8]

The Krays dominated the East and later the West End of London, while the turf south of the River Thames was under the control of their rivals, the Richardson family, led by Charlie Richardson and his brother Eddie. The Richardsons and their associates ruled with menace—electroshock treatment, bolt cutters, bare-knuckle punches—and made money from the scrap metal trade after the Second World War, eventually added gaming machines, mines, parking lots, and pornography to their portfolio in crime.[9]

While Reader, a professional thief, eschewed the limelight, the Krays owned nightclubs and mingled with politicians and prominent entertainers, such as Frank Sinatra, Diana Dors, and Judy Garland, and relished being splashed on newspaper front pages and interviewed on television. Not Reader, however, who inhabited the London "underworld" of fellow criminals, bent cops, and solicitors, but craved the outward signs of middle-class respectability. While he avoided clubs and discos, he and Lyn adored jazz and American crooners Ella Fitzgerald and Frank Sinatra and even attended one of Sinatra's London concerts, according to a longtime former criminal associate.

"Reader was the antithesis of the gangsters, who adored Warner Brothers B movies, Hollywood, and Cary Grant, wanted to be like Al Capone, drive Cadillacs, and wear cashmere overcoats," explained Dick Hobbs, Britain's leading sociologist of crime, who himself grew up on the mean streets of east London, and was a professor in the sociology department of the London School of Economics. "Reader would have known them and seen them in pubs and clubs, but he would've kept a distance. He wasn't taken in by violence and he didn't like drama."[10]

Reader preferred a quiet life, and was almost unfailingly loyal to Lyn. The associate, who has known him for four decades, recalled that while Reader was handsome and popular with the ladies, he had only one dalliance outside of his marriage. "All the time I known Brian he wasn't a woman chaser," he said. "I only know one instance where he, he, whatever, had a blow job or a fuck or whatever and that was because it was put on his plate. He wasn't a queer or nothing. He'd look at a woman and go, 'oh yeh,' but that was about as far as he ever did."

He also wasn't ostentatious. The Reader family behaved outwardly like a typical aspirational middle-class family, taking camping trips in the countryside near East Sussex, before graduating to a more bourgeois life of fine wines, French cooking, ski lessons for the children, sprawling suburban homes, and vacations on the continent. Eventually, the family moved to 40 Winn Road, an attractive four-bedroom house in Grove Park, in southeast London, and lived under the alias McCarthy.

According to old friends, Reader was good at cultivating and keeping friends, including friends from his childhood, a rare trait among thieves, who didn't trust anyone. And even as his criminal career took off, friends say he remained proudly working class and leftwing, admiring Tony Benn, a pugnacious and outspoken left-wing member of Parliament known for his unreconstructed socialism.

In the 1980s, there was an armed robbery nearly every week in London, with vast sums taken, as thieves targeted security vans, security depots, or poorly guarded banks. But Reader studiously avoided violence if he could help it, recognizing early on in his criminal career that violence meant longer jail sentences.

Reader had long been attracted to Hatton Garden, and he tried repeatedly to make an honest living as a jewelry trader. But each time, the lure of quick money yielded from burglaries proved too alluring. Nevertheless, he held a series of legitimate jobs, which law enforcement officials say provided a cover for his more illicit work. For a time, he ran a jewelry wholesaler in Leather Lane Market, next to Hatton Garden, and acted as a middle man in the gold trade, buying large quantities of chains and bracelets, and then selling them to dealers.

He also dabbled in the art world, and teamed up with "Little Legs" Larkins, one of his gang of thieves, to buy seventeenth-century Dutch masters and resell them to collectors. He would hang out at a bar in Hatton Garden called Pussy Galore and eat lunch at a Jewish deli, frequented by gangsters and orthodox Jews called the Nosherie.[11]

"There was a jewelry boom—I think most young ladies will remember—about that time when people were buying bracelets and necklaces," Reader later recalled when questioned about his life while he was on trial for his role in laundering gold from the 1983 Brink's-Mat heist. "I was purchasing them from a wholesaler to sell to private persons. I suppose you could call it a bit of pin money," he said, referring to a small amount of money to spend on nonessentials.[12]

The world of commercial crime in London had been turned upside down with the advent of the "supergrass" in the 1970s, criminal informants who ratted on their fellow criminals in return for reduced sentences. One theory is that the term "supergrass" originated in the nineteenth century when criminals in London sometimes used Cockney rhyming slang to refer to a policeman as a grasshopper, or "copper." Others ascribe the term to the Virgil quote, "There's a snake hidden in the grass." Whatever its origins, the supergrass would prove a disaster for Reader.

One of the pioneers of the supergrass was Tony Lundy, a former senior member of the Flying Squad, dubbed "the Andrew Lloyd

Webber of the Old Bailey" by his biographer Martin Short since he was so adept at catching thieves and would usually have three or four high-profile criminal trials going on at the same time. He later traveled to South America and worked with the FBI to help put the legendary cocaine kingpin Howard Marks behind bars.

Lundy was so successful at catching thieves that some critics questioned whether he had attained knowledge by illicit means. But he has never been charged with corruption, despite multiple police investigations. A former boxer and marathon runner, Lundy retired from Scotland Yard in 1988, citing stress, and has since lived in Spain. Decades later, he remains embittered by accusations he called "diabolical."

Lundy excelled at getting robbers to confess their crimes, in particular during the 1980s when armed robberies in the capital were epidemic. Lundy's "supergrass" was a notorious gangster called Roy Garner, whose fingerprints were on some of the greatest heists of the era. He also made a grass out of Micky "Skinny" Gervaise, Reader's associate, who had been involved in some thirty commercial robberies, including the daring hijacking of ten tons of silver bullion on its way from London to East Berlin in 1980, then the largest-ever heist in England.

According to Lundy, Reader had been doing "cutting jobs" for years, East End slang for breaking into safes. He described Reader as a criminal of the old school, who wouldn't cross certain lines—for example, shooting a policeman or hurting a bystander to a robbery. "For villains like Reader," he said, "crime is like smoking cigarettes. They just can't give up."[13]

In 1980, Gervaise "grassed" to Scotland Yard that Reader had been on several commercial burglaries. Reader was arrested and questioned but released on bail. Eager to avoid jail, he decided to skip town in 1982 and go to the south of Spain—known among the British criminal fraternity as the Costa del Crime. It was a popular destination for English criminals since Britain and Spain did not have an extradition treaty at the time. Reader would later complain that being stitched up by Gervaise was "the most devastating time of my life." During his European sojourn, he took Lyn and the family to Venice and a resort in France to learn how to ski. A photograph of Reader at the time shows one of Britain's most daring thieves sitting on a plush couch surrounded by his young family in the lobby of a luxury Méribel hotel in France. There is an animal-skin carpet on the floor, and his face is tanned and relaxed. A bon vivant with a penchant for sailing and skiing, Reader had come a long way from his days as rough-edged criminal from southeast London.

"I was on my own recognizance and I decided that I had had enough and went abroad," Reader later recalled.

It was a nice bourgeois life—traveling to southern France in the autumn, and the French Alps in the winter. The Reader family spent two years there—camouflaged as an expatriate English family—but returned to England in July 1984. The family felt restless and homesick, in particular Lyn, who hated being on the run and craved some stability. "I felt that I should come back to England and to sort things out," Reader would later recall. "My family were being fed up being away from home as well and we decided to come back home. I was also running."[14]

After arriving back in Britain, Reader was arrested and received a twelve-month prison sentence for having absconded on bail. After getting out of jail, he tried to resume a quiet life, buying and selling jewelry at Hatton Garden and keeping a low profile. But it didn't last long. He hungered to get back in the criminal game.

* * * *

A Whole Lot of Gold

At around 6:40 a.m. on November 26, 1983, six armed men in balaclavas entered the warehouse of Brink's-Mat, a security company, at

Heathrow Airport. One of the men, Micky McAvoy, was wearing a trilby hat atop his yellow mask, giving him the appearance of a dapper thug. The robbers had been tipped off that there was about £3 million ($4.4 million) in cash and valuables in the vault. The men were armed, and McAvoy and his associate Brian Robinson gathered the petrified guards together. They tied them up and doused them with gasoline. They threatened to light a match if they didn't hand over what they wanted. Thanks to Anthony Black, a Brink's-Mat security guard who also happened to be Robinson's brother-in-law, the crew knew which of the guards kept the keys and the combinations for the vault where the safe holding the gold was located.

But when the gang gained access to the vault, they could barely believe their eyes—or their luck. In total, there were seven thousand gleaming gold bars, packed into more than seventy cardboard boxes. About £26 million ($38 million) worth of gold. The crew's van was so overloaded, its tires looked deflated as it sped away.

While the robbery was daring in its plotting and execution, the criminals were foolhardy. They quickly began to spend the money, including on lavish homes. McAvoy, full of misplaced bravado, named his Rottweiler guard dogs Brinks and Mat. Robinson's and McAvoy's clumsy transactions were being monitored by Scotland Yard and they were soon arrested.

But not before the thieves helped set in motion an operation to smelt the stolen gold, with the aid of a then little-known petty criminal named Kenneth Noye and his pal John Palmer, a notorious gangster, who ran a Bristol-based gold dealership called Scadlynn. The company was used as a cover for the gold-smelting operation with the end product being sold on the lucrative scrap market. But the duo needed a middleman to help launder the gold—someone who was adept at being inconspicuous and who had contacts in the deeply secretive world of Hatton Garden.[15]

While in Spain, Reader had read about the audacious Brink's-

Mat heist in the London *Times* and his appetite was already whetted. So when Noye approached him to help fence some of the gold, he readily obliged. Reader and Noye were united by their upbringing in working-class southeast London and by their love of money and the finer things in life. At one point, Noye kept a pet lion, and his home doorbell played the theme song from *Goldfinger*.[16]

Reader's role was to help spirit some of the gold bars to Bristol in an elaborate and sophisticated scheme during which the bars were melted down and mixed with copper coins and brass to try to disguise it as scrap gold, before it was resold. He was eventually caught and sentenced to nine years in prison for his role in laundering the gold.

After Reader went to prison, Duncan Campbell, the *Guardian*'s veteran crime reporter, interviewed Lyn Reader, whom he recalled as being intelligent and possessed of a sharp sense of humor. Lyn lamented that being the wife of a man on the run had taken its toll on her and the family. "People think it sounds glamorous, but it was awful changing homes all the time," she said. "I used to get plants and flowers whenever we went to a new place, to try and make it look like a home."

She said she had been harassed by Britain's feverish tabloid press, for whom Reader—then a handsome young cad—had become an enigmatic but fascinating antihero. According to Campbell, she recalled that, during the Brink's-Mat trial, one paper had offered her £1,000 ($1,440) for a photograph of Reader drinking champagne. She declined. The British media had also breathlessly reported on the trial, describing how she had reacted to the verdict by crying out to her husband, "I'll wait for you darling!"

"I think if I'd actually said, 'I'll wait for you darling,'" she told Campbell, "Brian would have jumped out of the dock and punched me on the nose."[17]

Chapter 3

The Making of the Firm

Planning and Pubbing

This being England, the idea for the Hatton Garden Heist was hatched at a pub amid diners downing pints of beer and eating plates of fish and chips. During the three years leading up to the crime, the four old friends met at the Castle pub on Pentonville Road in Islington, north London, a conspicuously bright green gastropub with an outdoor terrace that was popular with locals and tourists alike. The aging thieves were not there to discuss their backaches and joint pain, although they were talking about a form of retirement. They were focused on pulling off one last heist that they hoped the world would never forget—and that would get them out of the crime game once and for all.

"That could be my pension!"[1] one of the gang members, the birdlike Terry Perkins, later exclaimed. The Firm's many meetings, which Scotland Yard say began as early as 2012, took place most Fridays at the pub in an area that had long since gentrified. The pub, about a fifteen-minute walk to Hatton Garden, was a fitting place for the men to meet and plot—a diamond ring logo adorned the door of the women's bathroom; a Go to Jail sign was on the gent's. At their table near the back, they could be inconspicuous. Or so they thought.

A blackboard on a wall listed specials alongside the regular dishes on the menu, such as treacle tart with vanilla ice cream, an impossibly sweet and beloved British pudding, and wild boar and apple sausages. Another sign advertised the rooftop terrace upstairs, which the pub boasted, with typical British understatement, was "possibly the finest roof terrace in Angel." The bustling and noisy pub, thronging with tourists and young professionals from the neighborhood, was decorated with lamps made with globes, which appealed to its well-traveled clientele. Old-school criminals though they were, the men seemed to like the good life: Angel was the surrounding bourgeois neighborhood in the north London borough of Islington, which has hosted, among others, former prime minister Tony Blair, Salman Rushdie, and the former London mayor-turned-foreign-secretary Boris Johnson. It was the kind of place where you could find French gourmet cheese shops, Bauhaus furniture stores, and the flagship restaurant of the star chef Yotam Ottolenghi.

But while the men sought out discretion toward the back of the pub, they could be easily seen as they sipped their beers and bantered. Their idea of discretion seemed to be studiously avoiding the Castle's Tuesday Quiz Night, or special evenings such as "National Talk Like a Pirate Day," when the Castle regular with the best pirate outfit got his or her second beer free.

Perkins, who was then in his early sixties, had only recently been released from prison, having been sentenced to a twenty-two-year stint for a sensational £6 million ($9 million) robbery in 1985.

Reader, seventy-six at the time, was known by his cohorts as "the Master" or the "Guv'nor," the would-be chief executive of their "Firm." He had joined forces with Daniel Jones, the eccentric fitness freak with a wiry frame, who clocked in at a sprightly sixty years of age, and John "Kenny" Collins, a pot-bellied fireworks salesman with a rap sheet dating back to 1961, whom Reader knew from prison. Collins was seventy-four years old at the time.

The cumulative age of the four men was 277 years when the caper took place in April 2015—that is, if you don't include Basil, a technology wiz and alarm man with a red wig who was in his fifties. Reader had known Basil for at least two decades and recruited him to help with the planning. His identity was shrouded in mystery.

While Reader was the one who gave orders, the others, including Jones, were the "laborers" who obeyed, albeit sometimes grudgingly; they thought him smug and condescending.

While Perkins dreamed of using the loot from the heist to buy a house for each of his four daughters, and Reader also wanted to support his family, the men seemed to be motivated by a mix of ambition, adventure, and the urge for one last great hoorah. Jones also had other ideas of what to do with his share, including raising his partner Val's weekly allowance by a "fiver" to £125 (about $190). Perkins was more generous and noted that he gave his "old woman" a weekly allowance of £150 (about $225). Jones also told the others he wanted to buy a Volvo with a big back seat for his beloved dog, Rocket.[2]

Perkins hadn't been impressed: "I'd get rid of that dog!" he chided him. "I wouldn't let him in that fucking motor, that's for sure!"

Collins and Jones would later muse while they were driving in Collins's white Mercedes that holding down a regular job just wasn't enough to eke out a living, enjoy the Christmas holidays, and go on vacation. Why work for a living when you could come by millions with the spin of a power drill?

"If you have to work for a living—you know, an ordinary job, not a good job, how you manage to get by during Christmas and then start fucking take the kids on holiday. Fuckin' hell!" Collins said to Jones.

"You get a straight man who goes to work for £25,000 a year. That's the average, ain't it?" Jones asked.

"I suppose they get a bit more now but I would say £25,000 'cause a lot of them get fucking worse," Collins replied.

"My Matthew works for the dust, he brings home £260 a week," Jones said, plaintively, referring to his son's job as a street cleaner.[3]

* * * *

OVER THE MONTHS OF planning, after discussing the relative challenges of different targets in central London, the gang eventually set their sights on 88–90 Hatton Garden. The reason was simple: hundreds of millions of pounds in diamonds, jewels, sapphires, gold bars, rare coins, and cash were stored there.

But the debates had sometimes been fraught. The building had been at the center of London's jewelry district since the 1940s. Reader knew the neighborhood and safe deposit company from his decades operating there as a professional fence and grifter and he had been casing out the seven-floor building for years. Yet perhaps because he was conditioned by his years in jail and was no stranger to the intoxication of greed that had led to past follies, he was deeply cautious. Hitting such a well-policed area could end in disaster and land the men behind bars. The rest of the gang were no strangers to prison, either.

But Reader saw an opening after the building's management, in a moment of cost-cutting folly, decided to lay off its longtime caretaker, ensuring that it would be unguarded after working hours when the Firm visited the storied vault during the long Easter weekend of 2015.[4]

Even in the unlikely event they were caught, they appear to have reasoned that they were getting old and, at most, would spend three or four years in jail, after which they could retrieve the loot. In the British justice system, those convicted of a crime typically serve only half their sentence in jail and the rest under supervised probation,[5] a legal vagary that Reader and his men would have been well familiar with, given their many brushes with the law.

While the vault in the basement required a four-digit pin code and was secured by two metallic gates, the Firm knew that the front door of the building was unlocked most of the day, that there now were no twenty-four-hour guards, and that the safe deposit boxes could be accessed, if only the gang could figure out a way of bypassing the vault, which was reinforced by twenty inches of concrete.

To attempt such a brazen crime in Hatton Garden, a tight-knit community of jewelers heavily patrolled by police, Reader knew his Firm would need a crew with diverse skills, ingenuity, and, above all, fearlessness.

The members of his crew were indeed getting on in years, and suffered from a range of ailments including diabetes, heart disease, and bladder-control problems. But among the men, they had more than enough experience picking locks, digging tunnels, cracking open safes, escaping from prisons, dousing guards with gas and threatening to light them on fire, melting down gold, and stashing loot. Reader and Perkins, the most experienced among the gang, had been involved in two of the most daring robberies of the twentieth century, and were no strangers to crimes that had turned violent.

All had wives or long-term partners and children and—in the case of Reader and Perkins—grandchildren. Beyond the glory, the glittering headlines, and the chance to take a break from the monotony of retirement, their banter and boasting, which was later surreptitiously recorded by Scotland Yard, suggests they were mainly motivated by the one thing that drove most old-school criminals of their generation: greed, and piles and piles of cold, hard cash.

* * * *

The Crew

Terry Perkins, the Pill-Popping Thief

By virtue of his age—he turned sixty-seven during the burglary—and his conviction for one of the largest cash robberies in British history, Brian Reader's number two in the gang in terms of seniority was Terry Perkins. He was a tough-as-nails career criminal, whose rough edges had been tempered somewhat by age, acute diabetes, and nearly twenty years behind bars.

Perkins had a grandfatherly demeanor, with blue eyes and a ruddy face. He had been sentenced for his role in a notorious 1983 robbery at the Security Express company in east London, which netted about £6 million ($9 million) in cash. The burglary took place over an Easter weekend—in this case, Easter Monday. Freddie Foreman, one of the robbers on that job, and the self-described "godfather of British crime," recalled in an interview that members of the hooded gang, which included a then thirty-five-year-old Perkins, wielded sawed-off shotguns and overpowered the lone guard at Security Express's offices at breakfast time.

During the robbery, the thieves poured gas over one terrified member of the staff and warned him that he would be set on fire if he didn't hand over the cash and gold, according to Foreman.[6] The gang loaded stacks of bank notes stored in the company's vaults into several escape vehicles. At the time, the Security Express holdup was the largest cash haul in British history.

Incredibly, Perkins did not serve the full twenty-two years for the 1985 Security Express heist. He simply failed to return to Spring Hill Prison in Buckinghamshire, about fifty miles southeast of London, in 1995 after a weekend visit approved by his probation officer. Instead, he remained at large for the next seventeen years. According to Scotland Yard and former associates, he had been living in a small apartment with his mother, and working as a bartender and cook at a pub called the Harlequin in Clerkenwell in central London that attracted aging thieves and was located in the same district as Hatton Garden. Collins, Reader, and other disreputable men liked to hang out at the Harlequin and it was there, among other places, that the men got to know one another and cemented their friendship.[7]

After police received a tip-off in 2012, possibly from a patron at the bar, Perkins was suddenly recaptured. When police arrived at his house to arrest him, he smiled and exclaimed, "I've been expecting you," according to Scotland Yard. Despite his ruse of having escaped from prison and all but living out in the open, he was released a few months later. After more than fifteen years in prison, he had done his fair share behind bars, and he was apparently seen as being too docile to be deemed a threat by police, even if his penchant for thievery had never left him.

He was a "hard worker." Freddie Foreman, who was an enforcer for the Kray twins, the legendary London gangsters in the 1950s and 1960s, recalled his old friend as a determined man, who never gave up and would never grass—or snitch. He said Perkins dressed sharply and had amassed a lot of money in real estate.

During the robbery, Perkins was diligent and dependable and was not averse to being one of "the heavies," if the situation demanded it. "He is not a leader," Foreman said. "He likes to joke, he is one of the chaps, the one who will stay all night long at the pub, even after closing." He added, "He is a good solid old boy, who keeps a low profile and does what he is told. He is a solid worker, a soldier. He wouldn't leave you to die on the pavement."[8]

For all of his accumulated wealth, Perkins lived in a modest house in Enfield, a gritty north London neighborhood, with his long-suffering wife, Jacqueline. Terri, one of his four daughters, lived nearby with her family, and he saw her frequently. He was a grandfather now, and, having spent so many years away in prison, appeared determined to make it up to his family. During his long criminal career, he had bought and sold properties, including in Portugal, and he had made hundreds of thousands of pounds in cash. But judging by the frequency with which money came up in his conversations with the rest of the Firm, he hungered for more.

He was a man of simple tastes—he liked fish 'n' chips. He liked to laugh. He appeared generous to his children and sweet toward his grandchildren, though he didn't hesitate to swear in front of them. He would drive his young granddaughter to her acting and dance classes, and fuss over his ill grandson. If he called you a "cunt," you were halfway to being friends.

Despite his harmless exterior, Perkins had a quick temper, and he could be competitive and jealous, especially of Reader, who was older than him, had accumulated an equally if not more impressive roster of robberies, and whom he resented for his bourgeois affectations and pretentiousness. Perkins was close to seventy. And he still wanted to be a player. Working class and seemingly proud of it, Perkins hated Reader's smugness. He was determined to show that age hadn't dented his thieving skills and complained to Jones that Reader behaved as if he was "past it."[9] grudging respect for the man the others called the Master. "But I will show him!"

Reader sometimes wanted the Firm to meet early so they would have time for lunch. But Perkins would have none of it, preferring to spend his free time with his family. " 'Let's make it early,' Brian said, the saucy cunt. 'Lunch?' I said, 'fuck off I have got somewhere to go, I got something to do,' I pick my daughter up and take her to work," Perkins told Danny Jones in the spring of 2015 as they were driving in Perkins's blue Citroën Saxo. "You go and have fucking lunch. Go where you want, you cunt."[10]

Despite a sometimes cantankerous manner, he was a man who kept a well-honed poker face, according to Tony Connell, a twenty-year veteran of Britain's Crown Prosecution Service, the main prosecution agency for England and Wales, who was once a member of Perkins's legal team when he was a younger thief.

A jovial Liverpudlian with a prodigious gift of gab, Connell was on Perkins's legal team after Perkins was accused of taking part in the Security Express robbery of 1983. That heist had yielded so much cash, Connell recalled, that Alan Opiola, one of the convicted, complained that they had tried to count the bills in a bathtub at his house but when they couldn't fit any more in the tub, they were forced to "squash" them into little squares.

When Connell met Perkins in 1985, he was sitting in a cell in the basement of the Old Bailey. He described Perkins as physically unremarkable. "He's not the leader or the strongman, more the guy who can carry the stash of goods to the van and drive away. In armed robberies, you need someone like that, someone you can count on not to panic."

Decades later, he recalled Perkins's defense with an uproarious, disbelieving laugh. "He said he was too old and ill to have jumped over the wall during the Security Express robbery, and he gave us medical files to show that he had a heart condition." It was eerily similar to the defense Perkins told the gang they should use during the planning of the Hatton Garden caper if they were ever arrested: that they were too old and infirm to lug heavy jewels, never mind wield a diamond-tipped drill that weighed eighty pounds.

During the Security Express trial, Connell was asked to write Perkins's application for bail, since he was the junior lawyer. He said it was a "lost cause"; Perkins had been linked to the scene of the crime, and he didn't have an effective alibi. After Perkins was sentenced to twenty-two years for the robbery, Connell recalled that he and another lawyer went to see him in his cell in the Old Bailey. When asked whether he needed anything, Perkins, unhappy but not unbowed—asked if he could have a cigarette. Perkins displayed remarkable composure for a man who was about to go to jail for the next two decades.

"I barely had a shilling in my pocket, and when I pulled out my cigarettes and gave him the pack, which was almost full, he replied, 'Thank you, Mr. Connell.' He was not very demonstrative. He had just been sent down. But he was a professional criminal and he knew the score. Perkins and his like just accepted long sentences like death or paying taxes because it was an occupational hazard that they tried to avoid. He was part of that generation of old school criminals who knew that if you did the crime and got caught, you did your time, and didn't complain. They gambled big and if you won, you won big. If they were scared, their code wouldn't allow them to show it."[11]

* * * *

Danny Jones, the Fabulist

Perkins's sidekick was Danny Jones, a fifty-eight-year-old marathon runner with white hair and a macho demeanor. The two had known each other for two decades, having met at Blantyre House, a prison for longer-term offenders located on the outskirts of Goudhurst in Kent. But while Perkins was old school and understated, Jones was far more flamboyant.

An experienced burglar, Jones was also an avid fortune-teller, who excelled at picking locks. "Danny is an eccentric, for sure, but don't believe everything you hear about him," warned Valerie Hart, his common-law wife and the mother of his two children, a trim and chic woman who looks at least twenty years his junior. "He is definitely eccentric."[12]

Hailing from Enfield like Perkins, Jones had a rap sheet as long as it was varied. His police records show four decades' worth of burglaries beginning in 1975, at the age of twenty, including stealing £80 (about $175) from a butcher shop in 1980 and £92,000 ($202,400) worth of jewelry from Ratner's jewelers in central London for which he was sentenced to five years in prison in 1982. He also did time for robbing a pawn shop with a shotgun.

While in prison in the 1980s, Jones came under the tutelage of an old-school burglar called Gerald Edward who took him under his wing, advising him that he was better off eschewing violence and instead doing burglaries since they typically generated more money and less prison time. It was an exhortation he seems never to have forgotten.

By the time he was fifty-eight, Jones had spent so many years in jail that he referred to 5 p.m. as "bang up," the slang used by prisoners to describe when a cell door is locked. After 5 p.m., he would rarely see friends, avoid picking up one of his four cell phones or accept guests at his house in Enfield. With its gabled roofs, richly decorated facade, large windows, and dark wooden and leather interior, his house looked every bit like a nineteenth-century Swiss chalet and reflected the vanity of a man who loved material objects, even as he led a somewhat Spartan life. The floors of the house were covered with Persian carpets, the expansive oak rooms filled with dark brown leather chairs, modernist sculptures, large ornate crucifixes, china plates, stuffed owls, and antique grandfather clocks. A replica of a skull adorned the banister at the end of a grand staircase. Befitting a man who prided himself on his athleticism, his closet was crammed with dozens of pairs of sneakers, and a tool shed near the back of the house overflowed with scuba gear and gardening tools; a black mountain bike hung from a hook.

Yet for all the outward signs of respectability, Jones misspelled words like a ten-year-old (one old friend said he used to ask others to read to him in prison) and could barely write a grammatical sentence. Proud of his physical prowess and clinging to the myth that he was in the army, he liked to boast that he offered survival training sessions to officers who wanted to learn how to survive in hostile territory.

His passion for physical fitness was matched by a love of crime and crime stories, and he enjoyed writing hilariously bad short stories and poetry in a diary labeled "The Master Thief," dated December 1994 and signed "Danny Jones." "Stroking the storage room door it gently opens. His heart beats like a small child as before him the diamond sparkles," the story reads. "He would caress them in some strange manner. Closing the storage door as he leaves. Why doesn't he take the booty and with a cat-like smile he says, because I am the master thief."

In another undated diary entry he wrote what appeared to be a letter to his young son, urging him to be strong as he was apparently leaving somewhere, perhaps heading off to prison: "Put your head on my shoulders, don't you shed a tear as cowboys don't cry. Pull yourself together give me a cowboy smile as cowboys don't cry. Be strong for mummy now daddy is gone and think of me and that cowboy song." He concluded with bravado: "Pull yourself together and you will become a man."[13]

* * * *

John "Kenny" Collins, the Sleep-Prone Getaway Driver

Every heist needs a lookout man and getaway driver and that task fell to Kenny Collins, an old prison mate of Reader and a break-in expert from Islington who sold tickets for football games and imported contraband fireworks and Russian cigarettes. His Staffordshire terrier, Dempsey, was never far behind him.

Burly with a florid complexion, Collins was an incorrigible blabbermouth; he was also going deaf and becoming increasingly forgetful. His sluggishness and inability to fend off the need to snooze would later prove a handicap.

Kevin Lane, a former boxer and bouncer who spent eighteen years in prison on murder charges, met Collins at Belmarsh Prison, a maximum security prison in southeast London. At the time, Collins was in jail for fabricating passports. Lane recalled Collins as a resilient and stocky character who was not easily phased, even when he was confronted with being "locked up with a couple of assholes," including a six-foot-seven-inch "geezer" who was threatening him.

When Collins told Lane about his tormentor, Lane said he offered to help. "I was 27, and he was a squat 50-year-old man. So I said to him, 'I'll sort them out.' I was the tough guy. You know what happened?" He added, "Kenny wrapped up the geezer no problem. He beat him up. He's a sturdy little fellow."

According to Lane, Collins was a family man, who had been married twice and had a grown son with Down syndrome from his first marriage, whom he adored. Apparently his son liked to drink and Collins, rather than reproaching him or coddling him, "used to let him drink two or three cans. He was a good father, who cared about his family."[14]

Danny Jones and the others liked to mock Collins for not being all that bright—Jones described him as a "wombat-thick old cunt." But the truth was that Collins was no dummy. In fact, he was a successful criminal—more dodgy businessman than burglar, his friends say—who had made millions by scalping sports tickets and selling stolen cigarettes. He lived well with his amiable and doting wife, Millie, in a leafy and posh part of Islington.

In 1975, Collins was arrested for handling stolen goods and received an eighteen-month sentence for stealing thirty-one dresses and two skirts. Another time he was arrested for trying to break into a shoe shop—a target that his friends Perkins and Jones found laughable. "He could not break into a shoe shop. The cunt doesn't know the price of anything!" Perkins once mocked him to Jones. "Fucking idiot, cunt."[15]

* * * *

Carl Wood, an Extra Pair of Hands

The least popular among the gang was Carl Wood, age fifty-eight, an unemployed and married father of two adult daughters. Lanky and strong but heavier on brawn than brains, he was to be an extra pair of hands during the heist. Wood, who had grown up in the poor neighborhood of Hackney, in east London, was mired in huge personal debts, living on welfare, and he needed money. He also suffered from Crohn's disease. He had become friendly with Danny Jones—both fanatical about fitness, they used to enjoy running together before Wood's illness became too debilitating.

With his receding brown hair, furrowed brow, and eye glasses, he looked like a librarian, albeit a menacing one. And indeed he could be a nasty piece of work. In 2002 he was sentenced to four years in prison for his involvement in an extortion racket with two corrupt cops. He had teamed up with them to help Robert Kean, a veteran criminal, recover £600,000 ($900,000) from a money launderer who owed him the money. The plan was to beat up the fellow and shove him into the trunk of a car. But undercover anticorruption police were secretly monitoring the operation and Kean and Wood were overheard saying that they planned to rough up the man and put his body in a car crusher if he didn't hand over the money.

"I'll just go smash, hit him straight in the head. I've got my blade. He ain't going home," Wood told Kean. "Don't worry about that." Surveillance equipment also picked Wood up boasting that he would "gouge out" the money-launderer's eyes and "shoot him in the kneecaps."[16]

More than two decades later, however, Wood was a shell of his former self. Married to his wife Paula for nineteen years, with two adult daughters, he suffered from Crohn's disease since he was twenty-four, and was afflicted with chronic fatigue, abdominal pain, diarrhea, and mouth sores. "It's like a mouthful of ulcers with a bottle of vinegar in your mouth," he would complain.[17] If that wasn't bad enough, he was also depressed, having accumulated £20,000 ($30,000) in debts. He would do odd DIY jobs but they weren't enough to scrape by, even with disability payments from the government. He needed money and he needed it quickly. Danny Jones would try to cheer him up by joining him for walks at a local garden center.

Jones appeared to feel sorry for him and recruited him even as he appeared to be skeptical of his old friend and his usefulness. He referred to him behind his back as a lunatic. When talking about Carl, "we say, 'you cunt,'" he would say to Perkins. A "fucking yellow cunt," Perkins would agree.[18]

*   *   *   *

Freddie Foreman, the Aging Heavy

In recruiting men for the job, toughness trumped age. Among those Perkins sought out was Freddie Foreman. A former enforcer for the Krays, the twins who had controlled swathes of east and west London, Foreman was eighty-two years old when Perkins came calling in 2014, he recalled.

Foreman said that in the summer of 2014, Perkins suddenly stopped by his son's pub, the Punchbowl, in the posh London neighborhood of Mayfair, ostensibly to recruit him for the heist. The two men missed each other, and it is not hard to see why Perkins would have thought of his old friend—he had been a ringleader during the daring Security Express robbery.

"Perkins came by as they were getting the Firm together to do some work, and he wanted me to join them. I hadn't seen him since Security Express. But we had broken bread together. We were mates," he said. "Of course, I would've gone."

Foreman recalled the Security Express job with no little pride. After overcoming one of the security guards when he went to get a bottle of milk at the entrance of the high-security building, Foreman tied him up, and forced him to sit at his desk near the safe to buzz the other guards in. To make sure he did as he was told, he added, he crouched under the desk and pointed a knife at his genitals.

"I held a knife at his balls," he recalled. "The other guards had to walk across a big space to get to the building where the safe was. It took eight hours for all of the guards to arrive and we had to be patient. The phone kept ringing and people were asking, 'Where the hell are you with the money?' which was needed to replenish cashiers across London. I picked up the phone and said the vans were having mechanical trouble."

When it was time to rob the safe at the company and none of the petrified guards produced the keys, Foreman said he put lighter fluid under one guard's nose and took out a match from a box of Swan Vestas. That spurred the guards to open the safe, their hands trembling with fear. The cash was then spirited into a van, before the gang sped away.

Foreman stressed that no one was injured or beaten up during the robbery. "That was a good job. We gave them tea, we gave them cigarettes. No one got hurt—they could massage their legs—and no one ended up in the hospital. They were just tied up and gagged. No one was hit over the head. That was a good job."

A squat man with dark darting eyes, a penchant for wearing gray jogging suits, and a fondness for red wine, Foreman grew up as one of five sons of a London black taxi driver and a housewife with Irish roots. His criminal career began in the 1940s at age sixteen when he lived in Battersea, in south London when he was recruited by a gang of female shoplifters known as the "Forty Thieves," who, dressed in specially tailored "bloomers" and hats sewn with hidden pockets, raided Harrods and shops on London's West End.

Following his shoplifting stint, he said he tried to do some honest jobs, working as a roofing scaffolder, as a porter at a cold storage facility for meat at Smithfield Market in east London, and trying a job on Southern Railway. But after holding up two people on their way to the bank to deposit money, Foreman said he was hooked by the thrill and the easy cash. Before long, he was as revered as he was feared in London's shadowy underworld.

As an associate of the Krays in the 1950s and 1960s, his job was to "clean up any messes" that arose in crimes that included robberies, arson, protection rackets, and murder. He also accumulated dozens of businesses including pubs, betting parlors, and casinos in both Britain and the United States. "There was sex, there were birds, there was money," Foreman recalled, adding, "I was a Mr. Fix it. The murder charges against me came from my time with the Krays."

During the Security Express robbery, he said the gang put on fake Irish accents and would refer to one another as Paddy, lest one of the guards remember their names. Perkins, he added, had been dependable and had not balked from conjuring the necessary menace to get the guards to open the safe.

Following the Security Express robbery in 1983, Foreman fled to Marbella, in southern Spain, where life in the Costa del Sol, or the "Costa del Crime" as it was known, was a welcome break from the pressures of the London criminal underworld. He and fellow Security Express robber Ronnie Knight, former husband of the actress Barbara Windsor, lived in Spain for more than a decade, soaking up the sun, sipping sangria, and "doing good business," before they returned to London to lengthy jail terms. Reader was there at the time, too.

Foreman's luxurious life in exile came to an abrupt end in 1990 after Ronnie Knight's wife photographed him and Knight at a wedding in Marbella, along with several other of the Security Express robbers. When the photo was leaked to the British tabloids, he said, it caused an enormous public outcry and pressure for his arrest. He was detained and taken to a police station in Marbella, where he demanded to see his lawyer. Instead, he said, he was "kidnapped" and spirited out of the country.

"I was punching and kicking, and the Spanish police say that my teeth marks are still on the door at the Spanish nick where they kept me," he recalled, referring to the jailhouse. "I remember seeing people sunning on the beach as I was being taken to the airport in a car and thinking that my life was about to change, that I was going back to face a terrible charge. I tried to smash my way out of the car, which was driving at 90 miles an hour. I remember the Gipsy Kings song 'Bambeleo' was playing on the car radio."

Back in London, he was never convicted for participating in the Security Express robbery, but he was jailed for nine years for handling stolen property. Prison had been miserable, and that explained why the gang, all thieves of a similar generation and no strangers to prison, were determined not to use force. "It was mental torture. I was only allowed to associate with six prisoners. There was barbed wire. When you had visitors, there were two screws on each side of the table. They used draconian methods, they treated us like rats in a cage."

He admitted that only a handful of people in Britain had the chops to pull off the heist Reader had in mind. "There aren't many who can do it. Young guys wouldn't do it. You need guys who are tried and tested, and who won't grass you out if you get arrested, people you have broken bread with." He added, "I admire them—they still had the bottle on their arseholes to do something like that at their age. You have to admire it," he said.[19]

Career criminals like Reader and the gang were always on the lookout for the "Big One"—robberies like the Great Train Robbery of 1963 that would forever remain in the history books.

* * * *

The Great Train Robbery:
Villains Idealized

As Reader and the gang began their preparations for hitting Hatton Garden, the Great Train Robbery—the granddaddy of every bold heist that came after it—served as both an affirmation of the romance and glory of the high-stakes heist as well as a cautionary tale about the perils of getting caught. Reader had a particular respect for the crime—if not its violent methods—as he had grown up in Bermondsey, southeast London, the area where several of the Great Train robbers—including Bruce Reynolds and Gordon Goody, two of its masterminds—used to hang out. In the 1950s he would run into them at the Chop House restaurant in Clerkenwell, a former working-class eatery for local tradesmen, where they liked to congregate. They had several friends in common. Reynolds would later boast that the Great Train Robbery was "my Sistine chapel."[20]

"For our generation, the Great Train Robbery was the one we all wanted to emulate and few have ever topped it," Freddie Foreman explained.[21]

Reader and his cohorts were young villains-in-training at the time of the Great Train Robbery, and thieves of their generation regarded it with a certain awe. Its elements of success and—perhaps, more importantly, its overwhelming gaffes—also offered up several lessons for pulling off a heist that Reader appears to have internalized as a young man: the need for grand ambition, the importance of the element of surprise, the consequences of using force, and the imperative of remaining under the radar if you wanted to avoid arrest. It also showed the British public's appetite for colorful villains who could be construed as working-class heroes, regardless of whether they were ruthless and motivated by greed.

The Great Train Robbery ringleader Bruce Reynolds, an armed

robber with a long rap sheet and a love of jazz, had wanted to become a journalist. He had worked in the accounting department of the *Daily Mail*, a tabloid newspaper—before he became bored and turned to petty crime. Nicknamed "Napoleon" by his fellow thieves because of his authority, he and his cohorts were pursued by a detective with another memorable name: Jack Slipper.[22]

"It was something I had been looking for all my life, the big one. As a career criminal, you reach a pinnacle and that was it," Reynolds recalled decades later, an old man using his infamy to raise money for charity to help fix a leaky roof. "Plus it had those elements of fantasy. I was brought up on Butch Cassidy and Jesse James. Other crimes have got their points, but for the audacity of it and the way it captured the public imagination it's up there."[23]

Inspired at least in part by the robberies of railways in the heyday of the American Wild West, Reynolds assembled a team to intercept a Royal Post Office train carrying millions of pounds in cash in Buckinghamshire, a county in southeast England. The robbery began on Thursday, August 8, 1963, when a gang of fifteen men wearing ski masks changed a signal to red before ambushing a traveling post office train that had left Glasgow Central Station at 6:50 p.m. the day before and was on its way to London's Euston Station, where it was scheduled to arrive at 3:59 in the morning.[24]

After boarding the train at around 3 a.m., a masked thief grabbed the train's driver Jack Mills from behind and soon men wielding clubs and pipes swarmed all over him.[25] Then they targeted the train's high-value packages carriage, grabbing about 120 bags of cash containing £2.6 million in used bank notes—equivalent to about £50 million (about $65 million) today.

The robbers then sped to their hideaway, Leatherslade Farm, a ramshackle farm about thirty miles from the scene of the crime. The men were so giddy after the robbery that they stopped to play a game of Monopoly, reportedly using real bank notes from the heist. It would prove a fatal error, as fingerprints left on the Monopoly board would later help lead police to the culprits. Money used in the Monopoly game by the gang later sold at auction for about £400 ($600) in 2015.[26]

It didn't take long before the Fleet Street media and the public at large were captivated by the sensational hit on one of the country's most dependable institutions—Her Majesty's Royal Post Office. The first member of the team to be arrested was Roger Cordrey, who was apprehended living with a friend above a flower shop in Bournemouth, a seaside resort on England's southern coast. The landlady, a policeman's widow, had become suspicious when her tenants paid three months of their rent in advance in ten-shilling notes. The rest were eventually apprehended and eleven of the men were each sentenced to between twenty and thirty years in prison.

At their sentencing, the judge, Justice Edmund Davies, keenly aware of the British public's fascination with the case and the idealization of the villains, sought to play up the violence of the crime and the toll it had exerted on Mr. Mills, the train's driver, who never recovered from his injuries and died six years later at the age of sixty-four of pneumonia.

"Let us clear out of the way any romantic notions of daredevilry," he told the court. "This is nothing less than a sordid crime of violence inspired by vast greed."[27]

Nevertheless, the culprits of the Great Train Robbery were celebrated as national folk heroes. It was a lesson that was, perhaps, not lost on Reader and his aging gang as they set out to outdo the Great Train Robbery.

Chapter 4

The Target

The Garden and the Criminal Underworld

LONG BEFORE READER AND HIS AGING COCONSPIRA-tors decided to pull off an improbable heist that would thrust "Hatton Garden" into headlines around the world, the area had occupied a special place in the popular imaginations of Londoners for centuries. To local jewelers, the street, which is also used synonymously as short-hand for the surrounding jewelry quarter, is known affectionately as "The Garden." The area was named after Sir Christopher Hatton, a handsome and debonair chancellor of the Exchequer, in the six-teenth century, who attained his post after he came to court to attend a masked ball, and Queen Elizabeth I admired his elegant dancing.[1]

The neighborhood hosted prosperous merchants in the eighteenth century, and later became popular with Jewish diamond traders who sometimes sold rough diamonds in local kosher restaurants. Today, more than fifty jewelry merchants and jewelers operate in the area, which borders the City of London, the capital's financial center. A magnet for intrigue, criminals, and law enforcement, Hatton Garden was the fictional setting where James Bond—in Ian Fleming's *Diamonds Are Forever*—trails diamond smugglers to the "neat white portals of the London Diamond Club."

At street level are dozens of jewelry shops, like New York City's

West 47th Street, many of them family owned and marked by kitsch neon signs offering discounts on gold wedding bands, diamond engagement rings, and watch repairs. For decades, coming to Hatton Garden to buy an engagement ring was a rite of passage for Londoners of a certain class, a place to win over a recalcitrant heart with a glittering diamond. Oasis's Liam Gallagher bought Patsy Kensit her wedding ring here.[2] The quarter also hosts the workshop of famed silversmiths Smith & Harris, who design Ascot trophies, rings based on sculptures by Anish Kapoor, and, perhaps most famously, a life-size eighteen-karat gold sculpture of the supermodel Kate Moss, called "Siren," that is thought to be the largest solid gold sculpture ever made.

In the Garden, the real wheeling and dealing takes place behind closed doors in gray Victorian buildings with labyrinths of small rooms that are off-limits to most casual customers, or on the bustling trading floor of the clubby London Diamond Bourse at 100 Hatton Garden.

Hidden London, which chronicles the streets and neighborhoods of the capital, notes that after the last Hatton descendant died in 1760, the area—with its handsome mansions and quiet streets—became a desirable place to live by the city's upper classes. But it has always lived in the shadow of the criminal underworld and its neighboring gritty streets became the backdrop for the petty crooks and miscreants of Charles Dickens's *Oliver Twist*, according to Rachel Lichtenstein, whose parents and grandfather worked in the district. Fagin resided in a slum near Hatton Garden next to the river, and Oliver was tried at a police court at 54 Hatton Garden after being falsely implicated in the theft of a handkerchief. (Dickens knew the Garden's streets intimately; at age fifteen, he did a stint as a clerk in a lawyer's office in Holborn in central London prior to becoming a writer.)[3]

During the Elizabethan era, Clerkenwell—the long-since gentrified commercial area of which Hatton Garden is a part—was outside the jurisdiction of the city's Puritanical rulers and consequently attracted, among other things, dilapidated tenement houses, beggars, brothels, and taverns. The area has such a rich history of criminality that in the eighteenth century there was a nearby prison where officers would tie prisoners to the railings and throw them in the River Fleet, where they would drown.[4] Hatton Garden also includes Ely Place, a sleepy street with its own gatehouse and beadles, which was privately owned by the bishops of Ely and part of the Diocese of Ely in Cambridgeshire, about sixty miles away. Despite its London location, it was a refuge for criminals over the centuries since it was not under the jurisdiction of London police. As a result, thieves fleeing robberies at Hatton Garden would sometimes hide out at Ye Olde Mitre, a tiny pub founded there in 1546 and all but hidden in a narrow passage, to escape detection and avoid arrest. London's Metropolitan Police would then have to ask the landlord's permission before they could enter and handcuff the wily villains.[5]

In *Diamond Street*, Lichtenstein describes Hatton Garden in the early part of the twentieth century as a mix of mercantile dynamism, criminality, and poverty. "There would be a setter in one room, a polisher in another, an engraver in another and if you opened a door sometimes a rat would run out."[6]

The district was long populated by so-called Frummers, orthodox Ashkenazi Jews, who learned the craft of diamond cutting in the shtetls of Eastern Europe. The first wave arrived in the nineteenth century, fleeing pogroms. Another wave brought their skills with them when they fled Hitler in the late 1930s and early 1940s, including Jewish jewelers from Antwerp, at the time the global center of the diamond trade, who fled Belgium after Nazi occupation in May 1940. Refugees from Antwerp, some of whom escaped with their precious gems by sewing the diamonds into the lining of their garments, set up the London Diamond Bourse in 1940 on Greville Street, inside a restaurant called Mrs. Cohen's Cafe. After 1945, an influx of Holocaust survivors arrived, swelling the Bourse's ranks, which eventually moved to several buildings on Hatton Garden, where it still resides today.[7]

Over time, the Jewish traders were joined by Indian diamond merchants, some of whom send their uncut diamonds to Gujarat, India, for cutting and polishing, and have used the economic advantage of lower labor costs to expand. Jewish cultural influence over the trade remains profound. When a diamond deal is completed, the two traders, whether Indian or Jewish or African, utter the word "*mazel*," or luck, to seal the deal. There is no paper, and no contract. It is a tight-knit community of jewelers, diamond traders, and watchmakers that operates on trust and where everyone knows one another.

This insularity and hypervigilance makes it a daunting challenge for a thief to snoop around unnoticed, and it influenced the decision by Reader and his cohorts to commit their crime over a long Easter weekend and in disguise. Even then, avoiding the prying eyes of the Garden's many yentas would prove elusive.

* * * *

Modern-Day Yentas

George Katz's jewelry shop E Katz & Co Ltd occupies the ground floor at 88–90 Hatton Garden, home of the safe deposit that Reader and his Firm planned to target. Katz & Co was founded by George's father Emiel, a jeweler, in 1947. A Czechoslovak Jew and refugee from Prague, Emiel fled the country in 1938, ahead of the Nazi occupation. He arrived in London penniless, with a few diamonds sewn into his clothes. His father quickly found work at Hatton Garden, working as an apprentice with another Jewish refugee. He sold the diamonds he had smuggled into Britain and used the proceeds to find a small apartment near Paddington, where George was born, and then he opened his shop.

George began to work in his father's shop in the 1960s when he was a teenager. The Garden teemed with immigrants, a majority of them Jews, who peddled their diamonds and precious stones from the tables of corner cafés or even on the street. He has been working in the shop for the past fifty years. Today, he said, concerns about security made selling precious gems on the street impossible.

"Hatton Garden back then was a big center for jewelry trade and people came from all over the United States and Europe to buy antique jewelry," he said. "Back then the dealing was very informal and everything was based on trust."

Because of the culture of trust, strangers, interlopers, or thieves were hard-pressed to remain invisible in an area where everyone knew everyone and where people liked to gossip like those old Jewish women in nineteenth-century Eastern European shtetls, known as yentas, who would keep tabs on the Jewish ghetto, matchmake, scold, kibitz, and report anything—or anyone—that appeared out of place.[8]

Jacob Meghnagi, thirty-nine, an Italian Jew with dual Israeli and British citizenship, has worked in the Garden for more than a decade, and exudes the swagger of someone who seems to know everyone in the Garden. With a buzz cut, leather jacket, yarmulke perched on his head, and a noticeable gift of gab, the father of six divides his time between London and Tel Aviv.

Every day, he said, he sends tens of thousands of pounds worth of gems in sealed envelopes to clients on spec, with the implicit understanding that payment will be received in kind or the gems will be returned, if they aren't able to sell them. But he added, unsold gems are always sent back; not doing so in the Garden means professional suicide.

"All we have in the Garden is words and trust. Everyone knows everyone, and everyone talks. Everyone borrows from one another. It is a very small village," he said. "You can have the same query for a stone from four different people, and then realize they're calling on behalf of the same person. The street is small. If someone is stung, it will soon make its rounds around the street. There is an expression here, 'If you sting once, you don't do it again, 'cause no one will ever do business with you again.'"[9]

* * * *

The Hatton Garden Safe Deposit Company

As the Jewish community prospered, many of the diamond traders moved to enclaves in north London such as Golders Green and Hendon—suburban, tree-lined neighborhoods where they could raise families away from the commercial center. In the absence of a safe place to store their diamonds, many dealers would take their goods home with them in their long black coats.

After several jewelers were robbed on their way home from Hatton Garden in the 1940s, demand grew for the creation of a safe deposit in the area where jewelers could leave their gems and cash before going home for the day. The origins of the Hatton Garden vault can be traced to 1948 when a local jeweler, George Edward Gordon, who had a business at 88–90 Hatton Garden, realized that his fellow jewelers felt jittery about the threat of being attacked when they walked on the streets with their gems.

Safekeeping has a history going back centuries. But remarkably— given the hundreds of millions of pounds worth of gems circulating at Hatton Garden, there was, until the 1950s, no safe deposit there. After Gordon realized the gap in the market, he spent nearly £20,000— the equivalent of roughly $630,000 today—to build his vault, which included a thick, seemingly impenetrable door that its owner boasted was resistant to both bombs and burglars.[10]

George Katz recalled that when the safe opened its doors in

1956, dozens of jewelers, many of them Holocaust survivors, lined up to rent a box.[11] People who had been very reluctant to part with their assets and livelihoods suddenly had a trusted place they could store them.

Nevertheless, Hatton Garden's jewelers were an easy target, and some insisted on keeping their gems on them at all times. On February 28, 1978, Hatton Garden diamond trader Leo Grunhut was suddenly attacked by two men with sawed-off shotguns and shot in the back outside his home in Golders Green as he tried to flee. He was carrying more than £250,000 (about $487,000) in diamonds. He died three weeks later, and for twelve years his murderer's identity remained a mystery until the Flying Squad, an elite unit of Scotland Yard that investigates commercial burglaries, arrested a sixty-one-year-old man named John Hilton in 1990 in a botched jewelry heist and he confessed to the killing.[12] Grunhut's murder only added luster to the mystique—and necessity—of the Hatton Garden vault.

But the security at the Hatton Garden Safe Deposit Company had hardly changed since the 1940s, beyond the addition of intruder alarms and CCTV cameras.[13] If members wanted to visit their box, one of the security guards would allow them in past two locked sliding gates. Once inside, a second security guard would log their visit in a book and escort them to their box, secured by a ten-ton door custom-made by Chubb. The door has two combination locks and two key locks. Two keys were required for box holders to get to their safe deposit boxes, and the keys would need to be turned clockwise simultaneously. Each box holder had his own key and the safe deposit guard kept the other master key. Even to this day, no thief has ever infiltrated the ten-ton door.[14]

But the Garden has long been a target for wily criminals and the scene of countless crimes, including sensational armed robberies.

As much as the vendors in Hatton Gardens would like to see

themselves as a close-knit community of honest, trustworthy businesspeople, the Garden has hardly been immune to nefarious practices or criminal interlopers.

Roy Ramm, a former head of the Flying Squad, who was once one of Europe's most renowned hostage negotiators and now works as a security consultant, recalled that the Garden was always awash with "*shvartz* money," or "black money," in Yiddish. "It is a pretty incestuous market. There are some very honest, very decent businesspeople. But there are also dubious businesses. There are some heavy duty Israeli organized crime there. It is difficult for honest people to operate there and not be ensnared by it."[15]

For decades, members of the criminal fraternity liked to hold court at 12 Greville Street, off Hatton Garden, a bustling Jewish restaurant called Nosherie, that served heaping plates of potato latkes, which doubled as a discreet venue for diamond trades and hosted an unlikely mix of Orthodox Jewish diamond traders, petty criminals, Italian mobsters, and local ladies who lunch. Among them was Brian Reader, who, according to law enforcement officials and veteran British crime reporters, was a regular at the Nosherie throughout the 1970s and 1980s.

* * * *

The Garden of Villains

The Garden also has not been immune to violence. In late December 1778, in what was dubbed "The great robbery of Hatton Garden," a gang of twenty thieves stormed a house on the street after pointing a pistol at the occupants. In a fate that has ensnared many a Hatton Garden thief, they were arrested two days later after trying to resell the goods they had stolen.[16]

Paul Lashmar, a veteran investigative crime reporter, spent decades investigating the Garden's hidden underworld. Stolen jewelry flowed so freely through the Garden that in 1994, he observed that several items filched from Prince Charles at St. James's Palace in Kensington ended up there. According to Lashmar, the jeweler who acquired the royal booty, Geoffrey Mann, thirty-nine, said he had bought the four pairs of cuff links and a tiepin within a few hours of the burglary, without realizing their origins.[17] When he saw the items in a newspaper, he called the police, and they were returned to a thankful prince. The jeweler had paid £450 ($675) for £10,000 ($15,000) in stolen goods.[18]

Thieves of every stripe had long been drawn to Hatton Garden's shadowy underbelly. In 1993 burglars armed with pistols and concealed by face masks stole jewels valued at £7 million ($10 million) from Graff's workshop, the biggest jeweler theft at the time.[19] But there have been dozens of other burglaries in the area.

Most memorably, in 2003, the Garden was reeling for months after a six-foot-four-inch man in his fifties, disguised as an Orthodox Jew, stole at least at least £1.5 million ($2.4 million) worth of diamonds from the safe deposit box at 88–90 Hatton Garden, which Reader and his men were targeting.

The man, who variously called himself Philip Goldberg, Luis Ruben, or Ruben Luis, was dressed in a dark suit and tie. He had spent months ingratiating himself into the community, opening a shop, trading diamonds, and winning the trust of his fellow dealers. He would frequently travel to and from 88–90 Hatton Garden to the basement safe deposit where he had rented four boxes in different parts of the vault, an apparent pretext to case out the place, and a similar modus operandi that police believe the gang of aging Hatton Garden thieves likely used.

One Saturday morning, while other Hatton Garden dealers were in synagogue for the Sabbath and the area was deserted, the man disappeared down the staircase to the safe deposit. It was only on the following Monday that a customer noticed that his box had been glued shut; the jewelry and gold inside had disappeared without a trace, along with the mysterious man. He was caught on CCTV cameras, entering the safe deposit with a black bag, but was never arrested. By the time the police saw the footage, he had fled.

Subsequent conspiracy theories swirled around the Garden, including whether the thief had used hypnosis to pry the jewels away. A gemologist at the time told the *Guardian* that the Garden had been shocked to the core by the burglary. "If he could get away with it in the safety deposit no lock in the world is safe," she said.[20]

For decades, there had been a special crime squad in Scotland Yard deployed to police the area, but in recent years, specialized policing in Hatton Garden has been cut back as national crime-fighting budgets have been squeezed. Many of the jewelers today rely on private security firms that began to appear in the late 1990s. Burly men from Eastern Europe with thick necks and menacing glares can be seen on patrol. As a result, the area has not suffered the proliferation of smash-and-grab jeweler heists that have become commonplace from Paris to Tokyo.

Meghnagi, the young jeweler, said, "You see them hanging out on corners, Eastern Europeans, Romanians, who look like wrestlers, not people you want to mess around with."[21]

The area that once hosted down-and-out ale houses as well as dozens of brothels has given way to modernist lofts housing Internet start-ups, media companies, and dozens of architectural firms, including the nearby offices of the late British-Iraqi architect Zaha Hadid. Between the changing demographics of the neighborhood and the private security, most of the jewelers thought that the days of the big-time heists were over.

They would soon discover they were wrong.

Chapter 5

The Firm Plots

Pubbing, Drilling, Planning

If Tony Soprano, the fictional New Jersey mobster, had lived in London, there is a good chance he would have felt at home in Enfield, an area about ten miles northeast of London that has hosted its fair share of thieves and gangsters and is known for its beer-fueled aspirational working class and its population of temperamental poltergeists. It was also the neighborhood where much of the Hatton Garden heist first took root.

Tree-lined with parks, churches, and pubs with names like The Moon Under Water, handsome middle-class homes, and drab government-subsidized housing, Enfield has a mix of tradesmen and teachers, Polish and Turkish grocery stores, the world's first ATM machine,[1] a large Victorian cemetery, and more than a few well-heeled gangsters and career criminals. It has also been the long-time home of Terry Perkins and Danny Jones.

Jones, the acrobat with a penchant for bodily contortion, resided for years in a sprawling gated house at No. 115 on Enfield's aptly named Park Avenue. It was a fitting venue for a professional thief with out-sized ambitions—the animal skin rugs and the modernist art conveying the swagger of a man whose ego could never be contained by a prison cell. The ostentatiousness of the house also inevitably raised the question: How did he pay for it?

Far less flamboyant than Jones, Perkins lived in Enfield with his wife Jacqueline. Terri, one of his four grown daughters, lived about ten minutes away. Perkins's gray house on nondescript 6 Heene Road was far more modest and discreet than Jones's large pile, befitting the understated character of someone used to confined spaces. Small and unremarkable, it was adorned with shabby and outmoded black vinyl chairs in the living room, a faux antique clock on the fireplace, old-fashioned black and white tiles in the kitchen, and kitsch brown and orange floral carpeting on the stairs. A red and yellow child's toy car was perched on a radiator next to a small dining table. A ladder on the second floor led to a messy attic full of plastic bags.

Only a few blocks away was a plumbing workshop located in a Dickensian-era nineteenth-century shelter for sheep that was owned by Hugh Doyle, a loquacious Irish plumber, an old friend of Collins's. It was ideal for those seeking a place away from prying eyes. His large house, not far from that of Perkins, is worth close to £1 million ($1.5 million), perhaps not that surprising for a friendly hustler who was constantly drumming up business, not only to support his wife and young children but also to entertain his love of yachting and flying planes. Glowing reviews on the website of his plumbing firm Associated Response laud his jovial manner in dealing with elderly ladies despondent about their dodgy boilers. "Such a good egg!" one gushes.

On any given Saturday, the pubs slowly fill up with men wearing Enfield Town Football Club soccer shirts. Local residents walk their dogs in front of small identical semidetached row houses. Those striving English suburbanites from the 1950s and 1960s who came in search of a suburban escape from the city have been joined by Polish, Turkish, Cypriot, and South Asian immigrants.

Residents are quick to tell you that Enfield has more than a few claims to fame, beyond hosting several of the Hatton Garden Firm. The Lee-Enfield rifle manufactured in the area was standard issue for the British Army until 1957. The world's first solid-state circuitry color televisions were also made here, along with the world's first mass-produced dishwasher. The Barclays Bank branch in Enfield was the first place in the world to have an ATM or cash machine, still marked by an English Heritage blue plaque.

If Britons know Enfield, if they know it at all, it is because of the small house at 284 Green Street where an eleven-year-old girl called Janet Hodgson, who spoke with the raspy male voice of a dead neighbor, came to national attention in August 1977. Her mother, Peggy, called the police after two of her children claimed that furniture was moving on its own, and neighbors heard knocking sounds coming from the house.

Soon, policemen, psychics, experts in the occult, and hardened reporters all descended on Enfield to investigate rumors that demonic voices were emanating from the house. Some wondered whether the children were pranksters or acting out (Peggy was spotted by a psychic researcher banging a broomstick at the ceiling). More than thirty years later, locals still dispute whether the Hogdson family was really possessed or whether the whole affair was a hoax.

Behind the Wheatsheaf pub, next to Enfield's main train station, is the parking lot and sheep shed where Hugh Doyle has his plumbing workshop. In the years leading up to the heist, Hugh gave Collins a key to the shed, which Collins kept on a key chain, along with the keys to his white Mercedes. Toward the end of 2014, neighbors of the pub said they heard strange sounds coming from the shed. This was no poltergeist, but, rather, the sounds of a power drill boring through concrete.

Once the gang had set its eyes on 88–90 Hatton Garden, figuring out how to breach the twenty inches of reinforced concrete separating the vault from the safe deposit cabinet remained perhaps the biggest challenge. Neighbors recalled seeing a small group of graying men going in and out of the sheep shed next to the Wheatsheaf, and then hearing loud drilling at all hours of the day and night.

While infiltrating seemingly impenetrable bank vaults has long been the stuff of Hollywood capers, real-life heists at bank vaults are a rarity. The brute force, dexterity, and know-how required to out-smart modern-day technology—including motion-triggered alarms, heat sensors, and vaults that open only with timers—has stumped even the wiliest thief.

In the United States, bank vaults emerged during the Gold Rush in the nineteenth century, when gun-slinging criminals began to hold up banks, perhaps mindful that it was less arduous than digging in the ground for gold. Banks responded by building ever larger safes and by the 1920s, many had constructed hulking vaults, with thick walls embedded in concrete.

By World War II, bank vaults had become so indestructible that two Mosler bank vaults at the Teikoku Bank in Hiroshima sur-vived after a nuclear bomb was dropped on the city in August 1945, despite the vault doors being severely damaged.[2] Fort Knox in Ken-tucky, which houses a good chunk of the United States' official gold reserves, is protected by, among other things, a twenty-two-ton vault door and four-foot-thick granite walls held together by 750 tons of reinforced steel.

Of course, clever bank robbers have sought to outmaneuver such constraints by, among other things, using explosives to blast through safes, drilling holes through combination locks, threatening bank staff with force, or, as was the case during the Baker Street caper of 1971, tunneling underground into the vault.

As thieves have become more determined and creative, vaults have been built underground or even under mountains, such as the Svalbard Global Seed Vault on the Norwegian island of Spitsber-gen, which was bored into the middle of a frozen, snow-covered arctic mountain to conserve a variety of plant seeds for genetic research and posterity.[3] As faith in bank vault security expanded, so too has the range of valuables held in vaults, from priceless diamonds and art works to Colonel Sanders's secret recipe for producing Kentucky Fried Chicken, which is stored in a safe in Louisville, Kentucky, at the company's headquarters, and Edison's patent for the light bulb, which is stowed under Iron Mountain, in western Pennsylvania, two hundred feet below ground.

Vault technology has become so advanced that, by the time Reader and the Firm had decided to hit Hatton Garden Safe Deposit, bank robberies were increasingly rare. According to the British Banker's Association, there were 847 robberies in 1992. By 2011, there were 66. Nevertheless, in and around 2012, the Firm came to the conclusion that getting into the vault at 88–90 Hatton Garden was doable, if only they could find the right tool to outmaneuver the vault's door, by drilling through the wall instead.

The task for figuring out how to breach the vault's wall fell largely to Jones, a man with a penchant for macho power tools. He kept several in his flashy Enfield home in a chaotic-looking tool shed. Beginning in 2012, Jones spent hours trawling the Internet on his ThinkCentre desktop personal computer for tips on how to penetrate the reinforced concrete in the vault. After Jones spotted a group of construction workers wielding diamond-tipped drills while driving near a construction site close to his home, Google led him to YouTube videos showing how to use the Hilti DD350 drill, a powerful diamond-tipped tool that can penetrate seemingly impenetrable surfaces such as concrete or steel, and retails for £3,475 (about $5,210). Such was his determination that he even watched "How-to" drilling videos in Korean. He also made multiple Google searches for "CCTV cameras," "price of diamonds," "gold prices," "gold buyers," and "Hatton antiques," and surfed the websites of diamonds.com and cash4mygold.co.uk.

Noel Sainsbury, the owner of Archers Financial Services in Enfield, whose business is adjacent to Doyle's sheep shed, said he recalled that it was sometime in November 2014 that the walls first began to shake, and he suddenly heard drilling that would continue for increments of thirty minutes before stopping. He said that, around that time, Doyle also installed water pipes outside the shed. It seemed no coincidence given that operating a heavy-duty diamond-tipped drill of the type needed to bore through reinforced concrete required a nearby water source so that the drill could be periodically cooled, or it would stop working. "The drilling would start in fits and starts, but then suddenly stop," he said. "They would drill in 30-minute intervals. It was as if they didn't want to attract too much attention."

He said that toward the end of 2014 four men would appear outside the sheep shed before disappearing inside. They were dressed as maintenance workers from the water company and wearing hard hats that seemed designed to hide their faces. He had also seen the men take arms into the attic of the sheep shed, an odd observation given that the gang was intent on avoiding violence.

"It was the same fellows, they made out they didn't know each other, but it was obvious that they did. I was in and out all the time, but I did notice them, and I thought it was a bit odd," he recalled matter-of-factly. "They were practicing for the heist. I have no doubt about that."

∗　∗　∗　∗

The Gardener and Basil

In the three years leading up to Easter 2015, the Firm reached out to an old friend and longtime associate of Reader's, a master locksmith and talented gardener, who had known Reader for decades. This was the man who had introduced Reader to Basil, the Firm's lanky and enigmatic key and alarm man about twenty years earlier. Reader and Basil became like a father and son, albeit a father and son who squabbled frequently. In the months leading up to the caper, Reader recruited Basil for the heist.

Reader told the rest of the Firm very little about Basil, who was particularly adept at remaining underground and evading police and he revealed little about himself to the others. Basil, who is middle aged, was Reader's protégé. Yet the Firm's respect for Basil at times surpassed their esteem for Reader. He appeared to earn their admiration for the speed with which he acquired a key for 88–90 Hatton Garden and learned how to disable the safe deposit's state-of-the-art alarm system. He would later vanish.

Jones observed to Perkins that Basil was a far quicker study than Reader, the so-called Master, who had decades of experience breaking and entering. "Basil learned in fucking two months what he had learned in forty years," he said to Perkins in the spring of 2015.[4]

In order to determine when 88–90 Hatton Garden was deserted, Basil planted an audio-listening device at the entrance of the building over Easter weekend 2013. As a result, he confirmed that the building was unoccupied from Thursday until Tuesday over the long holiday weekend. While an unused building one year didn't guarantee that it would be unoccupied a year later, the Firm considered it a valuable indicator. Reader was risk averse, and if something felt not quite right, he would freeze the planning operation for several months, and tell the others to stop what they were doing, before resuming work.

Basil was also charged with figuring out how to get into 88–90 Hatton Garden and access the safe deposit. There were more than sixty businesses on the premises and dozens of contractors going in and out during the course of the year, each with a front door key. And it proved remarkably easy for Basil to get a copy of the key from an elderly man who worked in the building. Reader's former associate, the locksmith and gardener, requested anonymity in order to be able to speak freely. Wiry and fit, "the Gardener" has hypnotic blue eyes. He exudes the quiet confidence of someone who has a secret but knows he is untouchable.

He tends the gardens of his neighbors on the street and has the keys to their homes, which he keeps in a bowl in his kitchen. He is an expert in handling keys. But he can break into a place, with or without them. He was, after all, one of the best locksmiths in London—that is, if you were looking to get in somewhere you weren't supposed to be.

"All the people I know are crooks," he said, with a hearty chuckle. "I say it now but on this street, I'm a boy scout, they don't know my past. I've got half their fucking keys. If they knew, their toes would curl up."

His rap sheet ended decades ago. He is careful. He prefers to work alone. He was asked by the others to go on the Hatton Garden job but he politely declined, or maybe not so politely. In any case, he never does jobs people bring to him—he prefers to find his own bit of work. It's more secure. No leaks. No gossiping. No fighting the impulse to tell anyone else.

The Gardener doesn't like to talk about himself. But when he starts recalling the past, little details slip out. He once lived in the southwest of France, downing oysters and laying low. He has a grand-son whom he goes to watch play in soccer matches. But these days he prefers to stay at home.

He said being old makes you philosophical, perhaps, because death is not so far away. Unless, of course, you need money or crave a little action. Just as old people don't stop enjoying sex, career criminals don't lose their taste for crime. But these days, he prefers to be seden-tary. "I used to look at my mother and she didn't go out of the house. I used to think, 'Strange woman, you don't go out of the house.' But now I could stay at home and read for days and days and not see a soul," he explained. "When you get old you change, accepting you're going to go. You know I've sat down with old people and I've heard them say, 'Yeah, I've had enough, I'd be glad to go.' And I can see that mentality now because I am coming to that stage."

Like many a young man on the make, he moved to London, lured back there after his family had fled the capital during the Blitz. He and Reader have more than a little in common, including fathers who abandoned them when they were young. The two became "business partners" in the 1960s. But they fell out over money, until they were reunited about four years ago at the funeral of a friend, a fellow thief. He recalled the falling out as a "ridiculous thing."

Basil had grudging respect for Reader. He always got the job done, and he wasn't a snitch. His greatest skill was his boundless patience and lack of excitability. He had a sixth sense if Scotland Yard was getting close (or at least he used to) and would call off a job for a few months if he had the slightest inkling something was amiss, and then he'd wait it out until he was convinced it was safe. It was a cautiousness born of experience.

Once the gang of retirees had chosen Hatton Garden as their target, the Gardener said that Reader, bossy and determined, divided up the work for the "Firm." Several times a week for three years, the men schemed and gossiped at old-school pubs and cafés in Enfield and Islington, among them the Castle, the Wheatsheaf, the Moon Under Water, and the Narrowboat.

They especially liked the worn but dependable Scotti's Snack Bar, a café in Clerkenwell that is peppered by converted industrial factories and gastropubs and is a short walk to Hatton Garden. The café had resisted the gentrification of the surrounding area and served a proper cup of tea. Crisps, or potato chips, were piled high in a wicker basket near the cash register. The men, carrying old supermarket plastic bags or cradling their dogs (Jones's ever-present white-haired terrier, Rocket; Collins's beloved Dempsey, a Staffordshire bull terrier), would have long strategy sessions while sitting on white plastic chairs on the outdoor terrace.

The criminal ecosystem where the gang operated suited men of their age. They needed to juggle their criminality with other duties, such as buying one's wife's arthritis medication at the pharmacy or doting on their grandchildren. Other than Reader, who lived about ninety minutes away from central London by bus, Jones and Perkins lived a half-hour drive or so from Clerkenwell. Collins, the getaway driver and all-purpose fixer, lived just minutes away. So they combined plotting the biggest heist of the century with their fatherly and grandfatherly duties—walking their dogs, and avoiding arousing too much suspicion among their wives or partners.

Befitting criminals of the analog era, the Gardener said the crux of the planning for the burglary involved old-fashioned shoe-leather reconnaissance. Reader and his team spent hours staking out 88–90 Hatton Garden and the surrounding area.

Except for trusting Basil, Reader was deeply suspicious of the rest of the group—even Perkins, just a few years his junior. The Gardener said he was particularly worried about Jones, whose admirable physical stamina was offset by a mouth that blabbed like a leaky faucet, making him a potential liability for a crime that depended on discretion and avoiding police surveillance. Collins, too, while avuncular and sweet, had a tendency to overshare that Reader feared could mean trouble.

"When you take someone like that Jones or any other laborer, you don't let them out of your sight even for a minute, in case they do something stupid," the Gardener said. "It's like doing any physical laboring job, when you have a construction business and each morning you pick up laborers waiting on the street corner. You don't tell them anything. You just take them to do the work when you need to do it."

Nevertheless, the rest of the gang became involved in recruiting manpower for the heist, and as the ranks of those involved expanded,

Reader and Basil grew increasingly worried that their cover could be blown, or worse, that too many other thieves could want in on a cut of the action. Freddie Foreman, Perkins's former associate and the one-time enforcer for the Krays, said that old-school burglars across London had sniffed out that something big was afoot. "Everyone wanted in on the action."[5]

Some muscle was needed to carry the tools, wield the heavy diamond-tipped power drill, and transport the wheelie bins stuffed with gold. Among those who say they were approached at the beginning of 2015 was Kevin Lane, a brawny, talkative, square-jawed former boxer who had recently been released from eighteen years in prison after having been convicted for the murder of Robert Magill, a car dealer. To this day, he vehemently protests his innocence.

But having barely tasted freedom, he politely declined. He said he wasn't surprised; Collins had talked about hitting Hatton Garden for years. "You know, the gang had worked together before the Hatton Garden job and they had been very successful. Ya' know, they had struck gold before and you want to tap into that."

Collins told him that, while the men were plotting the heist, they had established several cardinal rules—chief among them was that there would be no violence, even as he noted that some officers of Scotland Yard were armed. "They are good men. They didn't want to hurt anyone. They give money to charity, they stand up for women, these are old school criminals," he said, adding, "they wouldn't hurt a flea."[6]

* * * *

Reconnaissance

Reader decided that only he, Collins, and Basil would stake out the exterior and interior of 88–90 Hatton Garden and conduct reconnaissance, mapping and memorizing the layout of the area around the vault, the locations of the CCTV cameras, the comings and goings of the security guards. Collins, the designated getaway driver, was meanwhile charged with observing the area around the building and coming up with a nearby outpost where he could act as lookout during the crime. He chose 25 Hatton Garden, a building opposite 88–90 Hatton Garden, which hosts Madison Diamond and Wedding Rings, its name emblazoned on a black awning next to the front door. The venue offers a clear view of the entire street and was ideal for the designated lookout man, providing, of course, he didn't fall asleep.

The timing of a heist of this magnitude was everything and here Reader's experience as a young man on the Baker Street robbery proved to be instructive. The Baker Street heist of 1971 had taken place over a weekend, when the area was quiet and banks were closed. Reader and the Firm similarly decided that the Hatton Garden heist should take place over a long holiday weekend, given that Hatton Garden would be deserted and local dealers would be depositing their precious gems for safekeeping over the holidays. The Baker Street job had also involved hours of grueling tunneling underground with cumbersome equipment, impressing on Reader the sheer strength and athleticism needed to break through walls. That meant putting up with the sometimes petulant fantasist Danny Jones, who was strong and agile, and could slither through a hole in the wall.

During the Baker Street job, the thieves had communicated by walkie-talkies. Reader decided that that same method would work even better for the Hatton Garden raid. Mobile phones could be easily traced. (Never mind that, at Baker Street, a neighbor overheard the thieves' walkie-talkie chitchat on a ham radio, eventually leading to their undoing.)[7]

Jones had the book *Forensics for Dummies* in his home and was aware that a single fingerprint left at the scene of the crime could be disastrous. The men also decided they would wear surgical gloves.

The gang may have been analog criminals, but they were sufficiently sophisticated forensically that they foresaw the necessity of avoiding leaving behind DNA evidence in the building.

In the three years before the burglary, Basil and other members of the Firm traveled to the building at least a dozen times, observing when the last person left. It was usually the workaholic Lionel Wiffen, a grumpily avuncular jeweler, who had toiled in the building for forty years and used the fire escape door to exit the premises from the back.

During their snooping around, Reader and his team also observed that the safe deposit was left unguarded during the week, after 6 p.m., when the two security guards, Kelvin Stockwell and Keefa Kamara, left after setting the alarm. Moreover, the building's elevator did not go to the basement where Hatton Garden Safe Deposit was located—a security precaution after the safe deposit had been targeted by an armed robber in the 1970s—but the elevator shaft led directly inside the vault area. If they could figure out a way to climb down the shaft and breach the alarm, then all that would be left would be to access the safe deposit cabinet by breaking through the wall with Danny Jones's power drill. The ten-ton door protecting the custom-made Chubb vault was deemed too resistant—and risky—to infiltrate.

Hatton Garden Safe Deposit was open five days a week, from 9 a.m. until just before 6 p.m., when it was locked up. Repeated snooping during the weekend also showed that on Fridays, Saturdays, and Sundays, the building was unguarded altogether and largely unoccupied. Many of the resident jewelers lived in north London neighborhoods like Hampstead, Muswell Hill, or Belsize Park and rarely came in on the weekends, except for a pesky jeweler or two such as Lionel Wiffen.

The surrounding area became something of a ghost town on the weekends, its usually bustling and ancient pubs largely depleted of the jewelers and their customers who patronized them during the week. Workmen for the local council did conduct weekend maintenance work, but their loud drilling would provide a welcome diversion.

Police also have a theory that, in the months leading up to the heist, Reader hired an old crony to pretend he was a local jeweler and rent a safe deposit box in the building, perhaps armed with a body camera, that would have enabled the gang to case out the vault's interior and help determine how to outsmart the various alarms and CCTVs. In any case, Reader had worked for more than a decade in and around Hatton Garden, and had criminal associates who had used the safe deposit. That would have allowed him to draw a map of the building's exterior and interior and to memorize the interior layout of the vault.

The techniques used by the gang to plan the burglary did not require technological prowess, but rather the need for patient observation, which was in no short supply among retired senior citizens. Craig Turner, the Flying Squad chief, noted that it wouldn't have been difficult for one of them to rent a safe deposit box in the building in order to be able to visualize the interior of the vault and realize that drilling through the concrete wall was a way to avoid having to breach the giant Chubb lock on the vault door.

"There was definitely a level of commitment and planning," he said. "Everything they achieved you could achieve by just walking around that building. If it was many years in the planning, imagine how many times they could've walked into that building without being detected. It wouldn't have been difficult to go in and say they wanted to hire a box and to do so under a bogus name, and have a look. If they went a week before, maybe people would remember them. But not if this was years in the planning." He added, "There is a long tradition in British criminal history of doing heists on long holiday weekends when there aren't that many people around."[8]

To this day, the outside of the building remains unguarded.

* * * *

Something Suspicious Is Afoot

Trim with short silvered hair, Lionel Wiffen has fingers blackened from years of polishing diamonds. It is an occupational hazard for Wiffen, who began an apprenticeship in Hatton Garden in 1957 at the age of fifteen and started his own company specializing in fine jewelry just six years later. He works at his cramped offices in the basement of 88–90 Hatton Garden, often seven days a week, his loyal and studious wife, Helen, the firm's bookkeeper, never far from his side.[9]

Among the five-dozen businesses at 88–90 Hatton Garden, Wiffen was often the first to arrive, at 7:30 a.m., and the last to leave, sometimes after 9 p.m. Occasionally, he arrived so early that the front door hadn't been unlocked yet by one of the security guards. The incessant blabbing and wheeling and dealing of some of the other diamond traders were not for him. He liked to get to the point.

While most of his business derived from selling diamond rings, he also restored antique jewels that had been in a family for generations. He spent about six months working on Kate Middleton's royal sapphire engagement ring, a point of pride. That the rich and famous were among his clients was proudly advertised on his website, though he was abidingly discreet. In private, he might boast that he once received an order from a store to supply a ring for Victoria and David Beckham, engraved with *D* followed by *V*.[10]

Most of the jewelers at 88–90 Hatton Garden enter through the front door to get to their offices, walking through the building's lobby, and then down a long staircase to the basement, where Wiffen's company Lionel J Wiffen Ltd Fine Jewellery, is located a few doors down from Hatton Garden Safe Deposit and its 999 deposit boxes, where he also rented a box. (There are only two other jewelry businesses in the basement.)

But Wiffen, a creature of habit, often preferred to access his office from the fire escape stairs, which were reached from the side entrance to the building on Greville Street, and led to a courtyard. It was a more discreet place for his clients to leave with their $10,000 diamond rings. As the main door of the building closed at 6 p.m., the back entrance was also more practical.[11] Seen from the street, the back entrance is nondescript and inconspicuous, and conceals the secretive world of diamond trading inside.

In the months leading up to the burglary in March 2015, Wiffen, a guarded man with sharp eyes and an acute sense of his surroundings—the product of decades of dealing with very dear gems—felt like he was being watched. He would see the same white van drive up and down Greville and then park outside. He also noticed a blue Citroën Saxo and a Land Rover. Someone appeared to be casing the building. He was sure something suspicious was going on.[12]

He had sensed that something was wrong as of January 2015 when he felt eyes on him as he was escorting customers outside of the building. "I have felt uneasy," he told police. "I have noticed vehicles watching me or the door. I may be paranoid. But in this industry we are very conscious of who is around us, and during this period I often felt that there were too many vehicles parked on Greville Street with people in them."

He wasn't the only one to become suspicious of people appearing to be staking out the building.

A few weeks before the burglary, Katya Lewis, who works for Deblinger Diamonds in the area, observed something odd at 88–90 Hatton Gardens. She was on her way to deliver some gems to L & R Josyfon Ltd on the third floor, and noticed that the elevator was taking an "extraordinarily long time."

Just as she was about to leave, about ten minutes after she pressed the button, the doors suddenly opened. There before her, she recalled, was a white-haired man, with sideburns, about sixty years old, six feet tall, dressed as a workman in blue overalls, a blue fleece, and carrying a ladder. He smiled apologetically, as the floor of the elevator was covered in power tools and there was nowhere for her to stand. She took the stairs instead.[13] The man she described bears an eerie resemblance to Terry Perkins, perhaps on a reconnaissance mission. But it seems doubtful that Reader, risk averse as he was, would have allowed Perkins to jeopardize their plans. Who was it?

Lewis would later tell police that she had felt impressed that someone of that age was still working and doing manual labor. "When I first saw this man, I thought, 'Wow he is doing well at his age to still be working,'" she said. "I looked at where he was standing and thought it must've been hard for him to get into the lift without someone loading the tools and stuff around him." She recalled he never spoke a word. As she walked down the stairs and left the building, she said she saw no other workmen. "I have never seen him before in the Hatton Garden," she said. The man, she added, just kept smiling.[14]

Chapter 6

The Heist

Pills, Fish and Chips, and Concrete

As reader was making his way to Hatton Garden on Thursday, April 2, 2015, just another anonymous senior citizen on a bus, the guards at 88–90 Hatton Garden, Kelvin Stockwell and Keefa Kamara, set the alarm, as they had every working day for the past twelve years, in the basement premises of the safety deposit. Stockwell was the last to leave, and he locked the safe deposit company's wooden front door. It was 6 p.m. This being a long holiday weekend, the two guards did not plan to return until Tuesday. Once the guards had left, the building's concierge, Carlos Cruse, locked the magnetic glass door at the entrance of the building and left through the front door, which closed behind him and locked automatically.

A relic of the 1940s, the security deposit was nevertheless trusted among Hatton Garden jewelers, many of them older Jewish men, who believed in its sturdy dependability. Like them, it had been in the quarter for decades, and the sight of jewelers traveling to and from the safe deposit, their precious diamonds hidden in small plastic bags in money belts or concealed in their underclothing, was a part of the rhythm of daily life in what was a modern-day shtetl and commercial center. Reader and his gang were preying on elderly men and women of their same generation, men and women who valued God over technology, and who thought nothing of leaving their precious valuables in a safe deposit that had barely been updated in decades.

By early Thursday evening, Reader reached the inconspicuous seven-floor building on the handsome, manicured street. A large plaque on the outside said HATTON GARDEN SAFE DEPOSIT LTD. The rest of his crew was already there: John "Kenny" Collins, Daniel Jones, Terrence Perkins, and Carl Wood. The men had arrived in Hatton Garden at 8:25 p.m. in a white Ford transit van driven by Collins.

A few minutes earlier, Collins parked the vehicle on Leather Lane, around the corner from 88–90 Hatton Garden, where Jones and his old mate Carl Wood exited. They cautiously walked around the building and around the block to conduct reconnaissance. After three years of planning, the moment had finally come. One wrong move and everything would unravel. One wrong move and the millions of pounds in jewels they had been fantasizing about for months would be out of reach.

Lionel Wiffen, the busybody jeweler whose office was in the back of the building, was still there, dealing with a customer, and the men returned to the van on Leather Lane and waited until 9:21 p.m. when Wiffen finally emerged, delayed by a last-minute phone call from his wife. Wiffen left from the fire escape door in the back of the building. For the gang, the wait must have felt like an eternity. They had been observing Wiffen for months and worried that the pesky workaholic could prove an obstacle. He always seemed to work late and had a perpetual look of suspicion on his creased face. The tension must have been palpable, though the men at this stage of the caper appeared to be confident.

Most of them were dressed as maintenance workers; Collins, the lookout man, wore casual clothing. Wood sported a dark shirt, a surgeon's mask, dark-colored gloves, a high-visibility fluorescent vest, a navy baseball cap, and his ever-present glasses. He was also carrying a black backpack. Jones, the extroverted narcissist among them, had opted for flashier heist attire: a hooded sweatshirt, trousers with bright blue vertical stripes, a high-visibility vest, a navy baseball cap, and bright red running shoes. His face was also obscured by a black mask. The men carried walkie-talkies.

Along his way to Hatton Garden, Reader had discarded his over-coat and was now wearing a yellow hard hat and fluorescent jacket with "Gas" written on the back. He wore brown shoes, distinctive striped socks, and a colorful scarf.

Perkins, a diabetic, had brought with him a three-day supply of insulin shots, apparently mindful that the Hatton Garden job could take days. They knew they could use Good Friday to their advantage. "Fucking 20 pills a day!" he would later tell the others. "If I don't take the insulin for three days," he said, "you'd a had to carry me out in a wheelie bin."[1] But Perkins had sought to downplay his illness. Acknowledging his frailty did not appear to be in his character, and, judging by his reticence, he didn't want the others to worry that he could be a liability if he fell ill during an operation that required both nerve and stamina, the former of which he possessed in abundance, even if the latter was waning.

Basil walked casually down Greville Street and entered through the front of the building, having acquired a key from an elderly tenant there. The immediate area near 88–90 Hatton Garden was largely deserted. But as he walked, a black taxi with its lights drove by. There were also people from the neighborhood walking their dogs. It was nightime and nearby pubs were busier than usual with denizens eager to begin taking advantage of the long holiday weekend.

All residents had a key to the front door, which was fitted with a mortise night latch that could not be jimmied by a credit card. Even if Basil hadn't managed to acquire a key, he would've noted that there was a mail slot immediately next to the front door and that a nimble intruder could access the door's inside handle by putting his or her hand through the slot. Inside there was a glass door with a four-digit coded lock, which police say was opened with the correct combination of numbers. Basil, it seemed, had insider information.

After hours, the basement premises at 88–90 Hatton Garden, where the safe deposit was located, were reachable through a fire escape door accessible on Greville Street, adjacent to the main building. A locked gate on Greville leads to about twenty stairs that descend to a courtyard at the end of which is a door leading to the basement businesses, including the safe deposit. Only a handful of people had a key, including Lionel Wiffen.

Once inside the building, Basil observed a small, dimly lit and worn-looking lobby with beige-colored marble walls, and a list of the companies on the premises on a wall next to the elevator: among them E Katz & Co Ltd, Savvy+Sand, Hattons Antiques, Vicky Gems, and Hatton Garden Safe Deposit, next to which was written "Basement." From inside the building's main lobby, a flight of stairs led to the basement and the safe deposit company. Access to the flight of stairs after hours required a key to another door. Only a select few—including the building's caretaker, the safe deposit's two security guards, and two cleaners—had one. There was no visitor's book recording people coming in and out of the building. But there were eight doors between the front door of 88–90 Hatton Garden and the fortresslike high-security vault. Getting past all eight, with the risk of triggering the alarm at any moment, would have made even the most experienced burglar jittery. Basil descended the interior staircase leading to the basement and then opened the fire escape door—pulling back the two bolts on the basement door—to let the others in.

He carried a large black bag slung over his shoulder, apparently designed to obstruct his face from the CCTV cameras. He had the codes to the interior doors of the building and it was his role to disable the alarm.

With the Greville Street entrance now open, Collins slowly drove the van to the gate leading to the fire escape and let the men out. Jones and Wood carefully exited and unloaded bags, tools, metal joists, and two plastic trash cans with wheels, which they took into the building, walking through the basement door. The trash cans were full of tools for the job and were heavy. But a younger strongman was conspicuously missing among their ranks. Age and wisdom would need to trump brawn and bluster.

The men had turned off their mobile phones and communicated only by walkie-talkie (Reader, the proud Luddite among the gang, didn't have to bother turning off his cell phone since he didn't own one).

Collins, dressed in a green quilted jacket with buttons down the front and a flat cabbie's cap and carrying a brown briefcase, walked purposefully toward his position in the office building, his arm swinging back and forth as if to propel him forward. As he did, cars and pedestrians passed by, underscoring the brazenness of the men beginning the crime on a busy Thursday evening, even if the immediate area around Hatton Garden was relatively quiet. He entered through the front door at 25 Hatton Garden, on the other side of the street, which housed Madison Jewellers. How he had a key remains unclear. But once inside, he had a bird's-eye view of both doors to 88–90 Hatton Garden, assuming, of course, his tendency to fall asleep on the job didn't interfere.

Once inside 88–90 Hatton Garden, the gang called the elevator to the second floor and disabled it, ripping off the elevator door's sensor so that it remained open. They left an OUT OF ORDER sign next to the elevator on the first floor, taping it on the left side of the elevator over the down button. Then, in an adrenaline-fueled feat of athleticism that defied diabetes, arthritis, and bladder-control problems, members of the crew climbed about twelve feet down the elevator shaft from the lobby toward the basement. They had removed the metal barrier that had been installed in the 1970s after an armed robbery in the building. Prior to the burglary, the Firm had learned that the elevator didn't go to the basement since a man with a shotgun had tried to enter the vault some forty-five years earlier.

After they landed in the basement with a slight thump, Basil cut a gray telephone cable jutting out of an alarm box, as well as the GPS aerial and the wires of an electrical box. The men used a hammer to break off the lock to the exterior wooden door. So far, so good.

It took another forty-five minutes to bring the rest of their tools— including the essential diamond-tipped power drill that weighed seventy-seven pounds—down the elevator shaft by rope. They moved slowly.

To get to the vault required getting past two sliding iron gates. The first one could usually be opened from the outside by entering a four-digit code on a pin-code box (or by a foot switch manned during the day by a security guard). The second gate was locked manually with a key. The gang reasoned that once they had deactivated the alarm, cutting through the iron gates was just a matter of brute force—and power tools.

At around midnight, as Friday dawned, the gang opened the outer iron gate, which they had disabled when they cut the wires. It would take several more hours to cut through the second iron gate.

Between the two gates was a small office containing CCTV recording equipment where the security guards could monitor five cameras—two inside the vault, two outside, and a fifth pointed at the safe deposit's front door. The office appeared dated, and sparsely outfitted with worn furniture and a Union Jack flag. Another CCTV camera belonging to a jewelry company called Berganza Ltd— triggered by movement—was aimed at the fire exit leading to the premises from Greville Street. Basil was charged with smashing all of the building's CCTV cameras—which he thought he did. After getting past the gate, Basil removed the CCTV hard drive and began to destroy the other cameras with a hammer.

The 999 safe deposit boxes in the basement safe deposit were pro-

tected behind the Chubb vault. After entering the safe deposit company's entrance, a person had sixty seconds to deactivate the intruder
alarm by entering a five-digit code—1930Y—on an alarm box. Basil,
who was schooled in electronics and alarms, had figured out how to
disable the alarm just a few weeks before the break-in, according to a
person familiar with the planning of the burglary.

When the men were finally ensconced in the vault, they didn't
waste any time and began the long and arduous task of drilling
through the vault's wall, which was twenty inches of reinforced concrete. Jones, who had spent months watching hours of video footage
on YouTube to know how to handle it, was the main driller, helped
by Basil. Jones would later recall the responsibility bestowed upon
him with a mix of bravado and exuberance. But Reader must have
known from his experience tunneling underground toward a vault
during the Baker Street burglary that they were a long way from
accomplishing their goal.

The Hilti DD350 power drill, which cost £3,475 ($5,210) can rotate
667 times per minute in its highest gear. But even Jones struggled as
the hours elapsed. The drill was so cumbersome it had to be anchored
to the floor. Jones and Basil took turns aiming it at the wall. The
air was thick with smoke as the cement flew everywhere with each
thrust of the drill, and produced a loud humming sound. So loud, in
fact, that several neighbors next to the safe deposit said they heard the
commotion. But it was the gang's good fortune that the area had been
under construction during the previous several months, and Cross-
rail, a £15 billion ($22.5 billion) project to build a high-capacity, high-
frequency railway line for London and the southeast, had sent out
letters to local residents warning them about upcoming construction.
No one thought anything was amiss.

Reader was the commander, and he and the Firm would have calculated how long it would take before the sun rose and they had to
flee. Each passing hour brought with it the risk of getting caught. But

Jones's and Perkins's later boasting suggests that they had been running on pure adrenaline, barely able to conceal their excitement that
they were back in the game. They were giddy at the recollection of
the slowly widening hole. Perkins and Jones were urging each other
on, no doubt determined not to let Reader's grumpy mood undermine
their high spirits. The gang allowed themselves periodic bathroom
breaks; at one point Collins escaped from his lookout perch across the
street to buy fish and chips.[2]

As Jones wielded the drill and he and Basil struggled to breach
the reinforced concrete, Perkins would later recall that he had taken
a seat in the safe deposit, away from the others, at some points taking
a break to inject a shot of insulin. He also suffered from heart problems; the stress of the job was intense.

The neighborhood outside was eerily quiet because it was the
holiday weekend, but the area's private security guards and the local
Camden police were on duty. Across the street, the getaway driver
and lookout man, Collins, was fast asleep, snoring. Perkins pressed a
button on his walkie-talkie and called out to him. No answer. At one
point, Basil had to interrupt the burglary, walk across the street, and
wake up Collins.

But the gang had bigger problems to worry about besides Collins's
propensity for napping.

Shortly after 12:21 a.m. on April 3, Alok Bavishi, whose family
owns the safe deposit company, received a call that the intruder alarm
had been triggered. The alarm managed to send a text message to the
Southern Monitoring Services alarm company, which in turn notified the police. Bavishi was told that police were on the scene, giving
him a false sense of security; in fact, the police had not come. Bavishi's concerns were also tempered by the fact that a previous alarm
had been triggered by an insect. But he still called Keefa Raymond
Kamara, one of the guards, who said he couldn't come as the trains

had stopped running and he didn't have a car. Then he called Stockwell, his other trusted security guard, but the call went to voice mail.

He kept trying, and finally reached Stockwell, who agreed to go to the safe deposit to see what was happening. Stockwell arrived nearly an hour later by car at 1:15 a.m., just barely missing Carl Wood, who would later be seen on a CCTV camera at 12:51 a.m. at the top of the basement stairs, before he went down to rejoin the others. Stockwell's arrival also went unnoticed by the gang since Collins was blissfully asleep. After three years of meticulous planning, and more than five hours inside the claustrophobic safe deposit, the men were enticingly close to the shimmering jewels they had been coveting. They had braved fear and anxiety, CCTV cameras and high-security alarms, and a heavy power drill that would've challenged some men half their age. Now, they were just moments away from being discovered.

Alok Bavishi was initially so nonchalant that he decided not to accompany Stockwell. But he then changed his mind since Stockwell was by himself. After examining the front door and peering through the mail slot of the fire escape door, Stockwell called Bavishi, who by then was only five minutes away, to say it was a "false alarm."

"It's all locked up," he told him; the main door of the building and the fire escape door exit were locked, so there was no reason for Bavishi to come. There were no signs of forced entry, so Stockwell decided that the building was secure. If he was bewildered as to why there were no police at the scene, he didn't show it. Perhaps the lack of police response had reinforced the impression that there had been a technical glitch, and there was nothing to worry about. He left without going inside, and both men returned home.

Notified of the alarm, the police decided not to respond, as "a grade was applied to the call that meant that no police response was deemed to be required," according to Scotland Yard. They would later issue the statement that the "call-handling system and procedures for working with the alarm-monitoring companies were not followed."

All the while, Jones continued to wield the drill, oblivious that the security guard was only feet away, outside the vault. Oblivious to the fact that the alarm had been triggered and that their plan was perilously close to being undone, they continued to bore three adjoining circular holes through the vault's thick wall. The men had brought jugs of water because, as they knew from their prior practice with the technology, the drill periodically needed to be doused with a coolant to keep it from overheating.

After several hours of drilling, Jones was getting tired. Perkins and Reader, the consummate professionals, were adept at keeping their emotions in check. Basil was also proficient at maintaining a professional distance. But Wood paced in circles with nervous anticipation.

"Carl, do something for fuck sake!" Perkins scolded Wood, whom the others regarded with barely concealed contempt. By then the men had been in the vault nearly six hours. Despondency and fatigue had begun to set in. Nevertheless, Perkins and Jones continued to egg each other on as Jones pushed the drill through the wall.

After hours of exhausting work, they had finally managed to drill three holes, twenty inches deep through reinforced concrete. It was the moment they had all been waiting for. They were just inches away from the jewels, inches away from their audacious goal.

Except there was an obstruction.

It took a few seconds for them to figure it out, but the metal cabinet holding the safe deposit boxes, on the other side of the concrete wall, was bolted to the floor. Their moment of glee quickly disintegrated into disbelief. What could they do? If they drilled through the cabinet, it might destroy the very jewels and valuables they had come to steal. In any case, the cabinet wouldn't budge. They tried to use the ten-ton hydraulic ram they had brought with them to push it over. They hadn't anticipated the cabinet being locked into place.

"Smash that up!" Jones commanded. "Smash that up! Smash that up!" as Jones pumped the ram with the aim of pushing over the cabinet.

But the pump "pinged back," Perkins would later recall, and Jones fell to the floor with a thump. Jones and Perkins then secured the pump to the floor. But it was no use. As Perkins and Jones tried to push over the cabinet with the ram, the ram wouldn't remain in place, and then shattered into dozens of pieces.[3]

They had broken into a secure location, shimmied down an elevator shaft, disengaged the alarm system, and drilled through concrete—and they were nowhere. The jewels were just inches away but remained out of reach. There was nothing that could be done. Their frustration was intense, only slightly tempered, perhaps, by exhaustion and the resignation of aging criminals who were no strangers to stubbornly impregnable vaults that had eventually yielded to brute force and even more brute human will. But for now, their three years of planning had come to nothing. Reader, the "Master," had proven anything but. Age appeared to have caught up with them.

The men lugged the heavy equipment back through the back passage to the fire escape door near the back of the building on Greville Street. Meanwhile, Collins, newly refreshed from his nap, left his hideout at 25 Hatton Garden and walked cautiously though determinedly toward the white van, parked on nearby Leather Lane. He was carrying his briefcase. He approached the vehicle, suddenly stopping in his tracks, looking left and right before getting in. As he arrived at the Greville Street entrance, a large green Carlsberg truck was pulling ahead, just a few feet in front of him. One by one, Reader, Jones, Wood, and Perkins exited the building, and loaded up the van with carrier bags and tools. But Basil, seemingly a loner, left the building from the front door entrance, walking away, carrying a dark bag that concealed his face from CCTV cameras.

The men left the premises on Friday at 8:06 a.m., empty-handed, some twelve hours after they had first arrived. They had worked through the night and were overcome with sleep deprivation. Their heads must have been pounding. Like many golden agers, they needed their sleep and, judging by their later grousing about the aborted mission, they were even more irritable if they didn't get it.

It was a typical cloudy and rainy London day. Collins had activated the windshield wipers in the white van. The fresh air, daylight, and drizzle assaulted their senses after so many hours stuck in the cavernous, dimly lit, dusty basement, drilling. Daylight also brought with it a sense of reality that had been absent in the vault and once again the fear of getting caught intensified, at least for some members of the gang.

Collins, the only one who was well rested, drove Perkins and Jones to their homes in Enfield. Then Collins drove Reader to Collins's house on Bletsoe Walk in Islington. From Collins's house, Collins's brother-in-law, Lincoln, drove Reader to London Bridge station, where Reader took a train back home to Kent. It was morning rush hour as Reader slid his senior citizen pass through the turnstile at the train station.

It turned out that human will had its limits, at least for one old man. In the hours after leaving 88–90 Hatton Garden, Brian Reader did something the others thought unimaginable: he abandoned the heist, deciding that it was too risky to return to the scene of the crime. Jones and Perkins would later express how they had felt exhaustion, disbelief, and anger that Reader was abandoning them when they needed him most. Of the gang, Collins was the most sympathetic to Reader, whom Jones and Perkins resented. But Reader had made up his mind. He was out.

Perhaps the years he had spent in a jail cell flashed through his mind. He had a lot to consider. He wasn't the spring chicken he once had been. There was his ill son, who had high blood pressure. His dead wife. Perhaps he couldn't face another day behind bars.

The others were now bereft of the Master, both the chief strategist and curmudgeonly cheerleader. And they were irate that he had pulled out, angry at his cowardice and unwillingness to follow through on what they had started. Following the bungled burglary, Jones, in particular, was intent on going back in, convinced that they could infiltrate the vault, if only they could get a stronger battering ram to push over the cabinet.

Rather than return immediately to Hatton Garden, the remaining members of the gang decided to go home to gather their strength. Collins went back to his wife, Millie, at his home in north London, and, one imagines, took a nap. Carl Wood, ailing and perennially irritable, was, by all accounts, feeling skittish and nervous.

Jones returned to his north London home where he kept his drilling videos. At that point, there were no television reports of the break-in. Did that mean it was safe to go back? As for Reader, his decision to walk away meant that he could now be cut off from any booty. But the rest of the gang needed to make sure that Basil, Reader's associate, and the one with the keys and codes to get into the building, didn't ditch them. They proceeded to lobby him not to give up. "I'll tell you something now, if we never proceeded me and you, Basil would have walked away," Jones later recalled.[4] The remaining team members decided to plod on.

Meanwhile, Reader was at home in his country-style manor in Kent. His last big job had imploded. He was out of the game, but at least he remained a free man.

* * * *

Vinnie Jones on a Mission for Power Tools

They were an eccentric duo: the athletic fabulist who imagined himself as a would-be soldier and the pot-bellied senior citizen who made a killing selling smuggled cigarettes. But Jones and Collins were nevertheless united by a common adventurous zeal, a love of their canine companions, whom they both talked to, and a determination to finish what they had begun.

So it was that on Sunday, the day after the first bungled burglary, the two men used Collins's Mercedes to go shopping and buy another hydraulic pump. First, they set out for D & M Tools, a tool store in the affluent west London suburb of Twickenham. Wearing a gray-hooded sweatshirt and no disguise, a jovial-looking Jones entered the store and casually asked the woman at the cash register about the store's inventory of pumps.

When D & M didn't have the model of pump they were looking for, they went next door to Machine Mart, another tool store, where Jones paid about £100 ($140) for a new red Clarke pump ram and hose. He used his last name for the invoice but with the initial *V* for his first name, which the British media would later breathlessly conclude was a reference to Vinnie Jones from the 1998 heist film *Lock, Stock and Two Smoking Barrels*. Less glamorously, it was a reference to his long-standing partner, Valerie Hart. A store attendant recalled that Jones, appearing calm and relaxed, had put his own street address on the invoice.

A CCTV camera outside D & M also recorded video footage of the two men, along with Collins's distinctive black Mercedes with its white roof and black alloy tires. Collins, apparently giddy with excitement about the prospect of going back in, called Perkins to update him on the purchase. Then he called Wood. Returning to the scene of the crime was fraught with risks. But if they were nervous, they managed to overcome it, and decided to proceed.

* * * *

Returning to the Scene of the Crime

When the remaining members of the gang returned to Hatton Garden Safe Deposit Ltd—a full forty-eight hours later on Sunday, April 4—Perkins's sixty-seventh birthday—they found that the fire exit door at the back of the building, which they had left unlocked, was now engaged. Lionel Wiffen had stopped by his office on Saturday with his wife to prepare for a visit by an electrician the next day. After noticing that the fire exit door on Greville Street was unlocked and ajar, he locked it, and went to his offices. He had a feeling that something wasn't quite right. He was the only person to visit the premises on the weekend. Most of the neighboring businesses were, as the criminals hoped and suspected, closed for the Easter weekend. Wiffen then checked the door leading from the courtyard into the basement. It had been bolted from the inside after Basil had left the building after the first night. After cleaning his office, Wiffen departed the building at 9 p.m.

At 9:17 p.m., Collins left his home in north London, and with Jones, Wood, and Perkins, drove his white Mercedes to Hatton Garden to check out the area. They got out of the car and walked carefully toward the fire escape door near Greville Street. They looked around. The coast was clear. Satisfied with their preliminary reconnaissance mission, the men left Hatton Garden before returning, around 10 p.m., only this time in the white van.

It is not clear how the others had convinced Basil to return to the scene of the crime, but he did. As the men waited for Basil to go to the front of the building, unlock the door from the inside and let them in, as he had done on the first night, this time Carl Wood got cold feet as he tried to open the locked fire escape door at least two times. The others were already fed up with Wood, a whiny man beset by illnesses and debt, always complaining. They were also probably calculating in their heads how much Wood's departure would enlarge their share of the loot. Collins nevertheless urged him to stay.

"He thought we would never get in," he later told Jones and Perkins. "The cunt I said, 'Give it another half hour; fuck, we've done everything we can do; if we can't get in, we won't be able to get in, will we?' "[5]

Evidently spooked, Wood scuttled back up the stairs near the fire escape and fled on nearby Leather Lane, "His arsehole went and he thought we would never get in," Collins added.

They were now down two men. With Wood and Reader out, only three remained. It was half the crew they'd planned for, but Jones, Basil, and Perkins remained steadfast. They wanted what they'd set out to take. And when you want something strongly or for long enough, it can begin to feel like it's already yours.

After Basil let them into the building, the gang returned to their posts inside the vault. The men carried their equipment, including several wheeled trash cans, back into the safe deposit. Jones carried a black Nike bag and the new pump and hose, enclosed in a red box that matched his shoes. Collins, for his part, returned to his lookout post at 25 Hatton Garden, this time determined not to snooze.

As Collins scanned the empty street below, Basil, Jones, and Perkins set about dislodging the cabinet, anchoring the new pump with metal joists on the wall opposite the vault.[6]

Once again, Jones said, "Smash that up!" Jones began pumping aggressively. This time, the pump did not "ping" back. The men were urging one another on.

"It's fucking working!" Perkins cried out. "It ain't ping back. It ain't fucking come back." He egged on his friend as Jones continued to pump. The pump hissed violently and suddenly there was a loud bang.

"We're in! We're in!"[7] Perkins hollered, abandoning his usual calm. They had succeeded, at last.

"It was hissing, that pump, bang, didn't it?" Jones would later recall. The noise, he complained, had given him a massive headache.[8]

Jones slithered through the narrow figure-eight-shaped hole in the concrete. It was just as well Collins was the lookout man; he was portly and would've struggled to wiggle through. Once inside the vault, Jones used heavy cutting equipment to jimmy open 73 out of 999 safe deposit boxes to ransack them. The usual method to open a safe deposit box was for the box's owner and a security guard to individually turn two separate keys clockwise at the same time. But in the absence of keys, brute force could do the trick.

Jones focused mostly on the boxes at eye level on the right-hand side. Dislodging one box would loosen the box next to it. But in a sign of his frantic state of mind or lack of experience, he chose boxes randomly, significantly slowing himself down and reducing the gang's final booty. "The safety deposit boxes at Hatton Garden were the difficult ones—they were made in the 1950s," a person familiar with the heist's planning recalled. "In other places you could do a box per minute—or 60 boxes an hour. But then Jones was saying, 'Oh, I'll do that one, now I'll do that one.' So it took longer. That's why they only opened about 70 boxes." And of the 73 boxes they opened, about 29 were empty. Among the nearly 1,000 boxes, dozens were empty because they belonged to box owners who had defaulted on their rent, according to a statement the safe deposit company gave to police.

Nevertheless, the men quickly filled several bags and two large trash bins with jewels, gold, precious stones, and cash. The bags were so weighted down with jewels, that they struggled to carry all the loot up the stairs to the fire escape. As they emptied the boxes and stuffed jewels into wheelie bins, Perkins, at one point, nearly collapsed. Had his blood sugar gone too low? Wielding a drill while shooting himself with insulin had apparently taken its toll. But he was nevertheless elated and managed to bring several bags stuffed with jewels to the fire escape in the back of the building where Collins was waiting nearby in the van, its front lights on. Jones and Perkins loaded the trash cans into the van. The men, though exhausted, tried to work quickly. Greville Street was deserted, save two pigeons on the street, oblivious to the historic burglary unfolding before them.

Before they left, Jones brought the red pump he had bought earlier that day in Twickenham back to the van. He left behind the Sealy pump that had malfunctioned. Jones had apparently studied his copy of *Forensics for Dummies*, and the men scrubbed every inch of the safe deposit with bleach, ensuring that Scotland Yard wouldn't find even a trace of DNA evidence.

At 6:44 a.m. on Sunday—more than ten hours after they'd entered for the second time, and more than two days after they'd initially broken in—exhausted and out of breath, the men sped away in the white van. Collins dropped them off at each of their homes. Later that day, William Lincoln called his nephew John Harbinson, a taxi driver, and asked him if he would be willing to collect some goods for him for storage. He did not say what they were.

The next day, Jones and Perkins met at Collins's house in north London to take stock of the loot before Harbinson spirited away three bags stuffed with jewels in his taxi. It was a good haul. At least £14 million, or $21 million worth of gold, gems, diamonds, and cash, most of which was stored at Collins's house. They would meet the next day to divvy it up.

It was more than they had even hoped for.

Chapter 7

Paul Johnson

A Modern-Day Sherlock Holmes

THE THEFT WAS DISCOVERED ON THE MORNING OF Tuesday, April 7, 2015—a full two days after the Easter weekend—when Kelvin Stockwell, the guard who had walked away from the building over the weekend, came to work at around 8 a.m. He looked at the door leading to the vault and saw that the lock was missing. He slowly ventured into the unlocked heart and soul of Hatton Garden Safe Deposit Ltd. There were tools and safe deposit boxes strewn all over the floor, along with piles of glittering sapphires and diamonds that had been left behind as the gang frantically fled the scene of the crime.

As Stockwell surveyed the vault where he had been coming to work for some twenty years, the shock was visceral and breathtaking.

"It was like a bomb had hit the place," he would later recall, and no doubt he must have felt some of the explosion's impact, as the company's main security guard. He called the police immediately.[1]

It didn't take long for the heist to make its way all the way up the chain of command. Later that day, Detective Superintendent Craig Turner, the restless and indefatigable forty-four-year-old chief of the Flying Squad, was sitting at his desk at Putney, the squad's blocky headquarters in southwest London, when he received a phone call. Paul Johnson, one of his two deputies, was on the line.

At the time, Turner was preoccupied running "Operation Yena," an operation that was closing in on a gang of dangerous armed robbers who had been hitting post offices in southeast London.

"There's been a burglary at Hatton Garden, there are three holes in a wall, it looks like a lot of jewelry had been taken and we have no idea who did it," Johnson told him, with little discernible sense of urgency in his Manchester-accented voice. "I'm going down to the scene." As usual Johnson wasn't fazed, and, if he was, he wasn't showing it.

After decades of battling drug dealers, armed robbers, kidnappers, and contract killers, Johnson was no stranger to violence or menace. But the only violence here was three adjoining holes drilled into a wall. No one had been hurt. There were no dead bodies to contend with. And even if millions of pounds in jewelry had been stolen, he had seen what he considered more brazen crimes.

Johnson would eventually see the humor in the fact that the most high-profile case of his career—the one that he will always be remembered by—was the work of a group of seemingly harmless and hapless retirees. When he picked up the phone to tell Turner what had happened, he betrayed no particular sense of urgency or alarm. At this point he had no inkling that the plot of *Sexy Beast*, a British film featuring a cantankerous criminal who recruits a retired safecracker for one last job, had more or less landed on his desk.

"There's no point in getting excited until you see with your own eyes what has happened," Johnson recalled. "Everything sounds exciting at first. For me, it was just another job. I have seen violence and people shot and this was three holes in a wall. It was audacious what they did. But it was reputational risk to Scotland Yard more than anything else. No one was going to get hurt."

Initially, Johnson thought Hatton Garden was going to be just another burglary in a long catalog of burglaries he had seen in the capital. He had been attending a conference on the future of the

Metropolitan Police—presided over by the commissioner—when he excused himself from the room to take a call from one of his field officers, Jamie Day, who had been on duty the weekend of the burglary and had gone to the crime scene to investigate. "He was very matter-of-fact," Johnson said, recalling the conversation. "He said, 'There are three holes. It's a complete mess.' I thought it sounded interesting and I said 'Let's get on with it. It sounds like a good one for the Flying Squad.'"

Johnson, a lanky, laconic, and square-jawed fifty-six-year-old detective inspector with Scotland Yard's Flying Squad, has Hollywood good looks and the self-effacement of an undercover cop adept at being invisible. A native of Manchester, in England's former industrial north, he is affable but somewhat intimidating. In a nation of stiff upper lips, his reserved demeanor stands out.

He had worked as a detective constable at Tower Bridge, in east London, and spent nearly two decades fighting crime across the capital—including leading a team of officers investigating drug dealers, armed robbers, kidnappers, and contract killers. He had also been an officer at the scene of the daring Millennium Dome heist of 2000, when a gang of thieves armed with a bulldozer had tried to infiltrate an exhibition center and steal nearly half a billion dollars' worth of gems.[2] The theft would be immortalized by a headline in the tabloid newspaper the *Sun*: "I'm Only Here for De Beers."

Yet even after all of that, Johnson recalled that seeing the Hatton Garden crime scene with his own eyes for the first time made an impression. When he entered through the fire escape door of the seven-story building to see for himself what had happened, he knew immediately that this was no ordinary crime. To get to the vault, the thieves had managed to descend through an elevator shaft before drilling twenty-inch holes in the shape of a figure eight through reinforced concrete, suggesting a professional job requiring prodigious stamina and physical strength. A seventy-five-pound hydraulic pump lay in the middle of the floor. Empty safe deposit boxes were scattered about—on them were written the numbers 140, 141, 179, 182.

Local jewelers kept their jewels and most valuable belongings in the safe deposit overnight, and as police slowly counted the number of empty boxes—fifty-five, fifty-six, fifty-seven—the magnitude of the burglary slowly started to dawn on Johnson. It would eventually become clear that as much as £27.5 million ($41.25 million) in gems, diamonds, emeralds, cash, and rare antique coins had been spirited away, along with family heirlooms and World War II medals. Entire life savings were wiped out.

In total, seventy-four boxes had been emptied. Johnson just stood there, confounded. How in the bloody hell had this happened? Why had the police not caught this before it was too late? Making matters worse was the fact that the alarm had been triggered during the burglary and then ignored by police, while the owners of the safe deposit and their security staff appeared to have been lulled into a sense of complacency by an errant insect that had set off the alarm months earlier.

The Flying Squad would need to move quickly. The perpetrators could already have skipped town with their booty, dozens of victims were irate and starting to demand answers, and millions of pounds were at stake—along with the vaunted reputation of the Flying Squad.

* * * *

The Flying Squad and the Crime of the Century

Johnson was a proud member of the Flying Squad, an elite unit within London's Metropolitan Police, which was formed in October 1919 and originally consisted of twelve officers who gathered intelligence on robbers and pickpockets from atop horse-drawn carriages, with secret holes pocked in the canvas to allow for spying. Named for the unit's mandate to ignore geographic boundaries and "fly" all over the capital, the squad was never limited to a single borough.

The Flying Squad, also known as the Robbery Squad, or SDC7 for Specialist Crime Directorate 7, investigates commercial armed and unarmed robberies and other serious violent crimes. It has long held a special place in the British popular imagination, its members depicted as debonair heroes on television and radio in the 1960s and 1970s. Known as the "Sweeney"—Cockney rhyming slang for the murderous barber in *Sweeney Todd*—members of the Flying Squad would zip around London in Granada or Cortina sedans, decked out in suits and ties, emblazoned with the symbol of a screaming eagle ready to swoop in on its prey. In a 1970s British television show called *The Sweeney*, the squad was epitomized by a hard-boiled inspector called Jack Regan whose signature phrase was "Shut it!"

The Flying Squad's officers are also known for their nimbleness at remaining undetected; they work in civilian clothes and when they are armed and undercover, they keep their Glock firearms carefully concealed in a belt holster underneath their suit jackets.

Among the squad's most legendary officers was Jeremiah Lynch, an Irish-born cop who played a key role in ferreting out German spies during World War II and outmaneuvering a confidence trickster and member of Parliament named Horatio Bottomley, who lined his pockets with money skimmed from government-issued war bonds.

In July 1946, the squad successfully disrupted plans by a gang of thieves to drug the guards at a security depot at Heathrow Airport and steal nearly a million dollars' worth of gold and jewelry. Learning of the plot, the squad disguised themselves as guards, and ambushed them. Initially a small elite unit, the force grew to have dozens of officers in its ranks and by 1956 was making one thousand arrests per year.

The Flying Squad went head-to-head with many of the country's most cunning criminals. After the Great Train Robbery of 1963,
it hunted fugitive Ronnie Biggs for three decades, before Biggs finally
turned himself in in 2001; it ended the Kray twins' reign of terror over
east London; and it also foiled the attempt by a gang of thieves to steal
£350 (about $490 million) worth of diamonds—including the flawless
203-carat Millennium Star—at the capital's Millennium Dome in 2000.

The squad became known for its success in infiltrating London's
shadowy underworld through police informants called "supergrasses,"
for its adeptness at catching armed robbers, even if that meant shooting them dead, and for its success at foiling some of the biggest heists
the world had ever seen. It has also had its dark moments, including
the 1970s, when Operation Countryman, an internal probe, revealed
that officers from the unit were taking bribes from Soho pornogra-
phers. In 2001 three Flying Squad detectives received seven-year jail
sentences after springing a police informant from prison to carry out
a robbery on their behalf. But the episodes of bribery and corruption were offset by the Sweeney's reputation for doggedness, heroism,
and courage.

Among its ranks, Johnson was a modern-day Jeremiah Lynch:
inscrutable, indefatigable, with a well-honed instinct for the thought
processes of the criminal mind and a limitless patience that had
allowed him to outsmart criminals of every stripe—time and time
again. He knew from experience that catching a thief was usually just
a matter of waiting for him or her to make a mistake. And if you
waited long enough, they nearly always did.

Above all, he had an unwavering confidence in the methodology
of the Flying Squad, confident that its empirical approach would nab
the bad guys, in the end, even if Johnson doesn't like to dwell on past
successes. The squad's playbook had proven remarkably reliable over
the decades: methodically gathering evidence, whether that meant
secretly putting a listening device in a suspect's Peugeot or under-

ground hideout; finding a telltale DNA sample from a discarded hair or Coke can left at the scene of a crime; working a network of informants; or sending a team of undercover officers to track a suspect's every move without being detected.

It was a mix of old-fashioned beat policing and modern-day technology that took advantage of the capital's law enforcement resources—the millions of CCTV cameras that peppered the city in the aftermath of Irish Republican Army bombs in the 1980s and the 1990s that had made Londoners among the most watched and monitored citizens in the world, the automatic number plate recognition technology that secretly photographed millions of vehicles each day and allowed officers to track terrorist suspects or armed robbers, the teams of undercover Flying Squad officers who camouflaged themselves in underground tube stations or ancient jewelry quarters or shopping malls—until the moment was ripe to strike.

"There has long been a myth and mystique about the Flying Squad. There is something about wearing that tie with the eagle on it and saying you served on the Flying Squad," says Roy Ramm, the former Flying Squad chief and head of special operations for Scotland Yard, who has investigated some of the leading robberies of the century. "The Flying Squad is probably the best known of the Metropolitan police's various branches. It is also a tough and demanding beast, and to get there, officers have to be among the top in the country."

In law enforcement lore, Flying Squad officers were also revered for their ballsiness. In the 1980s the squad became far more aggressive in using force after a succession of robbery suspects managed to evade prison on the grounds that evidence—a stolen car used during the crime, a mask left at the scene, a gun found in a hideout—was circumstantial. As a result, the squad began taking suspects out "on the pavement," swooping in and ambushing armed robbers just moments before they were about to commit a crime—at the risk of their own lives. It cemented the Sweeney's reputation for employing fearless and brawny tough guys.[3]

In 2004, after the squad got its first female commander, Sharon Kerr, the BBC mused that the image of the "Sweeney as the haven of the rugby-playing, beer-swilling bruiser" was giving way to a "more family friendly, feminine, post-modernist Flying Squad."[4]

Either way, the Flying Squad was not a place for second tries or second chances. There was too much at stake. Money. Lives. The safety of one of the world's biggest capitals. Being part of the Flying Squad required physical and mental stamina, and a stubborn determination to solve crimes and bring criminals to justice. Overachievers filled the unit's ranks. "Members of the Flying Squad are very fit and motivated individuals. They are start to finishers," Turner, the Flying Squad chief, explained. "Even when you have only asked them for A and B, they normally come back with A, B, C, D and E, and even F. They deliver beyond what is expected."[5]

By the time the Hatton Garden case landed on Johnson's desk, undercover surveillance operations were already his specialty. During a long career, he had dismantled gangs of ruthless armed bank robbers, foiled a honey trap plot in which a contract killer tried to kidnap a millionaire businessman by installing an attractive secretary at his office to seduce him, and helped put dozens of the capital's most wily thieves behind bars.

At the time of the caper, he had recently been promoted to detective chief inspector, the number two spot on the squad, and was in charge of west London, which was a cauldron of burglaries and commercial crime. He was just two years away from retirement. The Hatton Garden job was to be the last big case of his distinguished career. It was to be his last job.

Johnson was a man of action, who gave little away, preferring his work to speak on his behalf. He exuded quiet authority and was always immaculately dressed in civilian clothes, a dark jacket and muted navy blue tie, adorned with the yellow sweeping eagle of the Flying Squad—the bird of prey. After decades of long days and nights, he was ready for a change.[6]

His next move would be to join the Serious Fraud Office, investigating fraud, bribery, and corruption from a grand building near London's Trafalgar Square. It was a job that would satisfy the imperturbable moral compass that had guided him to do good in the world since he was a novice police officer. Chasing financial corruption was probably better for your health than chasing dangerous armed robbers, and the hours would be less punishing. He could retire his Glock. He could spend more time with his family.

Since joining the Hendon Police Training School, the London Metropolitan Police Service's main officer training center, when he was twenty-three years old, he thought he had seen it all—that is, until he saw those figure-eight-shaped concentric holes bored into a reinforced concrete wall, in a basement in central London, that would soon take on iconic status across the country.

* * * *

A Media Frenzy Begins

On Thursday, April 9, 2015, two days after the police discovered the crime, Johnson convened a hastily arranged press conference, and announced that Hatton Garden had been hit. By the time he arrived, a scrum of Fleet Street reporters had already formed a large semicircle outside 88–90 Hatton Garden. There was already a sense of excitement that something big had taken place in a country that relished the theater of dramatic heists.

"They forced open shutter doors into the basement where Hatton Garden Safe Deposit is based and then made their way to the vault area. Once outside the vault area, they used a Hilti DD 350 drill to bore holes in the vault wall. This wall is two meters thick and is made of reinforced concrete," Johnson said, in a matter-of-fact voice to the crowd of reporters. "The vault is covered in dust and debris and the floor is strewn with discarded safety deposit boxes, numerous power tools," he continued. "We are in the process of identifying the owners of the safety deposit boxes that have been interfered with." He refused to say how much had been stolen.

This being England, the tabloid media reacted with barely concealed glee turning what little information they had in the days following the crime into sensational headlines. "HATTON GARDEN RAIDERS PLUNDER UP TO £200 MILLION FROM SAFE DEPOSIT," screamed the headline in the *Daily Telegraph*. "HATTON GARDEN JEWELRY ROBBERY: POLICE LAUNCH MANHUNT AFTER EASTER WEEKEND HEIST," declared the *Mirror*. "PERFECT PLANNING OF £200 MILLION BLINGO HEIST REVEALED," the *Sun*'s headline blared.

The tabloids went into overdrive. Dominated by the *Sun*, owned by Rupert Murdoch, and the populist *Daily Mail*, edited by the combative Paul Dacre, they feasted with barely concealed delight on a story that had it all—an old-school caper out of Hollywood, a whodunit mystery, and a crime committed in central London, over a long weekend, under the nose of Scotland Yard.

The revelation that the police had somehow missed the alarm particularly whetted the appetite of Fleet Street, which had recently been in a simmering battle with Scotland Yard in the aftermath of a salacious phone-hacking scandal that had rocked the media and law enforcement establishment. In 2014, London—and the world—had been captivated by a trial during which key protagonists in the tabloid media, including the former editor of the *News of the World*, a now defunct Murdoch tabloid, were accused of illegally bribing police and intercepting voice mails in the pursuit of stories, including the voice mail of a kidnapped teenager, Milly Dowler, who was later found dead.

The June 2014 trial exposed a culture in which journalists were paid six figures for celebrity scoops and sifting through garbage bins, along with the systemic eavesdropping on the cell phones of British luminaries, including the royal family and leading politicians.[7]

During the scandal, several Scotland Yard officers were accused of leaking some of the confidentially acquired information to journalists and the sometimes cozy relationship between journalists and police came under intense scrutiny. In July 2011, Scotland Yard's police commissioner, Sir Paul Stephenson, resigned after coming under criticism for hiring a former *News of the World* executive, who had been questioned by police investigating phone hacking—as an adviser. A year later, the Yard's communications chief, faced with a disciplinary hearing over his link to the same executive, also resigned.[8]

The result was that, by the time of the Hatton Garden heist, the access and information provided by Scotland Yard to journalists had been severely circumscribed and the relationship between the British media and London's Metropolitan Police, strained in the best of times, had become fraught by mutual distrust and suspicion. The lack of information whetted appetites even more.

Meanwhile, as news of the burglary began to spread, frantic owners of the safe deposit boxes from across Hatton Garden began to mass outside the building, desperate for any information regarding their valuables. It quickly emerged that many of them were not insured, believing the Hatton Garden Safe Deposit to be impenetrable. Photographs of the gaping holes drilled through the wall and grainy CCTV footage of the four thieves were soon splashed on the covers of Britain's newspapers.

Thanks to the media frenzy, news of the crime soon reached all the way to No. 10 Downing Street, the residence of the British prime minister, and David Cameron called the Scotland Yard commissioner, Bernard Hogan-Howe, to stress that the reputation of the Yard was on the line. A group of villains could not walk into a vault in the center of London in broad daylight on a holiday weekend—steal millions worth of gold, jewels, and cash—and be allowed to get away with it.

Hogan-Howe, a tough-on-crime police commander in the old-fashioned mold, was known for taming gangs when he was chief constable in Merseyside, a county in northwest England, and respected for having successfully policed the 2012 London Olympics. He wanted results.

Theresa May, then the no-nonsense head of the Home Office—Britain's internal affairs ministry—and now the prime minister, was also keeping close tabs on the case. British law enforcement came under the global spotlight as the *New York Times*, *Le Monde*, and others piled in on a case that seemed conjured from the pages of a crime thriller.

With the British media engaged in a guessing game of "Who done it?" people the world over were fascinated by reports of a heist that seemed to hark back to a different era.

"There was concern from the highest levels at Scotland Yard from the commissioner downward, who wanted to know, hour by hour, what progress was being made," Turner, the Flying Squad chief, recalled. "From the onset, there was huge pressure to solve the crime. I would certainly rate it at the top of the biggest challenges I have encountered in my career. It was one of the most notorious crimes of the century. The world was watching."

A failure on a case of this magnitude, and the legacy of the Flying Squad would be irreparably shattered. "You want to perpetuate the Flying Squad's legacy," Johnson said. "In this business, you're only as good as your last case."[9]

The Flying Squad faced huge pressure to solve the crime, while at the same time keeping a covert police operation secret amid intense media scrutiny. The Sweeney ordained itself the most fit and able to take on the case since the Metropolitan Police in Camden borough, in northwest and central London, who were charged with policing Hatton Garden, didn't have the capability or the resources. Besides, they had missed the initial alarm.

The case quickly became Scotland Yard's top priority, having seeped into the public imagination: The large holes drilled through reinforced concrete. The mystery of who was behind it. The insatiable appetite of the tabloid press ensured that it dominated the headlines.

At the inscrutable Flying Squad each covert operation is given a name, chosen from a chronological list, and the investigation was unceremoniously dubbed "Operation Spire." The name for what would become one of the most notorious crimes of the past three hundred years was randomly chosen, according to Turner, and had no particular significance.

Beyond the pressure from the highest levels of Scotland Yard and the government, the Hatton Garden investigation was also complicated from the beginning because of the scale of the crime: 999 safe deposit boxes, 73 of which had been emptied. All the stolen jewelry, gold, and gems had to be meticulously documented and identified, a task made all the more difficult by the fact that dozens of safe deposit boxes had been thrown on the floor during the mayhem of the burglary, and many of the hundreds of gold chains and rings strewn on the floor looked alike.

* * * *

Dowries, Family Heirlooms, and Life Savings

Safe deposits are repositories of lives lived, where treasures and family histories are kept under lock and key—children's birth certificates, the deeds of houses, black and white family photographs, war medals, engagement rings, memories of loved ones long since departed—

and while the millions of pounds in stolen gems would eventually be quantified, the emotional cost of the heist was incalculable.

Entire life savings were wiped out in the burglary, along with cherished heirlooms. There were millions of dollars' worth of fine jewelry, valuable antique coins, and wads of cold cash spirited away for retirement and to start new businesses. University funds for grandchildren. Money for long put-off vacations for hardworking men and women who worked nearly one hundred hours a week at Hatton Garden and relied on the safe deposit as a storehouse for their dreams.

The victims of the heist included people from all walks of life: Holocaust survivors; young entrepreneurs; retirees; immigrants from the Middle East, Asia, and Africa, who had arrived penniless to Britain in the 1960s after fleeing strife or civil war and had rebuilt their lives, and started flourishing businesses. One Afghan diamond trader was so shaken by the burglary that even though he spoke excellent English after decades in the country, he brought an Urdu translator to his police interview. Other elderly safe deposit box holders were reduced to tears as they recounted their losses to the police.

Among the victims were dozens of Jewish traders, who had been working in Hatton Garden for decades, and some of whom were storing their jewels in a box first rented out by their great-grandparents after World War II. Many didn't have insurance for their stored valuables, believing, as one embarrassed box holder put it, that "the use of the safe deposit was my best insurance policy and that they would be safe." One trader whose family had survived the Holocaust and had come to Britain with nothing but smuggled diamonds hidden in their clothes, woke up to discover his box had been targeted. He was devastated. Rick Marchant, an insurance loss adjustor who had seven clients who had lost more than £2 million ($3 million) worth of gems stored in the vault, told the BBC that it had mainly been small family-run firms that had been ruined by the heist. He warned them that the chances of ever recovering their gems were very limited. For some,

the theft would bring bankruptcy and financial ruin. "We are dealing here with mainly small businesses and they are not making huge
profits," he said. "These aren't extremely wealthy people, for a lot of
them their livelihoods have gone."[10] The media might applaud the
audacity of the criminals, he added, but the lives of many lay in ruins.

They had been lulled into a false sense of security every time they
entered the safe deposit, walked through two metal gates, into the
imposing-looking, seemingly impenetrable Chubb vault, with its two
combination locks and motion-triggered alarm system. The burglary
also proved devastating for the Bavishi family, owners of the safe
deposit company, who quickly became objects of derision, fury, and
little sympathy. A visibly shaken Mahendra Bavishi, at home in Khartoum, told the British media that he believed the heist was an "inside
job," given that the thieves seemed to know which CCTV cameras
were not working in the building. He said the police had called his
son Manish, who had been in Sudan at the time of the burglary, and
had asked him to return as soon as possible to London. "The police
want to know from Manish if he suspects someone inside who could
have contact with a gang," he explained. "There must be suspicion on
everyone who worked in that building."[11]

Mr. Bavishi was furious that the police had not responded
to the alarm, and complained that the safe deposit, which was
already struggling financially, would likely go into bankruptcy,
which it soon did. Manish Bavishi would later tell the police that
the burglary had cost the company an estimated £401,000 (about
$601,500) in lost annual income, never mind the damage done to
the premises and the irreparable damage done to his family's—and
company's—reputation.

"To many this robbery is like something out of a Hollywood fiction film, but to my family it is a tragedy," he told the *Daily Mail*. "It
is the end of the business my son has worked so hard to build slowly
over the last seven years." After pumping money into it and taking

out loans, he lamented, "Now business is finished. Who will trust their valuables with us after this?"[12] The answer was no one.

As the brazenness of the heist became the talk of the town, and Britons everywhere asked who could be responsible, John O'Connor, a former head of the Flying Squad, joined the loud chorus of law enforcement professionals, amateur sleuths, and conspiracy theorists calling it an "inside job."

"You're gonna have to have a detailed layout of the whole of the business. So clearly they got that from somebody on the inside," he told Sky News. "You've got a major strong room, there's no sign of a forced entry, they've apparently been able to abseil down the lift shaft to get access to the vault—I just find it astonishing that it was that easy. The fact that there is no sign of forced entry, what does that mean? That someone left the door open? That someone left the windows open? It smacks all the time of inside aid, all of the way through it. This doesn't look to me like a genuine sort of smash and grab raid by determined criminals, this looks like they've had accomplices on the inside. You wouldn't go to attack a building like that unless you knew you could gain access."[13]

Suspicions also were aroused by the fact that days before the heist a fire had raged in the High Holborn area, just a few blocks from the vault, causing power outages. Fire experts said the blaze had been caused by an electrical fault in the underground Victorian tunnels near Hatton Garden. But O'Connor was just one of many who speculated that the fire may have been set by wily thieves to distract from the raid, or perhaps in an attempt to disable the alarm. "Yeah, I think that probably was deliberate," he told LBC, a popular talk radio show that was a favorite of Jones's and Perkins's. "I've never heard of an outage of electricity like that causing a fire that lasted as long as that. That seems to me as too much of a coincidence."

Whatever had caused the fire, the feverish speculation offered cold comfort for the hundreds of box holders. Most, but not all, had meticulously recorded the contents of each box, which they would later relay to the police. But some had hazier memories, presenting a difficult challenge for police trying to assess, catalog, and value what was stolen.

Among the long lists of stolen items given to the police by dozens of Hatton Garden traders was an eighteen-carat gold antique pocket watch heirloom that had belonged to a grandfather; a gold bangle worn by a box holder's great-grandmother at her wedding one hundred years ago; an art deco green emerald and diamond broach valued at about £7,000 ($10,500) that had been worn by a box holder's now deceased mother; a rare Distinguished Flying Cross Royal Air Force medal that had been awarded to a box holder's father-in-law; a flip-up silver matchbox belonging to a great-uncle, long since departed; an eighteen-carat enameled pocket watch by Thomas Grignion, the celebrated eighteenth-century French clockmaker, handmade in 1784, with a fusee movement; and a silver enameled Edwardian butterfly brooch from 1910 valued at about £30 ($45); hundreds of blocks of gold; and as much as £1 million ($1.5 million) worth of rough diamonds of the type used in diamond-tipped power drills such as the one the gang had used to penetrate the vault.

Then there was the inventory of gems, valued in the tens of millions of dollars, and currency—stacks of pounds, euros, dollars, Krugerrands, sovereigns, and half-sovereigns, and a 1908 American Indian head $2 gold coin among them, now valued at about £200 ($300).

One jeweler, who rented five safe deposit boxes, lost more than £1.5 million ($2.25 million) worth of valuables, including 1,000 gold bars from the United States, Britain, China, Switzerland, and Canada; more than 1,000 gold coins; and dozens of pure platinum bars. A third-generation immigrant Indian family that ran a jewelry business at Hatton Garden lost nearly £3 million ($4.5 million) worth of valuables, including fifty-eight pearl necklaces and earrings, diamonds,

packets of sapphires, and mounted stones. But there were also sentimental objects, including fake gold bracelets, that prompted a police
officer to scrawl on his report next to one box: "Primark crap!" referring to a retailer selling kitsch costume jewelry. Nevertheless, police
initially estimated that about £14 million ($21 million) worth of valu-
ables had been stolen, an amount that was eventually determined to
be much higher.

Most of the safe deposit box holders had saliva swabbed from their
mouths so that Scotland Yard could check that their DNA didn't
match any traces potentially found at the scene of the crime, and they
could be eliminated as suspects. Police interviewed box holders who
were no longer using their boxes, including one former jeweler, who
gave a police statement via e-mail since he had moved to the United
States. He had emptied his box of thousands of dollars' worth of jewelry a few weeks before the heist. "I have not had any of my property
stolen as a result of this offence," the statement said.

As is often the case for safe deposit boxes, where depositors eschew
a bank in search of more privacy and anonymity, the safe deposit had
also attracted black money. One box is said to belong to a well-known
north London drug lord and contained a million dollars in thousand-
pound notes. Another box was rumored to contain a taped murder
confession of a crime boss, spirited away and held in a rival gangster's
box for extortion at some future date.

One Jewish jeweler, elderly and ailing, had kept a safe deposit box
at 88–90 Hatton Garden for decades. He told police that fifteen years
ago, he had remortgaged his home to raise £100,000 ($150,000) in
loans to help keep his jewelry business afloat. The capital on the loan
was due in 2016. "Because of my age and infirmity I have become
semiretired," he told police, evidently shaken. "The jewelry in the safe
deposit represented my life savings and I had intended to use it to
repay the mortgage loan in 2016," he said.

The widow of an Indian jeweler had meticulously stored away

her gems in an Indian sweet tin and a chocolate tin in the shape of a heart. The gang had taken more than £230,000 (about $345,000) worth of her jewelry. She told police she was devastated since "all the items have memories" and she had treasured the jewelry since much of it had been designed by her late husband.

In another case, the dowry for a young Indian woman—collected since she was a young girl and stored in the vault—had been stolen by the white-haired thieves and now her family worried she would never find a suitable husband.

Yet another jeweler, this one of Greek heritage, who had worked at Hatton Garden for many years, told police that for nearly twenty years he received his bonus in diamonds rather than cash, so he wouldn't spend it. He stored the diamonds in the safe deposit box to bequeath to his children for their future.

The family of one Danish box holder had been in the jewelry business for more than a century. After fifty years in the business, the box holder had decided to finally retire. Just months before the burglary he had sold the lease on his jewelry store back to the owner. All that was left was for him to transfer his remaining stock to the safe deposit, which he did just weeks before it was hit. He was so sentimental about his years in the trade that he had asked his staff to move the goods; he couldn't bring himself to remove the jewelry himself from his company's showroom. Each piece was like a child, and nearly half had been designed by his company, for which he meticulously and lovingly oversaw the workmanship. In total, he lost an estimated £550,000 (about $825,000) worth of jewelry, including platinum rings, sapphires, rubies, and emeralds. The financial loss threatened to unravel his retirement plans.

One box included thousands of pounds worth of gold ingots that belonged to a Ghanaian man, whose late mother was a tribal chieftain. When the family had tried to sell her ceremonial gold jewelry and was unable to find a seller, they melted it down into several small blocks of gold, which were meant to provide a financial lifeline to the family and had been stored at the safe deposit.

One British jeweler with Indian roots, whose grandfather had started a jewelry business in London in the mid-1960s, supplying fine diamonds and jewels from Belgium, Hong Kong, and India to diamond traders, said the burglary threatened to undermine his business. "The main ethos of the jewelry industry is integrity and trust which we feel has been damaged by this incident," he said. His company had rented a safe deposit box from 88–90 Hatton Garden for more than forty years, and had lost diamonds, emeralds, and pearls.

Jacob Meghnagi, thirty-nine, the Italian Jewish jeweler who had been working in Hatton Garden for more than a decade and stored tens of thousands of pounds worth of diamonds and gems there, said the heist had reverberated across the Garden because the profit margins on gems were small, and dozens of dealers lost all of their stocks.

Meghnagi said he had long felt apprehensive that the safe deposit was vulnerable, since its alarm system was outmoded and it was unguarded in the evening after office hours. "People trusted Hatton Garden Safe Deposit. But I always had a bad feeling about that place that it could be robbed. I didn't trust it," he says. "But since it was across the street from our building I kept my stock there for the sake of convenience."

On the Tuesday after the burglary, Meghnagi was on vacation in Tel Aviv, on the beach with his six children, when he received a call from a friend that the safe deposit had been targeted. "I was really nervous, I was going crazy," he recalled. "It was Passover weekend and I was on holiday when a friend called and said, 'Did you hear what happened at Hatton Garden?' I freaked out. I called my wife and she told me to calm down since I was insured." He also called his insurance agent, who assured him that he was covered up to losses of £250,000 ($375,000), and urged him to get back to his vacation.

"People who weren't insured were morons," Meghnagi said.

"They thought it was impregnable and they were wrong. Now they are embarrassed to admit it, because a lot of people keep stuff in the boxes that they don't declare on the books."

When he returned to London after his vacation, he learned from the police that his box had fallen out of the cabinet when the gang's pump pushed it over, and that it had landed on the ground, underneath another box. In the rush to loot the boxes, the thieves had missed it. Still, his diamonds and other stock were held by police for more than two months after the burglary, and he wasn't able to do any business.

"I had diamonds, all my stock, all my livelihood in that box. I was lucky my box fell out and went to the other side and was hidden under his box, which also fell down," he said, pointing to Boaz, his office mate. The two laughed. "But I couldn't trade for two months. I had to buy some gear. It was a huge problem and I lost a lot of money."

When he first heard about the burglary, Meghnagi said he was deeply worried about his stash of diamonds stored there, but was also impressed. "I laughed. They are fucking geniuses," he said. But he was also angry at their disregard for the lives they ruined. "I work hard for a living. The margins in this trade are small. I don't respect stealing. Fuck them. I thought, 'They deserve to go to prison and pay for what they did.'"

* * * *

Who Dunnit?

For Johnson and Jamie Day, the more junior officer charged with executing the day-to-day investigation under Johnson's command, the new case wasn't promising. The crime scene at 88–90 Hatton Garden that Tuesday offered up few obvious clues. There was not a single fingerprint. The building's multiple CCTV cameras had been disabled, apparently smashed with a hammer. And as the officers surveyed the scene, several questions remained: Who had the savvy to pull off such an audacious crime? Had the thieves already spirited the jewels out of the country? And was the Flying Squad swooping in too late? Was it a foreign job? An inside job? A group of Eastern Europeans? A former Navy Seal? Who would have the swagger, confidence, and experience to hit a high-security vault with a motion-triggered alarm in the center of London?

The public was captivated. Whether inspired by the glamour of heist films, like the original and remade versions of *The Thomas Crown Affair*, or the die-hard fondness for the country's original generous bandit, Robin Hood, Britons read the headlines with a mischievous smile. You had to hand it to whomever pulled this off. And that whomever quickly started to take many shapes amid a frenzy of speculation about the thieves' true identities.

Scotland Yard's telephones rang off the hook with members of the public calling in with tips pointing at wily Italian mafia leaders, Irish crime syndicates, and, above all, the Eastern European gang known as the Pink Panthers, a notorious group of Eastern European jewelry thieves who had been behind some of the most sensational heists of the past decade.

Others urged the police to focus on the Panama hat-wearing "Mr. Big," as he was known, who drove to jewel raids in his Bentley and was one of two dapperly dressed men who posed as wealthy customers to rob a Graff Diamonds store in London in 2007.

At least initially, the absurd notion that the theft could have been the work of a group of homegrown and wily thieves with joint pain wasn't even considered.

The Pink Panthers were once led by Zoran Kostić, a chameleon of a man with dark brooding looks who has variously disguised himself as a prosperous banker in a suit and a chic woman to outmaneuver security systems at some of the most heavily guarded jewelry stores in the world, including the luxurious Place Vendôme in Paris, where some of the glittering jewelry brands such as Cartier have their flagship stores. Kostić was arrested in 2009 at the two-star Hotel Utrillo, a short walk from the Moulin Rouge in Paris, with a stash of gold Swiss watches. But that didn't stop the rest of the roughly two hundred Pink Panthers, many of them with military and athletic backgrounds, from continuing their spree.[14]

They are believed to have snatched jewels worth more than $130 million in swift attacks that extend from Dubai to Geneva to Monaco. Their nickname was invented by British investigators when one suspect hid a $657,000 blue diamond in a jar of cream, a tactic lifted from one of *The Pink Panther* films starring Peter Sellers. Dozens of men connected to the Pink Panthers have been arrested, and police have tracked them to as far away as Japan, where robbers in suits and ties tear-gassed employees in a jewelry store in Tokyo in 2004, and then vanished, in a matter of minutes, with a sack of diamonds and the Comtesse de Vendôme, a 125-carat necklace of 116 diamonds. Then, in December 2008, suspicions were once again cast on the Pink Panthers when four men—three disguised as women with long tresses, sunglasses, and winter scarves—struck the fabled Harry Winston jewelry store on Avenue Montaigne in Paris, and walked away with $105 million worth of emeralds, rubies, and diamonds.[15]

"When Hatton Garden was hit, the British media was rife with speculation that the Panthers had struck," recalls Ed Hall, a leading prosecutor in the Hatton Garden case.[16] If it was the Panthers, it would mean that Scotland Yard might have to mount an international dragnet—and, owing to the Panthers's deftness at avoiding capture thus far, that didn't bode well.

But they would soon discover that solving the Hatton Garden heist would require looking far closer to home.

Meanwhile, a rumor was circulating among the criminal fraternity that the Firm had been hired by the Adams family, a feared north London crime family, to hit Hatton Garden and remove an incriminating murder confession, supposedly hidden in one of the safe deposit boxes owned by John Palmer, a rival gangster known as "Goldfinger." Palmer, who had been involved in the plot to launder Brink's-Mat gold in the 1980s—the same plot Reader was implicated in—lived in a sprawling mansion in an affluent suburb of Essex, outside of London, and had fallen out big-time with the Adams family.

In the weeks after the Hatton Garden heist—on June 24, 2005—Palmer, age sixty-four, was assassinated while at home, despite the mansion's high security that made it an impenetrable fortress. His bloodied body, shot six times, was discovered by police, and the perpetrator escaped, suggesting a professional hit. The circumstantial evidence linking him to the heist was compelling. Scotland Yard dismissed the theory as "nonsense." The contents of the tape have never been publicly disclosed.

For Johnson, only one thing was for certain. He needed to solve the crime and to find the perpetrators who had committed it. After all, it was the biggest burglary in the history of England.

Chapter 8

An Investigation
Takes Shape

THE FLYING SQUAD FACED THE DAUNTING TASK OF investigating the crime, while also trying to tame the very understandable anxiety of the Hatton Garden jeweler community. Dozens of jewelers in the area had stored millions of dollars' worth of diamonds, gold, and jewelry in the safe deposit over the weekend. They were desperate to get access to their boxes in order to see what had been stolen. Many were despondent and had broken down in tears during their police interviews. The human toll of the burglary was beginning to sink in, and Johnson was determined to hold the culprits, whomever they were, accountable.

Johnson and Craig Turner, the Flying Squad chief, quickly assembled a team: six Flying Squad officers led by Jamie Day, who would handle the day-to-day investigation. Johnson would effectively run the operation. They also put together a small brigade of about two hundred surveillance and forensic officers—including undercover cops and a deaf woman who read lips. The men and women of the Flying Squad would work day and night to solve the crime. Weekends off were not an option.

With his piercing blue eyes and stocky athletic physique, Turner looks like he could've been a wrestler or a professional rugby player if he hadn't chosen a career in policing. He and Johnson had worked together for more than a decade and risen together in the Flying Squad's ranks. As younger detectives they had been on the Flying Squad's special projects team in London, they had hunted Colombian drug cartels, managed hostage negotiations, grappled with Irish contract killers, busted drug smuggling and gun trading rings, and solved their fair share of sensational armed robberies.

A chatty extrovert, Turner, a family man, oozes authority and swagger. He was born at the Port of Tilbury in Essex, a county northeast of London that became synonymous in the 1980s with a generation of brash and aspirational hungry young men whose parents had planted roots in new towns of south Essex after World War II and had gone on to prosper. These self-made men, who came of age during the heyday of Thatcher's economic liberalism, are known, fairly or not, for working in the City of London's financial sector, voting Tory, driving fast cars, going to the gym, and being a bit scrappy.

Outgoing and ambitious, Turner likes working out and playing rugby, but he defies the easy stereotype of the "Essex Man." He is friendly but enigmatic. The only thing he offers about his family is that his father was a businessman who worked in The City, London's financial sector, while his mother worked as a secretary.

For all of his well-cultivated mysteriousness, a necessity of the job, Turner is the public face of the elite unit, and, like Johnson, he wears the swooping eagle of the squad with obvious pride. He travels periodically to Washington, DC, to compare notes with colleagues at the FBI. But he retains the easy informality of a beat cop, signing his e-mails "Craig." He offers to get coffee when guests come to see him. He is not without vanity, befitting a man who runs one of the most prestigious police units in the world. "I'm the one who goes on television to take the pressure off of the other guys on the team," he says, explaining the public relations aspect of his job. But it was ultimately Johnson who was running the investigation.

Turner and Johnson were effective foils for each other. Turner was the natural-born schmoozer, the extrovert, the leader respected by his officers for his ability to get things done. Johnson was the focused lieutenant, the one who ran the Hatton Garden investigation—but largely from behind the scenes. While Turner was wired and energetic, Johnson was decidedly caffeine-free. "Craig is great at networking, he is a people person, who knows how to work the bureaucracy at Scotland Yard and get things done," said Johnson. "Officers like him because he weighs risks but is not too risk averse." He added mischievously, "He usually has an orange tan."

Rounding out the team of Hatton Garden detectives was Jamie Day, forty-one, an amiable Flying Squad officer with the reserved demeanor and sharp mind of a would-be physics professor. With more than a decade of experience as a detective, Day was admired on the force for his strict adherence to logic and deductive reasoning. He was free from emotional flourish or grandstanding. He pieced together clues quietly and methodically like a would-be Hercule Poirot. Like Johnson, he was man who played it by the books. Colleagues say his evidence reports are as meticulous as they are thorough. He doesn't cut corners. He is the opposite of flamboyant or speculative.

"We follow the evidence, and see where it takes us," he explained, with typical understatement, carefully choosing each word. "Everything you handle may be given to another officer so you want to get things right the first time. So that anyone can rely on that work, no matter how small the detail."[1]

* * * *

The Investigation's First Big Break: The Anatomy of the Crime Scene

The Tuesday after the burglary—a full forty-eight hours after the gang had fled with wheelie bins stuffed with gold and jewelry—

Jamie Day was the first officer to arrive at the crime scene. Like his bosses, he wore the swooping eagle of the Flying Squad with pride. He was dressed, as was the custom of Flying Squad officers, in civilian clothes. He knew this was going to be an important case, but he betrayed neither nerves nor excitement. He had that same feeling he always got when he was about to visit the scene of a crime: he had a problem to solve. And his commander Johnson wanted results—and fast.

After surveying the sprawl of tools on the floor of the vault and scrubbing for evidence, it didn't take long for him to realize that it was a professional job. There wasn't a single trace of DNA. Whoever had committed the crime knew what they were doing. Or so it seemed.

"I was the first person in the building," Day recalled. "When I opened the door of the safe deposit company, it looked like an explosion had gone off. The inside of the building was completely ransacked. From the doorway of the corridor leading to the vault, you could see discarded items, including tools strewn on the floor and the contents of safe deposit boxes."

The team of about twenty police and forensics officers worked meticulously to gather evidence without disturbing the crime scene. It was slow, painstaking work, Day recalled, as the officers swept for fingerprints, tried to determine the point of entry, what had been taken or been left behind, and to reconstruct with as much precision as possible what had happened. The forensics officers of the Flying Squad were acutely aware that the crime had reached the top of the chain of command, and that each hour that elapsed was another hour for the criminals to get away. But if they rushed or were clumsy, they risked spoiling evidence or missing a vital clue. They needed to tread carefully.

"Crime scenes are very sensitive and you don't want to disturb any evidence," Day said, recalling the patience Scotland Yard needed to survey a crime scene that only days earlier had tested the patience of the cranky, but determined, drill-wielding geriatrics. "There weren't lives at risk. You don't just charge in and go and look at the vault. It took hours. You couldn't say how much had been taken."[2]

Narrowing down a suspect—or list of suspects—topped the list of priorities. Day spent several hours meticulously interviewing Kelvin Stockwell, the security guard, and Manish Bavishi, who was visibly distraught and had rushed home from Khartoum to survey the damage. At this stage of the investigation, no one could be ruled out. Could it be that the theft was an inside job hatched by the owners of a money-losing business? Given the family's despondency, it seemed unlikely. But that could also be an act. Both Stockwell and Bavishi explained to Day, with no little embarrassment, that they had left the crime as it was unfolding because they had been convinced that nothing was amiss. Their sense of frustration was palpable.

Stockwell meticulously described to the Flying Squad how the safe deposit's security systems and CCTV cameras operated and walked a detective through the premises to help the forensics team identify what the burglars had left behind and what had been damaged. He explained that one of the magnetic gates hadn't been working properly and so the security guards had been using an emergency button to manually lock it. He also noticed that a small yellow-handled screwdriver was missing from a tool case near one of the gates protecting the vault. "I know it should have been there as I used it on Thursday, 2nd of April 2015 before I locked up," he told the officer. He also observed that the number of new clients had been reduced to a trickle during the last year and that all members needed to provide a passport or driving license, a utility bill, a recent bank statement, and a personal reference.

But he also acknowledged that several nonmembers who had inquired about renting a safe deposit box had been given access to the vault. "I would say that I have only let four or five nonmembers into the vault in the last twelve months."[3]

As investigators took witness statements from security guards, the building's concierge, and maintenance workers and tenants who had access to the interior of the building, about a dozen forensics officers scanned the scene for fingerprints. Only two officers at a time could fit in the cramped vault area, substantially slowing things down. Day recalled that it took about twelve hours before he finally set eyes on the massive adjoining circles the gang had drilled through reinforced concrete. The hole resembled the figure-eight rings of the Audi automobile logo. Police also discovered markings on the wall that the thieves had drawn to indicate where to place the drill.

Meanwhile, the Flying Squad had to contend with angry, emotional, and, in many cases, elderly safe deposit box owners whose boxes had been emptied and were desperate to determine what had been stolen, but were not allowed to access because the box was now part of a crime scene investigation. By necessity, the investigation was shrouded in a secrecy worthy of the Garden itself, since the Flying Squad did not want to tip off the burglars about whether they were closing in. Even without that constraint, the vault door itself remained shut.

The safe deposit box owners "all wanted to know if their box had been broken into and we couldn't tell them at this point, and they were frustrated as they couldn't understand why we didn't have an answer," Day recalled. "The reality is that the vault's door wasn't open. The only access to the vault was the triple eight holes in the wall." It was not something a doughnut-eating police officer could easily slither through, but, luckily, Day was slim.

It was Tuesday, April 7, at 9 p.m.—nearly half a day after they began to investigate the scene—when a small group of forensics officers, including Day, finally poked their heads through the holes in the concrete wall. "I had personally never seen anything like that," Day said, laughing as he recalled the moment. "It is not an everyday occurrence. But the enormity of what had happened wasn't yet clear to us: Had one box or 999 boxes been broken into?"[4]

Among the dozens of potential clues, the CCTV camera footage held a vital key to solve the crime, assuming, of course, the Flying Squad could recover it. So Day was feeling a bit anxious as he checked the 120-plus cameras in and around the building, several of which had been smashed by "Basil" before the gang had entered. Now the magnitude of the case was dawning on Johnson and his team.

For the young officers working under Johnson's charge, botching things up on such a high-stakes case could prove devastating. As it was, the Flying Squad was a close-knit unit of type-A-plus personalities in which officers hungered for one another's approval, even if sangfroid was as much a badge of honor as wearing the squad's swooping eagle. Day invariably wanted a win. And solving the Hatton Garden case would be a win on an epic scale.

But he was also a creature of empiricism, not easily rattled, and, like Johnson and Turner, unflinchingly confident that the methodical approach of the Flying Squad would ultimately persevere. It had in the past. He just needed to be patient.

As journalists gathered outside the front of the building and irate safe deposit box holders lined up to give television interviews, Day went to the back of the building to check one last CCTV camera near the fire escape door. The natural point of investigation was the CCTV footage. The thieves had disabled most of the CCTV cameras in the building. But as Day approached the fire escape, his eyes widened. The camera there was completely intact. Somehow they had missed it. "Finding that CCTV camera was our first big break," he admitted.

The gang also hadn't realized that Berganza Ltd, an antique dealer on Greville Street, which has one of the finest collections of medieval rings in the world and faces the back of 88–90 Hatton Garden, also had trained a CCTV camera on them. Berganza was undergoing construction at the time and Day quickly collected the film footage and downloaded it. It could help solve the mystery provided the thieves had let their guard down.

Day returned to Flying Squad headquarters in Putney, in south-west London, Tuesday night. After taking off his jacket and rolling up his sleeves, he began the arduous and seemingly endless task of scanning through the CCTV footage, minute by minute, hunched over his computer, trying to reconstruct the crime. Meticulously going through the footage, frame by frame, required patience and perserverence, a keen eye for spotting clues, and a very high tolerance for monotony. It was going to be a long night.

He began by working backward from the moment the thieves had left the building on Easter Sunday, in order to retrace their steps and establish a timeline of what had taken place. This was made easier by the fact that the time was marked in a dark rectangle on the bottom of the screen by the CCTV video recorder. But the scale of the task was enormous given that he was not only sifting through hundreds of hours of footage from the CCTV cameras that the thieves had missed near the fire escape but also looking for clues from the dozens of CCTV cameras that peppered the jewelry quarter's streets. He was trying to determine how and when the perpetrators had entered the building and when they had fled.

Days turned into nights and nights turned into days as Day, running on adrenaline, trawled through the footage. Initially he saw nothing out of the ordinary. Johnson asked to be constantly updated. As Day zoomed in and out with a click of a computer mouse, the pressure for a break that could solve the crime grew intense.

That moment finally arrived on day three when, bleary-eyed and fatigued from lack of sleep, Day suddenly stopped the CCTV footage and froze the screen. Finally, he saw what he had been looking for: the grainy image of several men entering the building, with their faces covered, and then exiting. The frame showed two shadowy figures in fluorescent maintenance jackets.

"We were able to pinpoint what time the gang had arrived and the last person was inside. We could see that they had waited for the last person to leave for the long weekend before they arrived on the premises." But the men's faces were obscured. Who were they?

A CCTV camera had also captured in the darkness the team parking a car on Leather Lane, which runs parallel to Hatton Garden one block away. In a blunder, Collins had been undertaking reconnaissance in his own car around the neighborhood on the Saturday evening of the burglary. During the week, the street hosts a boisterous food, vegetable, and clothing market. But as it was the holiday weekend, it was largely deserted, making it easier for police to spot unexpected activity.

As the car's lights flashed in the video, Day noticed something else. He froze the frame and saw a distinctive white Mercedes. Its license plate was not immediately visible. He paused, squinting his eyes. Then he tapped on his keyboard to close in on the vehicle, and examined the model. It was a white Mercedes E200 with a black roof and alloy rims. Day knew that white Mercedes were common enough. So that wasn't a huge break. But a black roof and, more notably, black alloy rims—now that wasn't common at all. Armed with this differentiating detail, he now had something to go on.

As the images played out, Day saw something else. By reviewing the time stamp on the CCTV and seeing the men in fluorescent maintenance outfits walking out of a white van and then leaving the scene, he was also able to deduce that they had spent three days in the vault during which they had left and returned to the scene of the crime. What audacity! What balls they must have had!

With the evidence strongly suggesting that the Mercedes belonged to one of them, Day and the surveillance team, taking advantage of the dozens of hidden cameras peppering Hatton Garden, studied all the CCTV footage within a one-mile radius of Hatton Garden during the seventy-two hours the heist took place. It took several hours until Day saw what he was looking for: A camera had captured the license plate of the car. A background check then determined that it was registered in Wales and insured in Herefordshire, in England's west Midlands. But—nearly a week after the burglary had taken place—it still was not clear who the car belonged to. Finding the Mercedes, however, was a watershed for the investigation.

"It was a bank holiday and there weren't many people or cars around. So that made it easier to find the Mercedes, since the roads were quiet and there aren't many Mercedes models with roofs and tires that color," Day said. "By identifying the Mercedes, we were able to see that they had come to and from Hatton Garden three times that weekend," he said. "The imagery was fuzzy so we had to look at every angle. It wasn't as easy as it sounds."

Using the massive network of CCTV cameras across London that have made Britons the most-watched nation in Europe, Day and the rest of the team were also able to trace and track the Mercedes's movements throughout London during the previous several months. Just about a week after the burglary had first been discovered, the network of surveillance footage finally led them to the tool shop in Edmonton, where CCTV cameras had filmed the distinctive car parked outside, while Collins and Jones bought a new replacement pump to help them complete the job. They were homing in.

Automatic license plate recognition cameras, which photograph license plates and are installed all over London to help police fight crime, had also photographed the Mercedes. Armed with a positive identification on the car and the data on its movements, Day was then able to identify the car's owner: a portly career criminal called Kenny Collins, whom the Firm referred to as "a wombat-thick old cunt." The Flying Squad had its first suspect.

"Once we identified the car, it was a matter of following its trail and seeing where it led us," Day explained, with the typical deductive logic of a veteran Flying Squad officer and allowing himself a barely discernible soupçon of self-satisfaction. "By tailing Collins, we were able to piece the team together."

"Using the same car during and after the crime was a real clanger!" Johnson added, allowing himself to grin.

And while the aging thieves adroitly used walkie-talkies during the heist to avoid being traced, they continued using the same cell phones they had before the heist, providing the Flying Squad an opportunity to monitor Collins's calls. Soon it became apparent that Collins was talking to Brian Reader and Terry Perkins, men with long criminal records who were already known to police. Once they had been identified, the police were also able to determine their cell phone numbers, and to track who was calling whom.

The police had a list of about fifty suspects with the experience to have pulled off such a daring crime. But once they had identified Collins, they tailed him for days, and, before long, he led police to the other members of the gang. "We didn't go after Reader," Turner explained. "He came to us."[5]

With the list of key suspects in hand, the Flying Squad also traced the diamond-tipped drill left at the scene of the crime to a drill that had been stolen eighteen months previously in what Day said was a fraudulent purchase under a false name. If it was Jones who had stolen it, he had covered his tracks. But the date of the invoice for the drill showed that the heist had been in the works for at least two years.

As a picture of the men slowly began to emerge, Johnson assembled a team of more than a hundred officers—forensic specialists, surveillance experts, and officers specializing in burglaries. He also applied to Scotland Yard's Specialist Crime and Operations II Surveillance Command team to plant listening devices in Collins's Mercedes and Terry Perkins's Citroën Saxo, and in mid-May the vehicles were bugged.

Overhearing what the villains were saying was just the evidence he needed to ensnare the gang. It was to be an old-fashioned game of cat and mouse, though the quality of sound and ability to conceal covert listening devices had improved since the days of the Second World War when British intelligence agencies used bugs to monitor captured German fighter pilots.

Today, British police forces have regional surveillance units that can disrupt wireless Internet networks, surreptitiously install bugs in cars or properties, or monitor computers.[6] Such is the sophistication of surveillance technology that Scotland Yard reportedly has secret spy planes capable of eavesdropping on cell phone conversations from the sky,[7] while snooping local councils in London, Manchester, and Birmingham have tested spy cameras hidden in street lampposts that can monitor whether citizens are committing antisocial behavior after being triggered by loud noise.

For covert surveillance in criminal investigations, permission must be granted from either the home secretary, the chief constable, or the Serious Organized Crime Agency, among others, and must be justified on the grounds of "national security" or "detecting serious crime." Such evidence is admissible in court.[8]

Using undercover surveillance equipment was a method Johnson knew all too well. All he needed was to summon his vast stores of patience and hope that the gang of gabby elderly thieves began to blab. He didn't have to wait long.

* * * *

Brian Reader, a Cop Killer?

Once Scotland Yard homed in on Reader, thanks to the Firm's bungling, the Flying Squad had renewed motivation in bringing the perpetrators to justice, beyond just the scale and audacity of the crime.

Officers in the Yard still remembered the bone-chilling morning on January 26, 1985, when Reader had been seen standing over Detective Constable John Fordham, an undercover officer who had three children and was close to death. Two Rottweilers, Cleo and Sam, were barking ferociously. Only minutes earlier Reader, then forty-five years old and helping the gangster Kenneth Noye to launder millions in gold bars, had arrived at Hollywood Cottage, Noye's sprawling Kent mansion.

Scotland Yard had been tailing Noye for weeks, as part of a secret surveillance operation aimed at recovering the gold, some of which had been buried in Noye's garden. Police were finally ready to pounce. Fordham, known as "Gentleman John" because of his kindly manner, was part of a Scotland Yard special undercover surveillance unit, called C11, according to Noye's biographer, Wensley Clarkson.

After sundown on that freezing Saturday, two undercover officers, including Fordham, entered Noye's estate, when his Rottweilers began barking. "Dogs hostile," a panicked Fordham said quietly into his radio. Reader and Noye were in Noye's study when they heard the tumult, according to Clarkson. Then, Noye immediately rushed out. "What's happening with those dogs?" he screamed.

When he went to investigate the noise, armed with a knife, and was confronted with the sight of two holes peering out of a mask, Noye punched the man in the head as hard as he could, before Fordham jumped on him. The sequence of events was later disputed, with Noye claiming he had been attacked first. Noye then stabbed Fordham several times, including in the heart, killing him.[9]

As a team of officers stormed the estate, Reader fled. Neil Murphy, Fordham's partner, would later testify that Reader had kicked Fordham's body before he fled. Reader made his way to a country road and hailed a car, which turned out to be an undercover police car. He was arrested on suspicion of assaulting a police officer. Reader soon had a new label attached to him: cop killer.

Following the killing of Fordham in 1985, Noye was charged with murder and Reader as an accomplice. Prosecutors told the jury that Murphy had seen Reader making a kicking motion near Fordham's body. Throughout the proceedings, Noye acknowledged that he had killed Fordham but insisted that he had done so because he believed his life was in imminent danger.[10]

In a verdict that shocked members of London's law enforcement establishment and which is still bitterly remembered to this day, both men were acquitted of murder on the grounds that they had been acting in self-defense.

Now, Scotland Yard had been given a new chance to bring Brian Reader to justice.

Chapter 9

A Game of Cat and Mouse

The Hapless Accomplices

In the weeks following the burglary, the men reveled in their work. They may have pulled off a wildly daring heist, bypassing the latest in security—its software and hardware—but they were quick to break some of the most basic rules from old-school criminal handbooks. First, they returned to—if not the scene of the crime, exactly—the place where they were known and had most frequented in the run-up to the crime: the Castle pub. They were back to plates of bangers and mash at the same spot where they had hatched the plan in the first place.

Armed with a bravado perhaps conditioned by age—and blissfully unaware that police were already on to them—they went about their lives, shopping for groceries at their local Tesco supermarkets, eating curry at their favorite Indian restaurant, picking up their granddaughters from ballet lessons, and nattering among themselves about their nagging wives, the younger "birds" they fancied (among them a young woman called "Randy Mandy") their ungrateful children, their hapless sons-in-law, their ailments, their impending mortality, their real estate investments, the state of the country, British versus Portuguese sewage systems, the relative benefits of diesel versus gas, the relative strength of Margaret Thatcher versus Vladimir Putin, and, of course, their retirement plans.

There was also some unfinished business to attend to—the disposal of the white van used in the heist—a task, which, according to a person close to the gang, was handled by Perkins. Ever adept at camouflaging himself as a doddering and kindly old man, he drove the van to a scrap yard in north London where it was turned into scrap metal. Collins also contacted his sixty-year-old brother-in-law, William Lincoln, a burly lug of a man with bladder-control problems, and asked him if he would help transport some of the stolen goods and help conceal them. Lincoln, in turn, contacted his nephew John Harbinson, a forty-two-year-old taxi driver with whom he had reconciled after twenty years, to see whether he could provide transportation and store three bags of jewels in his garage. He told Harbinson that the diamonds, rubies, and emeralds were a "load of old shit."

Also rounding out the team was Hugh Doyle, an amiable Irish plumber who prosecutors suspect of offering up his plumbing studio in Enfield, north London, as a drilling rehearsal space ahead of the heist.

* * * *

"Billy the Fish" Lincoln

William Lincoln was known as "Billy the Fish" by the others because he made extra cash by supplying friends and family with fish and seafood he bought from Billingsgate Fish Market in east London—including eel every Sunday for his mother in Essex. Like many working-class criminals in east London, Lincoln had a taste for jellied saltwater eels, known as the "poor man's delicacy." High in fat, they were served cold and congealed in bars known as "eel, pie and mash houses."

With remarkable self-awareness, Lincoln conceded to the others that he was "not the sharpest knife in the drawer" but also said he was not a "divvo," or dummy. He was encumbered by bladder-control problems—which would sometimes embarrass him when arriving unannounced—and a hip replacement. At the time of the heist he was on government disability.

But for all of his perceived clumsiness, Lincoln was deemed to be trustworthy by Collins, who was married to Lincoln's sister, Millie. He had been a petty thief for much of his life and had been convicted for attempted burglary in the 1970s and 1980s. He was generally harmless but also had a temper, which could flare up from time to time. In 2013 he was convicted of battery after attacking a gang of youths with a chair because they were making a fracas on a street in Bethnal Green, the east London neighborhood where he liked to hold court with his cronies.

These days, when not selling fish, he would often go to the baths at a community center in Bethnal Green, and gleefully dunk his bearlike body in the water. Collins was a relative, if only by marriage, and Lincoln, who was always eager to help a family member in need, agreed to help him hide millions of dollars of stolen goods.

* * * *

The Plumber

Compared to the rest of the gang, Hugh Doyle, an affable Irish father of two with a white speckled goatee and sparkling eyes, was comparatively young, only forty-eight at the time of the burglary. He had driven a taxi and worked as a plumber and appeared to be in awe of the elder men and their storied careers.

Doyle was a natural-born charmer and bon vivant who had a pilot's license and liked to go yachting. Married with two young children, he was a popular neighbor in Enfield, north London, where he lived in a large semidetached brick house. Neighbors said he was always rushing from one place to another on his motorbike, servicing boilers, and engaging in chitchat. "Everyone knows Hugh," said a neighbor. "He's the kind of person who is always friendly, always offering a helping hand." His Facebook page shows him piloting a variety of small planes, taking his son to the National Maritime Museum, doing indoor skydiving, and yachting with friends.

He was friendly with Collins, Reader, and Perkins. They were drinking buddies he had met at the Harlequin Pub in Islington in the late 1990s and early 2000s, where Perkins had worked as a short-order cook after he went AWOL from prison. Doyle gave Collins a key to his plumbing workshop, behind the Wheatsheaf pub in Enfield, which prosecutors suspected the gang used to practice their drilling ahead of the burglary. Doyle said he gave Collins the key so he could "let himself in and make coffee."

After the burglary, the gang used his plumbing business as a meeting point and a place to store some of the jewels, including gold and gems. Collins trusted Doyle, but the others remained suspicious of him. They worried that their inner circle was getting too large and that Doyle would take some "cream" for himself.

* * * *

Catch Me If You Can

Once Collins was identified, the Flying Squad noticed that he kept meeting with the same three or four men, in their sixties and seventies, at the same pubs and restaurants in north London and Enfield, often huddled together, whispering.

While the tabloid media was feverishly reporting that the Pink Panthers were behind the crime, Johnson now knew the more embarrassing truth: the villains appeared to be homegrown and graying.

The Flying Squad faced enormous pressure to ensure that the covert operation wasn't compromised, even as the media continued to pry, and frustrated Hatton Garden jewelers clamored for the recovery of their stolen jewels. The media played an inadvertent and invaluable role by throwing the real thieves off the scent.

In the days after the burglary, the *Mirror* published leaked CCTV footage of the men as they fled the premises, giving them the nicknames Mr. Ginger, Mr. Strong, Mr. Montana, the Gent, the Tall Man, and the Old Man, and expressing alarm that the gang had already fled the country. But their identities were obscured and the public did not realize that they were older criminals. While it is not clear who leaked the footage, it could have been part of a deliberate strategy by Scotland Yard to destabilize the gang.

"We went quiet and it perpetuated even more media attention," Turner recalled. "For me, this was fantastic, as it was taking attention away from what we were doing. And the villains were watching and thinking: the police are looking over there—they are looking at Germany, they are looking at eastern Europe, they think it's an inside job—they are not looking at us. So we let the media run with their conspiracy theories as it worked to our advantage."

Keeping a lid on a covert operation that had all the delicious aspects of a homegrown thriller demanded discipline. No one could know. No other colleagues outside the Flying Squad. Not a spouse. Not a friend. No one. "The crime captured the public imagination and this was something we had to manage. There was so much interest and we had to run a covert operation, while satisfying the public and keeping what we were doing secret," Turner said. "There were quite a few people inside Scotland Yard who knew about this and the media were trying to dig in and you didn't know, did ya'?" he says, smiling widely. "I had concerns about the security of the operations given the massive press interest in what had happened."[1]

* * * *

As the flying squad patiently waited for the men to incriminate themselves, lying low was no little challenge for the Firm. They appeared to have felt reborn following the heist, and could barely contain their glee.

Accomplishing such a sensational heist would make even a young man feel giddy, never mind a gang that had had to contend with arthritis and diabetes. It was enough to make Jones want to do cartwheels down the street. They had just pulled off what some were already calling the heist of the century, perhaps even more daring than the Great Train Robbery fifty-two years before. Every thief in Britain was marveling at it. Punters at pubs across the land were toasting to their sheer gumption, and engaged in the national parlor game of trying to guess who they were. Images of three gaping holes in the concrete wall of 88–90 Hatton Garden were being flashed on news bulletins every hour, a testament to their bravura performance. Without the curmudgeonly Reader to shush them, the rest of the liver-spotted crew began to crow.

On May 15, on a sunny day, more than a month after the burglary, Perkins and Jones were driving in Perkins's blue Citroën Saxo near their homes in Enfield when the two began to boast about the heist. As far as they were concerned, Scotland Yard had no idea who was behind the caper.

Using the cockney rhyming slang word "tom"—short for "tom-foolery" or jewelry—and referring to the previous Security Express robbery Perkins had helped to pull off in the 1980s, when he and a gang of thieves stole £6 million ($9 million) from a security depot in east London, Jones was triumphant: "The biggest cash robbery in history at the time and now the biggest tom history in the fucking world, that's what they are saying . . . And what a book you could write, fucking hell," he said.

Perkins, less prone to hyperbole than Jones, was equally effusive. "And what are the fucking odds, what fucking odds!" he said. "We done the best bit of work of the whole century!"

Back at the Flying Squad headquarters, the officers surveilling the gang could barely believe what they were hearing as the boasts were picked up by the surveillance bugs in Perkins's car. Just minutes before Jones and Perkins had begun to talk, the bugs had been activated. "Positive identification of Perkins out of home address," reads Scotland Yard's audio transcript, recording its license plate EN51EUD and the date and time—14:43 p.m. on May 15, 2015.[2]

The log noted that he was wearing a beige jacket and sitting in the driver's seat. The radio was turned to LBC, or "Leading Britain's Conversation," a talk radio station that was a kind of poor man's BBC and was prone to vehement political discussions and uplifting soft rock ballads from the 1980s.

Over the din of the radio, always played at a loud ear-splitting volume befitting senior citizens whose hearing wasn't what it used to be, two of the key suspects were admitting they had committed the crime. The trap was yielding results. But Turner and Johnson were waiting to make a move. They wanted the criminals to become their own grave diggers—and they had now dug out about three feet of dirt.

It was old-school reconnaissance of the type the elderly gang themselves had used to stake out the Garden. Only this time, the gang didn't realize they were being watched and recorded, their every taciturn glance or reckless confession transmitted to the good men and women of Scotland Yard.

Eavesdropping on Reader and his cronies without being detected was hard enough. But the good men and women of the Flying Squad also faced perhaps an even greater challenge: deciphering the rapid-fire East End Cockney rhyming slang with which the men peppered their speech. The seemingly endless stream of "fucks," "arseholes," and "cunts" was much easier to parse.

"It wasn't always easy to understand what they were saying," Jamie Day recalled, noting with a chuckle that Reader and his team offered him a crash course in Cockney, which some scholars say originated in the East End of London in the nineteenth century as a code used by criminals precisely so the police wouldn't understand them.[3]

While Cockney is inextricably bound up in the identity of London, a 2012 study of two thousand adult Londoners commissioned by the Museum of London found that many Londoners were baffled by the famous east London slang, finding it increasingly incomprehensible in a throbbing multicultural capital where a babel of foreign languages has transformed modern usage. "OMG! Cockney Rhyming Slang Is Brown Bread," the British news agency Reuters intoned in mock horror at the time, using the Cockney rhyming slang for "dead."[4]

The survey found that about 80 percent of Londoners did not understand that "donkey ears" was Cockney rhyming slang for "years," and that "bacon and eggs" meant "legs" while they also struggled to parse "tommy tucker" (supper) or "spending time with the teapot lids" (kids).

Champions of Cockney, however, were relieved that, at least, many seemed to grasp that "apples and pears" meant "stairs" and that "tea leaf" meant "thief," while "porky pies" (lies) was the most commonly used expression. At the same time, experts noted that adolescents had developed their own Cockney lingo for text messaging, with David Crystal, honorary professor of linguistics at Bangor University, telling the *Daily Telegraph* that some were using "Barack Obamas" instead of "pajamas."[5]

Whatever its elusiveness in the age of Twitter, Cockney rhyming slang appears to have captured the imaginations—and lexicon—of the "tea leafs" Danny Jones and Terry Perkins, who spoke it with such abandon that the Flying Squad officers—and prosecutors—studying their speech sometimes consulted with colleagues from the East End of London to make sure they didn't miss anything.

* * * *

Following the Villains

In the weeks after the heist, beginning in early April 2015, dozens of undercover officers working in small teams and driving in unmarked cars tailed the men. Johnson was determined to gather enough evidence to ensnare them, even if that meant waiting months for an arrest. By the beginning of May, the surveillance officers had acquired a strong sense of their daily routines. They followed them to the pub and to their other favorite haunts, which betrayed a middle-class aspirational swagger worthy of aging thieves who had traded jail cells for handsome homes and took relish in enjoying the good life.

While Perkins appeared to be a fish-'n'-chips man through and through, the gang—save Reader—had embraced the national obsession with Indian food and chicken tikka masala. So they repeatedly returned to the Delhi Grill, a canteen-style Indian restaurant plastered with Bollywood posters on a quiet street in Islington.

On Friday, April 12, at 12:37 p.m., Reader was photographed, appearing tired and ruddy faced, as he sat with Collins on the terrace outside Scotti's Snack Bar on Islington Green. It appeared to be his favorite café in north London; it had first opened in 1967 and had barely changed since, offering dependable bacon fry-ups—that is, bacon, sausage, eggs, and coffee—and a vision of a 1960s Britain frozen in time. Surveillance officers noted that a man wearing a brown suit and carrying a Waitrose shopping bag had shown Reader and Collins its contents.[6]

On May 1, Perkins and Jones were surreptitiously recorded at the Castle pub, their favorite watering hole before moving on to the upmarket Bonnie Gull Seafood Bar in nearby Exmouth Market. A map on the blackboard showed where all the fish had been caught in England and Scotland, which appealed to men of their generation.

Collins, an avid dog walker who often did the grocery shopping for Millie, seemed to pass aimless hours wandering in parks in north London and stocking up on medicine at the pharmacy. On Friday, April 24, surveillance officers spied on him as he met with Perkins and Jones at Ye Olde Cherry Tree pub in Southgate, in north London, and then, later that day, feasted with them on steak at the Highland Angus Steakhouse on Cannon Hill.

Collins offered a particular challenge for the young surveillance officers due to the sheer monotony of his daily routine. Throughout April and early May, he was tailed as he went to take a "black and white dog" for a walk, talked in a hushed voice on his black Nokia flip-style phone, and frequently purchased medication for his arthritis.

"I could see there was a blue disabled badge displayed in the windscreen of the vehicle," one of the undercover officers following Collins wrote in his report, meticulously detailing the movements of Collins's white Mercedes with the registration CP13BGY, and observing its distinct black roof and black alloy tires. "I saw that John Kenneth Collins was wearing black rimmed glasses whilst driving," he added in a report dated Friday, April 17, 2015. Another officer noted that he had a gold bracelet on his right wrist.[7] The officer snapped photographs with a Nikon digital camera. No detail was too small. No meeting too inconsequential.

Meanwhile, during the first two weeks of May, Perkins was followed as he took his grandson to the doctor, put a large and suspicious-looking black bag in the trunk of the Saxo, and when he stopped by himself at 6 p.m. sharp at the counter of the Blue Mermaid fish-and-chip shop near his home in Enfield. Despite having a wife and four daughters, he seemed to like to spend time on his own when he was not with his old pals—perhaps a hangover from all those long hours spent in a jail cell. He was trim and wiry and didn't finish everything on his plate, the surveillance officers observed.

The surveillance operation was painstaking. "We were trying to get a sense of their lifestyle, who they met with, what they did on a daily basis," as Johnson described it.[8]

Turner, the Flying Squad chief, added that following the gang required a lot of patience since they were, after all, senior citizens, and continued performing the domestic chores of people their age. That meant that officers sometimes had to endure their endless squabbles over where to have lunch, their slagging off of relatives and neighbors, their deliberations on whether to buy granola or porridge at the super-market. At least their expletive-laced discussions about their wives and children did provide some relief from the banalities. The officers did not follow the men twenty-four hours a day, Turner explained, in order to ensure that the surveillance operation wasn't compromised.

"It could be very tedious to follow these guys around—we were not interested in observing them doing their shopping. You have to pick your moments," Turner said. "But we observed them closely and by doing so we could see when they were doing something out of the ordinary that didn't fit with their usual pattern. In that sense, every clue could help us."

A special police unit also monitored their phone calls, as they called one another with more and more frequency, shifting between boasts and chats about when and how they were going to cash in their booty. When the others called Reader, who didn't have a cell phone, they called his son Paul, who passed his father the phone. His phone, too, was being monitored.

"We followed them around for weeks, without being detected, which is not easy," said Day.[9]

One false move could blow open the investigation. Undercover officers had to blend in without being exposed. And while the gang was behaving with foolhardy exuberance, they were also experienced criminals who were used to being followed by police. Danny Jones, in particular, was an avid reader of crime books, and was very careful to constantly check whether he was being followed. At one point, in the middle of the surveillance, he left for a preplanned vacation, a walking trip in the English countryside with his sister.

* * * *

Boozing and Lip-Reading

In their arsenal of methods to ensnare the gang, the police also had another secret weapon: a deaf woman named Gillian Hadfield who was as adept at reading lips as she was at analyzing hand gestures. She had been helping Scotland Yard solve crimes for some forty years. Now she was hired by the Yard to decipher what the men were saying when they weren't in their cars and were being secretly watched. It was a classic combination of the Flying Squad's use of high-tech and old-school techniques to crack a case wide open.

Gillian Hadfield was born with her hearing but became slowly deaf in her teens. By the time she left school at age sixteen, she relied entirely on lip-reading, and at twenty-two, she could not hear anything. But because she was born with her hearing, she had a residual sense of speech, and spoke like a hearing person. Her hearing was also buttressed by a cochlear implant that allowed her to hear some sounds. She did not use sign language. Her ability to read lips was so acute and nuanced that she had often been used by both prosecutors and defense attorneys as an expert witness. In one case, a woman who didn't have a voice box and couldn't speak, witnessed a murder. Hadfield was brought in to read her lips and become her voice.

Racing against the clock to gather enough evidence to prove that the gang was behind the heist, the Flying Squad employed Hadfield to examine the audio evidence. Her ability to read their lips became a valuable asset, even though she was the first to admit that lip-reading was an inexact science. Context, facial expressions, small gestures, and body language were all needed to sort out words that sound the same but are spelled differently, like "tied" and "tide" or words that look the same on lips such as "quip" and "whip." Such challenges were made all the more difficult when observing a group of old-timers, who spoke in machine-gun bursts and used East End slang, peppered by expletives and outmoded Cockney rhymes from a different era.

But when Hadfield sat down at Flying Squad headquarters in May 2015 to watch a DVD showing video footage of the men from the Castle pub, the triumphant boasting and gesticulations were so animated that it didn't take long before she managed to decipher at least part of what they were saying. Old infirm men, some of them hard of hearing themselves, were outwitted by a deaf woman.

On a trip to the Castle pub at the beginning of May—about one month after the heist—Perkins and Collins sat hunched over beers in the corner, as they reminisced excitedly about the moment they finally broke through the concrete vault and used their power drills to make three large and adjoining holes. Reader was also there, appearing less grumpy than usual, sitting on the opposite side of the table as the two men filled him in on what had happened after he had abandoned the burglary. As usual, he remained seated, and it was Perkins who went to the bar to order another round of beers, taking out a wad of cash to pay.

Unaware that they were being secretly filmed by a Scotland Yard operative, Collins and Perkins recalled the thickness of the wall and how they used a hydraulic pump to force the cabinet down, after realizing it was bolted to the floor. Then, with a flourish worthy of a Charlie Chaplin slapstick comedy, Perkins mimicked the furious motion of the pump. The video shows him thrusting his right hand up and down in a pumping motion as he hollered, "Boom! Boom! Boom!" The men cackled appreciatively.

Watching the DVD, Hadfield noted that the three men were sitting in the pub in the back, trying to appear inconspicuous, if not entirely succeeding. She wrote, "Male wearing open neck white shirt with glasses" made "pumping actions and is making what looks like an explosive sound." "There is general hilarity," she added in brackets.[10] The jovial grandpas appeared completely unconcerned about the possibility that they were being watched.

Later, as they drove around London in Perkins's Citroën Saxo, Perkins and Jones patted each other on the back for the "bottle"— the Cockney term for "courage"—that had moved them to not walk away, even when the burglary seemed hopeless. Jones, ever the exhibitionist, was especially pleased by all the media coverage.

"Have you seen the headlines?" Jones bragged. "We are going to be famous! I tell you something now, if we never proceeded me and you, Basil would have walked away."

"Yeah, he would have," Perkins replied.

"So they put the work down to me and you," Jones recalled, displaying more than a little cockiness and once again reliving that sweet moment the drill had breached the wall.

"And you said, 'Smash that up!' "

"Smash that up!"[11]

Perkins, who had been distracted by his need to take his insulin shots during the burglary, nevertheless marveled at his role as cheerleader while Jones, the lithe athlete, got the job done. Now that the burglary was over, he nonchalantly informed Jones that he had been taking the insulin shots throughout the four-day heist, the whole time they were in the basement, a fact he seems to have previously neglected to tell the others.

Noting that he had recently turned sixty-seven, he finally let Jones in on his secret. "Fucking 20 pills a day, think of it, three injections. I had it all with me my injections."

Jones reacted with equanimity, if not a little shock. Perhaps he didn't want to embarrass his old friend.

"You never . . ." His voice trailed off.

"Course I had to take them in there for three days."

"What were they in your pocket?"

"Oh yeah, I had them in a proper pack in me bag, yeah." Jones could not help but be impressed by his pluckiness and courage. It was one thing to have pulled off the heist at their age—and to have wielded that heavy drill. But to have done all that while injecting shots of insulin suddenly made Perkins a king among thieves.

"And you've got Carl, whose been on massive bits of work, screaming like a pig!" Jones observed, referring to the hapless Carl Wood, at nearly a decade younger.

"Yeah, if I don't take the insulin for three days I could, you'd a had to carry me out in a wheelie bin!"

"Fucking hell!" Jones replied.

Perkins played it down. "You know like act drunk you know the side effects, well that never happened to me."[12]

Before long, Perkins's mind wandered back inside the vault and focused on their unlikely moment of triumph. "Smash that up now, put that down, it's fucking working cos you're egging one another on, it's working you got to take it off, it ain't ping back. Remember me saying, 'We're in! we're in!'" Perkins recalled. "And then you started pumping again. If I had been saying this ain't going to work, Dan, you're defeated you know."[13]

Jones seemed to relish the recollection. After all, it had been the pinnacle of their criminal careers.

The men also listened obsessively to the radio and just as obsessively read newspaper coverage of the heist. They were lulled into a false sense of security that the police were off of their scent. All the reports said that police had no suspects, and Jones assured the others that he was hearing that Scotland Yard believed the heist had been committed by someone who worked at the safe deposit company.

"That's a good thing if they think it's an inside job," Perkins told

Jones during another spin in the Saxo to discuss their plans to fence the jewels.

"They do, badly," Jones replied.

The police, Perkins mused confidently, would not put a lot of resources into investigating the crime if they thought the suspects came from inside the company. And they would surely never suspect that the culprits were a bunch of aging old men like them!

"They will not put 100 percent into it, 'cause they'll think, 'you mugging us off you cunts, you want us running all around London when it's fucking from the inside,' " he said.[14]

Meanwhile, back at the Flying Squad headquarters in Putney, teams of officers were hunched over computers, reviewing CCTV footage and recordings and sifting through the evidence. Officers, including Day, had been retrieving CCTV footage from the shops and restaurants, grocery stores, and pharmacies where the gang stopped to meet. It was one of the biggest Scotland Yard surveillance operations in decades.

The eavesdropping had yielded a wealth of confessional bravado, but Johnson wasn't yet satisfied. He knew that the gang could shrewdly try to shrug it off as if all the boasting was just the musings of a bunch of aging and senile fantasists. What the police needed was hard evidence.

Chapter 10

The Art of Snooping and Waiting

Known for his imperturbability and patience, Johnson was particularly skilled in surveillance operations. He had spent years running covert operations that relied on surreptitiously installing listening devices in the cars or homes of criminals and then pouncing when the moment was right. Hunting and outsmarting bank robbers was one of his specialties. "I have seen my fair share of jobs," he says, quickly adding, "no more than anyone else."[1]

The hunter and the hunted could not have been more different. Both were determined that their "last job" would be successful and burnish their legacies. But while the gang was loud and boisterous and urged themselves along with their incessant bluster, Johnson was calm, deliberate, and meticulous. He took nothing for granted. In many ways, his entire career had prepared him for this case.

Johnson grew up in Manchester where soccer is a religion and what team you support is tantamount to choosing a lifelong spouse. Johnson proudly supported Manchester City, a one-time beleaguered east Manchester club that was founded in 1880 and had been in the shadow of its more flamboyant and successful rival, Manchester United, the one-time home of David Beckham. His was the choice of someone with a natural inclination to root for the underdog.

He grew up watching police dramas and was particularly drawn to *Hill Street Blues*, the pioneering 1980s American police drama that was celebrated for its portrayal of the gritty realism of policing in an inner-city precinct in a fictional midwestern city. In some ways, the precinct captain on the show, Frank Furillo, bears a striking resemblance to Johnson, though Johnson is a far more understated and self-effacing character. Unlike Johnson, who is eminently English and even-keeled, Furillo barks his commands, but he is also an avuncular figure who remains deeply committed to his officers. Johnson disliked taking credit for anything and, with no touch of false modesty, attributed even the biggest wins of his career—and there have been many—to "teamwork."

Colleagues unanimously characterized Johnson as the kind of officer you wanted to have watching your back. In a country where police typically do not carry guns, he had intense firearms training, a prerequisite for officers facing down armed robbers and hit men. He is precise, reticent, and enigmatic. No one in the Flying Squad could recall ever seeing him lose his cool, even when lives were at stake.

Colleagues say Johnson could also be tough in his dogged push for results, and he was adept at letting others fill in the long gaps of silence in his conversation. His taciturn nature could be unsettling.

Philip Evans, a leading criminal prosecutor who has worked closely with Johnson, said he could be intimidating not simply as a result of his physical stature but also because of his forensic knowledge of London's criminal underworld that even a seasoned criminal prosecutor would struggle to match. He was the type of leader who empowered his subordinates by giving them space to do their jobs, and, as such, commanded loyalty.[2]

Whatever his reserve, Johnson's background in undercover surveillance operations was ideal preparation for his work on the Hatton Garden heist. He led a team of officers charged with tailing the men while avoiding detection and gathering enough evidence so that the gang would not be able to use their age and infirmity to claim that they could not possibly be behind such an elaborate crime. It was a cat-and-mouse game that pitted age against relative youth (Johnson was in his fifties; Reader nearly eighty), carelessness against cautiousness, a gang of thieves chasing the scent of money and a free pension against a man who wouldn't even dare have a drink on the job and who was determined to uphold the Flying Squad's legacy. Johnson was patient to a fault and prepared. After Perkins was fingered as a suspect, for example, Johnson read a book on the Security Express robbery Perkins had been involved with in 1983, and noted the parallels with the Hatton Garden heist. The Security Express caper also took place on an Easter Monday.

* * * *

The Millennium Dome Heist

One of the highlights of Johnson's career was the smash-and-grab robbery at the Millennium Dome exhibition center in Greenwich on November 7, 2000, an audacious crime straight out of a James Bond film.

At the time, Johnson had recently been promoted to detective inspector at the Flying Squad, and had joined the squad's Tower Bridge office, which was investigating the crime. The operation would prove to be one of the most challenging—and successful—in the history of Scotland Yard and would provide valuable lessons for Johnson more than two decades later when Hatton Garden was targeted.

Commissioned to mark the beginning of the twenty-first century, the sprawling Dome was designed by the star architect Richard Rogers as a celebratory one million square-foot exhibition space that was both lauded for its ambition but vilified by critics as a monstrous white elephant which cost about £800 million ($1.2 billion) to build and generated massive cost overruns.

During a De Beers diamond exhibition there, a gang of six burglars had planned to use a bulldozer to smash through the Dome's
walls, and then deploy smoke bombs, sledgehammers, and nail
guns to break through reinforced bulletproof glass display windows
and steal £350 million (about $490 million) worth of diamonds—
including the dazzling 203-carat Millennium Star diamond. With
the gems in hand, they would make off in an inflatable speedboat,
down the Thames. The last part of the ruse mimicked the Bond
movie *The World Is Not Enough*, in which Bond chases an assassin on
a boat to the Millennium Dome where she attempts to escape via hot
air balloon.

In what was then the biggest operation in the Flying Squad's history, a team of more than one hundred officers secretly tailed the
thieves in a meticulously planned sting operation. They had already
been under surveillance after the squad had received a tip-off from
a paid informer that a daring robbery plot was in the works. In an
operation code-named "Operation Magician," a Flying Squad surveillance team quietly monitored the suspects for months, undetected,
following them as they conducted reconnaissance at the Dome,
including taking video footage of the river and the jetty, from which
they planned to escape.

On the eve of the crime on November 7, 2000, Flying Squad officers switched the priceless gems with crystal replicas of the same size,
and the Dome staff was replaced with armed undercover officers,
who were disguised as cleaners and had their guns in black garbage
bins. Johnson was part of a team of Flying Squad officers who waited
outside the Dome in the nearby parking lot of a supermarket to conduct surveillance. The mission was to swoop in and arrest the thieves
after they had been immobilized by the team of officers inside the
Dome—assuming, of course, that the operation was a success.

"It was quite exciting, you could hear the chug chug of the bulldozer as it passed the parking lot on its way to breach into the Dome

and see smoke rising from it," Johnson recalled, emphasizing, with typical self-effacement, that he was just one of hundreds of officers at the scene.

The Flying Squad team rushed in and arrested four thieves, when they were just inches away from the gems inside a vault. If they had succeeded, it would have been the world's largest robbery ever. Two other men were arrested on and around the River Thames as they attempted to escape in a powerboat. Not a single gunshot was fired. The theft would be immortalized by a headline in the *Sun*, the tabloid newspaper: "I'm Only Here for De Beers."

Johnson said that the covert operation to catch the Millennium Dome thieves underscored what was required when conducting an undercover operation like the Hatton Garden probe. Surprising and capturing the thieves in the act was essential to bringing them to justice, as was jumping on their weaknesses, whether carelessness, an ignorance of forensics, or a tendency to boast.

"In Flying Squad ops, you try and catch suspects in the act," he explained, noting that criminals "typically won't talk to you after they are arrested, so you have to structure it in such a way as to amass as much evidence as possible. The idea is that when you arrest them, it is irrelevant what they do or say or don't say because you have caught them in the act," he added. "That is the whole ethos of the Flying Squad."[3]

Johnson's decades of crime-fighting skills now faced one last epic challenge. The hunter and the hunted could not have been more different. But each had the benefit of age and experience.

Chapter 11

The Flying Squad Is Listening

A Glimmer of Remorse?

In the weeks after the burglary, the gang talked about how they would spend their newfound fortune. If they had any moral qualms about what they had done, they didn't express it to one another. If the surveillance officers listening in expected to hear even a glimmer of remorse, they were sorely disappointed. As far as the elderly gang was concerned, the safe deposit box holders they had targeted had it coming to them. Never mind that many of them were retirees their own age who had been fleeced of their life savings and pensions as a result of the burglary.

They were "rich cunts," as far as the gang was concerned. Besides, Perkins was still fuming after discovering, with the aid of a diamond tester, that an engagement ring his daughter Terri had bought in Hatton Garden with seven small diamonds had one that was a fake. "It shows you what a con Hatton Garden is!" he had complained to his son-in-law Spencer, as if that fact gave him a moral get-out-of-jail card for stealing millions of pounds worth of gems. "Oh fucking, the most wonderful thing in the world. The diamond center of the world, that's what they think."[1]

On Thursday, May 7, 2015—general election day in Britain—Perkins was driving in his blue Citroën Saxo on his way to pick up Spencer. As usual, "Leading Britain's Conversation" was playing on the radio. The gang had been so consumed by the heist and the stress of how they were going to unload the jewels, that the burglary had trumped politics in their frequent conversations. Perkins seemed to take a particular interest in which leader would keep interest rates low. Perhaps not surprising for a man who had spent so many years in a claustrophobic jail cell, Perkins was obsessed with real estate. Property also offered an easy way to hide stolen cash.

As Perkins drove through Enfield, past Polish specialty food shops, Turkish restaurants, and council estates, the two candidates in the election, the incumbent prime minister David Cameron, and Ed Miliband, the challenger from the left-leaning Labour Party, were about to make their final pleas to voters.

Perkins was working class to his core, and Cameron, an Old Etonian who talked as if he had a plum in his mouth, irked men of his ilk. He told Spencer that he liked to vote conservative. He also loved Margaret Thatcher, he said. She had been one tough old bird, and he still credited her for low income taxes and a muscular foreign policy—invading the Falkland Islands, showing the French and Germans who was boss, telling Brussels to bugger off—that had made Britain a country to be reckoned with.

As the newscasters discussed the election, the broadcast suddenly broke off for an update on the Hatton Garden burglary. "Some victims of the Hatton Garden burglary over Easter say their livelihoods have been ruined," the male newscaster began. "The group representing diamond traders met earlier and advised those who weren't fully insured that the chance of recovering their losses are very limited." He then added, "No one has been arrested over the burglary."[2]

Perkins's breathing—picked up by the bug in the car—grew heavier. Perhaps the word "victim" jarred him, because he didn't consider the safe deposit box holders to be victims. Could it be that an image of the gems and stolen cash hidden in stacks underneath the gang's kitchen sinks was flashing in his mind, and, along with it, what seemed like a very short-lived pang, not exactly of remorse, but of hesitation? Was he having even a pang of moral gumption? If so, it quickly passed like a little and unexpected sneeze.

Nearby, a Flying Squad surveillance officer in an unmarked car followed him from a distance, but Perkins didn't notice. Writing in his log, the officer noted that Perkins wore a light-colored jacket and glasses and had a white carrier bag in the car. "Newscaster mentions Hatton Garden robbery," he jotted down, adding, "Sound of movement within vehicle."[3] The bug was picking up Perkins's every utterance.

"Shut up," Perkins suddenly said at the radio, dismissing the report in a barely discernible and husky whisper.[4]

* * * *

PERKINS REMAINED OBLIVIOUS that Scotland Yard was listening in, and his tone changed to a more congenial note as his car arrived to pick up his son-in-law Spencer. Spencer was the apparent favorite among his four sons-in-law, judging by the frequency with which they met. Spencer and his daughter Vicky lived just a few blocks away from his small, compact house in Enfield, in the same north London neighborhood. Now that he had come into all this cash, he seemed intent on making up for some of those lost years when he had been nicked and absent while in prison.

Spencer had barely closed the door behind him when Perkins began a tirade on one of his favorite subjects: how Britain was being invaded by foreigners. It was a frequent topic on talk radio and one that was fueled by the debate over whether Britain should leave the European Union. Enfield, Perkins's neighborhood, was just one of many in London where immigration had transformed the social fabric; only 35 percent of residents were now white Britons, and the local residents spoke 178 languages, among them Turkish, Somali, and Polish.[5]

"You know the Chinaman's house opposite, do you ever notice it's a dirty house, you never seen anyone going in or coming out of it, that is a dirty house," Perkins said, his voice suffused with disgust.

"No, yes," Spencer replied.

"It's up for sale because Terri Googled it—it's half a million pound," Perkins, who had long dabbled in real estate, said with grudging admiration.

"Amazing, isn't it?"

"You still you got to have 50 grand to put down on a half a million pound property," Perkins said, calculating how much it would cost to buy each of his daughters a house. "Then there's the fucking mortgage."

"Well it's like that Noel Gallagher," Spencer replied, alluding to the Oasis drummer whose name must've sounded alien to an old-school thief who had spent a good chunk of the 1990s in prison and for whom Tom Jones or the Beatles were contemporaries. But Spencer didn't seem to notice or care. "He was talking about that boy who left One Direction," he continued, referring to the defection of singer Zayn Malik from the wildly popular British boy band, whose members could be Perkins's grandchildren. "He says he's an idiot. He says if he thinks his 20 million is going to do him for the rest of his life, he's in for a shock. 'Cause once you've had a taste of the high life, you can't go back."

Was Perkins smiling inwardly? Did Spencer realize that the man sitting next to him would soon have his cut of millions in cash, gold, and jewels? Perkins's voice betrayed no change; he was behaving as if nothing had happened. He was adept at maintaining a poker face, honed during nearly four decades of facing down police, judges, and fellow prisoners. It had kept him out of trouble on the inside and made him a dependable member of his Firm since he would never blab or snitch on anyone.

"Yes, that is true," Perkins offered.

Spencer, warming to his theme, continued. "You can't go back, that's what kills people if you've had it all and you lose it all," he said. "If you think you got a big family like yours, four daughters, eight grandchildren, whatever it is, it is all the same. Even if you buy your four daughters a house, that's four mill, depending where they want to live, then you got to give them some money to maintain that."

"Yeah, but I can't see how the mortgage rate can keep going up though," Perkins replied. "I can't see it. This mortgage rate has only got to move, which it will do and fuck me, there will be a lot of people in trouble. Well, if wages don't go up in comparison, you know." He added, "You might as well live in your car." It was an astute macroeconomic analysis from a man who had somehow managed to accumulate a large real estate portfolio—even from behind bars—and whose love of his family was perhaps surpassed only by his other great love: cold, hard cash.

"You off to vote?" Perkins asked, changing the subject.

"Yeah."

"Who do you vote for?"

"Tory. Child of Thatcher, ain't I."

"Well, I wish she was back in," Perkins said approvingly, ignoring the fact that the Iron Lady had died two years earlier at the age of eighty-seven.

"She was a big fan of the old what's its name, getting on the property ladder," Spencer said, referring to the 1980s when Thatcher had introduced tax breaks so that working-class people like them could buy their state-subsidized council apartments, with the aim of creating a nation of homeowners and stimulating the economy.

Perkins indicated his approval. Like many working-class criminals, he liked her toughness. Like him, she was self-made. He suggested that Cameron was weak by comparison. "Well, you have more confidence in her if she had to meet Putin in a row or a war, wouldn't you?" Perkins asked.

"Ah definitely," Spencer replied. "I'll see ya' tomorrow."

"See ya' later."[6]

For the Flying Squad officer pursuing him, the discussion—boy bands aside—was instructive. Spencer seemed awfully intent on discussing a big purchase like a house, prompting the questions: Was he in on it? Did he know about the burglary? His suggestion that Perkins would need £4 million ($6 milllion) to buy homes for his four daughters seemed like a pretty fat wad of cash for a man who lived in a small house himself, and was only fairly recently out of jail and retired. But for now, the officer decided to omit that from his notes.

* * * *

A Fatherly Villain

Perkins appeared to have death and money on his mind a few days later when speaking with Terri in the Citroën Saxo on an apparent shopping excursion. He was worried that his wastrel sons-in-law would try to get their grubby hands on his jewels, gold, and cash. It didn't help that Terri was egging him on.

"It's been too long now they got comfortable, Courtney and Laura, because you have fucking paid for everything," she said, referring to two of her sisters.

"No, it's not happening anymore."

"I am glad that you are coming to your senses."[7]

For the Flying Squad surveillance officer tailing and eavesdropping on Perkins, the family banter was, at least, more interesting than watching Perkins scarf down fish and chips. He aimed his digital camera. Click. Click. Click. Click. Terri wore an oversized blue blouse with red diamonds, and a beige sweater, her peroxide blond hair pulled back with a clip. She had a fake Gucci purse hanging on her shoulder, and clutched a banana peel in her right hand. She looked worn out, tired, and stressed. Was she, too, in on it? After all, criminality often ran in families. Judging by the frequency with which Perkins met her, she seemed to be his favorite daughter. The two spoke often and Perkins took delight in driving her to work.

Perkins continued his rant. "Everything that I've got I am looking after. I am trying to fucking invest it for you lot when I am dead."[8]

Now that his pension was taken care of, it appeared he wanted assurances from Terri that the rest of his newly acquired fortune wouldn't be squandered. The two marveled that the pound was stronger than the euro, and credited the conservative government. Perkins planned to pay for Terri to go on a last-minute holiday in Portugal so the gang could use her house to divvy up the jewels. The strength of the euro was proving a good excuse to get her out of the country.

"It's 1.45 now you know," Perkins said approvingly, before returning to the subject of his will.

He had made up his mind: When he died, each daughter would receive £100,000 ($150,000). For a man who had just helped to steal millions in jewels, it wasn't exactly overgenerous.

But he wanted assurances from Terri that they would respect his wishes. "When I die, mum might change the rules because it all goes to mum. But I want a straight answer now. When I die whatever wealth I got, we just say it's hundred grand each alright; I want my four daughters to have a hundred grand each because I would not rest in my grave."[9]

He added, "And if your wishes ain't going to be carried out when you're dead what's the fucking point of being on earth!"[10]

For the Flying Squad officers monitoring the conversation, it was not clear whether Perkins, every inch an old-timer when it came to his thievery, had obeyed the old-school criminal code of keeping "business" and family separate. He was obviously close with his daughter and would want to protect her. But all the sudden banter about money, continental vacations, and six-figure inheritances sounded deeply suspicious.

* * * *

Bickering and Conniving

They began to fight among themselves over who got what. It had been such a mad scramble out of the vault that Perkins and Jones, in particular, were worried that they had been stiffed. Brian Reader and Carl Wood, meanwhile, sulked at home, out of the action.

Friday was their favorite day to meet, the day when most of the heist had been planned. So being creatures of habit, about a month after the burglary, Perkins picked up Jones in the Saxo on a Friday afternoon for what was becoming a daily ritual to chat, gossip, boast, and scheme about what to do with the jewels and to bitch about the others. It was about 11 a.m. The car, however cramped, seemed to be their favored venue to discuss business, perhaps because they calculated that moving around would help them avoid detection. It also got them out of the house, and away from their inquisitive wives. It was a foolhardy calculation.

On that day, however, they had other things on their minds. Perkins was speeding out of Enfield and the two traveled west through Southgate, in north London, a middle-class enclave with a subway station that looks like a space ship. Two retirees in a car, who had just managed to pull off the largest burglary in English history. But their initial giddiness had given way to anxiety. They were both fuming that they had been cheated out of the most valuable jewels during the mayhem that followed the heist.

"I wound up with none," Perkins said to Jones, referring to packets of large diamonds in several of the boxes. "He got the cream, fuck me, there's a lot of rings there," Jones replied, referring to Collins, whom they had decided would keep the bulk of the stolen goods, hidden in his house in Islington. They had divvied up the rest in little parcels that they stashed in, among other places, pots in their kitchen cabinets in their homes across London.

Jones, for his part, had buried some of the loot under a tombstone in a verdant Victorian cemetery near his house in Enfield. The rest he had put in a loft at his brother's house in a bag concealed by a plank of wood. When he went up to check on it in the days after the heist, he told Perkins, he nearly had a heart attack when his nephew Paul came up behind him, with his girlfriend in tow, and asked him, "What you got up there?" For a show-off like Jones, remaining mum about what he and the others had managed to pull off must have been sheer torture.

Now Jones and Perkins tried to parse what they could sell, fence, or melt down. "A lot of it is sellable," Perkins said.

"Sellable, yes. Necklaces all with stones, then you got the necklace with the fucking big emeralds in it with the matching earrings. There are hundreds of hundreds of rings," Jones said hopefully.

"We could chop all," Perkins agreed, suggesting the method of removing the stones and fencing the jewels to conceal their origins.

"Yeah, chop all that," Jones replied. But he was worried he had been shafted and that the carrier bag where he had put his stash had not been as filled up as the others. "The gear he give me I'd call them monkey rings," he complained to Perkins. "I said, 'What about that? Put some other in here!' There was a big heap, you know."[11]

The seemingly hapless Collins, who could barely stay awake during the heist, appeared to have been more than alert when it came to deciding how to apportion the booty. Now, they wondered, was his sweet demeanor all just a ruse to dupe them out of their fair share?

* * * *

What to Do with the Haul?

As with any large haul, the biggest challenge was how to dispose of it and turn the valuables into cash. Within a matter of hours after the burglary, nearly every jeweler in Hatton Garden had heard about the heist and so reselling it in the Garden—often the usual fate for stolen jewelry—was fraught with risk. They could try to spirit it out of the country, though that was also risky, or to melt it down and resell at least some of it as gold bars. They decided it was better to hide at least part of it and then lie low, or at least as low as was humanly possible, given their somewhat understandable pride in their accomplishment.

Tiny and easily concealed, diamonds have long been coveted by thieves seeking to move cash without being traced. Sew a ten-carat £1 million ($1.5 million) into a pair of underwear, fly out of the country, and the gem could quickly vanish into a global supply chain of millions of diamonds that extends from Hatton Garden to New York and Tel Aviv.

The gang's stash contained millions of dollars in both uncut and polished diamonds, leaving them with a few options. The uncut diamonds could be smuggled out of Britain and sent to cutting centers in Gujarat, Tel Aviv, or New York, where characteristics such as weight and size could be transformed out of all recognition. Even without that disguise, the chances of finding stolen diamonds once they left the country was very slim.

The dozens of tiny bags of glittering polished diamonds provided a bigger challenge, however, since some high-end diamond traders have their diamonds laser inscribed with a name or number, as a way to identify and authenticate the stone. But while the identifier, a sort of serial number for diamonds, could help police trace a diamond, there were unscrupulous diamond polishers in the Garden who knew how to make an inscription vanish. At the same time, there was no central global database that listed diamond ownership. A receipt from Cartier or Tiffany wouldn't help a desperate victim if her diamonds were cut, polished, and sold under a different guise.

Even as they discussed how to conceal the origins of the stolen gems, the gang was also mulling a way to unload them. One option was to find a criminal courier to spirit the jewels and gold out of the country. If they ended up at a dealer in Antwerp, or at a cutting shop in Gujarat, they would be harder to trace. An heirloom brooch made of rubies could be dismantled, its jewels ripped out and then recirculated in the Garden for resale by an illegal trader. Their stacks of gold necklaces, earrings, and rings could be sent to a foreign port like Rotterdam, where the gold could be melted down by a criminal trader. Or perhaps at a future date, it would be less of a hassle to melt down the gold at a scrap yard closer to home.

Another option to conceal such a large and high-profile haul was to bury it and hide it for a few months until the frenzy from the heist had died down. That option appealed to the adventurous-minded Jones. An avid consumer of crime thrillers and Hollywood heist films, he had already set his sights on a picturesque Victorian cemetery in Enfield, about ten minutes from his house. A reconnaissance trip there had given him the idea to bury part of his stash under the gray granite gravestone of his partner Valerie Hart's father. Had she known that Jones would be disturbing her father's grave, she likely would have not appreciated it.

No strangers to unloading stolen goods, the men also needed to find a fence, or intermediary on the black market, who would buy the jewels and not ask too many questions. That task fell largely to Perkins, who, with his grandfatherly demeanor, was adept at remaining invisible. The fence, in turn, could sell the stolen goods back to an unknowing seller.

With their shadowy handshake deals and paperless contracts, the world's diamond centers—Antwerp, New York, Tel Aviv, and Hatton Garden itself—all provided opportunities to find a fence who would buy the stolen goods. All that was left was for the Firm to find someone they could trust. Thieves typically lose up to 90 percent of the value of the original jewels when selling stolen items. But if a stash is big enough, such a hefty discount can be offset by the instant gratification of cold cash.

While Jones and Perkins appeared adamant about cutting out Reader, they nevertheless relented somewhat and, in the end, let him remain among their inner circle, cognizant, perhaps, that his contacts and experience laundering gold and stolen goods was now invaluable as the gang struggled with how to unload their goods. After all, Reader had played a pivotal role in fencing stolen gold during one of the most audacious robberies of the 1980s, even if that had eventually landed him behind bars.

After a group of thieves in 1983 had stolen £26 million ($38 million) worth of gold bars at Brink's-Mat, the security company at Heathrow Airport, Reader's role was to help convert the gold into cash after it was smuggled back into the country from the Netherlands and Belgium, sometimes hidden in Tupperware containers in trucks or the gas tanks of large Grenada and Austin sedans.

Reader would later recall how he met associates like "Little Legs" Larkins at a Turkish bath in Paddington, in central London, where the two would discuss where to sell the gold in Hatton Garden. Reader would receive half a percent commission on each shipment. He wasn't too bothered. He was a frugal sort[12] and he was careful to not attract suspicion by spending too much of his cut. Reader had developed key skills—and contacts—during the Brink's-Mat gold-laundering operation that would now prove helpful. It made sense for the other men to keep him around, as long as he didn't try to bully them into getting too big a piece of the action.

* * * *

Master of None

At another meeting at the Castle pub, the Firm discussed the challenges they faced. In an apparent nod to his expertise, Reader was present. But Wood was out of the game, judging by his absence at the meeting and the frequency with which the crew castigated him; he would not get a single pence.

As Jones and Perkins drove around London discussing how to divvy up the spoils—with Neil Diamond, Boy George, or talk radio amped up on the car radio—they seemed barely able to contain their glee that Reader's decision to leave in the middle of the heist had knocked him off of his perch. Their joy in his suffering felt as relentless as the drill they had used to break through the reinforced concrete.

Now that Reader had shown himself to be lily-livered and craven, the others who had persevered and now had millions in gold and jewels to show for it mercilessly mocked him for his stupidity and fecklessness.

The men already resented Reader for his cockiness, and for never offering to buy a pint when they went to the Castle. Perkins and Jones were stewing with animus toward him. He lived in a house that looked like a country manor. He thought his long rap sheet somehow made him superior. A bit of a "wide boy," as the expression went in working-class slang to describe an untrustworthy hustler. Now was their chance to kick the old fart back down to earth. It turned out that this group of aging thieves could be as vicious as American teenage girls. Provided, of course, the object of their scorn wasn't listening.

"Brian must be having a nightmare," Perkins mused. "I hope he fucking suffers."

"Fucking wanker, regardless of his age," Jones added.

"Fucking wanker," Perkins repeated. Perkins told Jones he was aggrieved that Reader behaved as if he outranked him, even though Perkins had been present at the 1983 Security Express robbery, a holdup that had yielded £6 million ($9 million) in cash—the largest cash robbery at that time—and for which he had been sentenced to twenty-two years behind bars. A badge of honor among thieves. Reader even decided where the gang would take breaks from plotting to get a bite to eat. When Perkins suggested Delhi Grill, favored by the rest of the gang, Reader would sometimes veto it. "He only has toast for lunch," Perkins raged. "Fucking lunch!"

Perkins fulminated that there were three "bits of work" he had done with Reader over twelve years and he was finally ready to tell "the Guv'nor" he had wrecked them all. "I am going to say 'You fucked every one of them up Brian, and the last one you walked away.'" As if Reader was in the car with them, he admonished him, "You gave up being a thief ten years ago you cunt!"[13]

Jones had been invaluable during the heist due to his Houdini-like physical flexibility and his impressive athletic endurance. But Reader appears to have done little to conceal that he considered Jones to be a fabulist and a blabbermouth. As far as Jones was concerned, he had been patronizing him for months. Now that Reader had been demoted from the top to the bottom of the gang, it was Jones's turn to vent and get even.

And Jones raged, "He was a thief forty years ago, they never took no chances, had it all their own way. Like all them thieves then." He ridiculed Reader as a friendless "old ponce" who spent all his time waxing lyrical about the past. In the pantheon of insults from men of their class and generation, "ponce"—an effeminate man—was up there. Criticizing Reader for his nostalgia was a rich rebuke coming from Jones, who spent ample time bragging about past exploits, imagined and real, to whomever would listen.

Jones mused that Reader was past his "sell-by date" and could no longer live off his past glories as one of London's most talented break-

The Firm plotted the crime at the Castle pub in Islington, north London, a gastropub that had a "Go to Jail" sign on the gents' bathroom door.

BELOW   Top row, left to right: Kenny Collins, Danny Jones, and Terry Perkins. Bottom row, left to right: Carl Wood, William Lincoln, and Hugh Doyle.

ABOVE   Brian Reader, known as "The Master," a veteran thief who has been involved in some of the most brazen heists of the twentieth century. Hatton Garden was his last job.

Known as the "Godfather of British Crime," Freddie Foreman, a former enforcer for the Kray twins, says he was approached to go on the heist.

ABOVE   To access the safe deposit, the thieves entered 88–90 Hatton Garden from the fire escape in the back of the building, largely hidden from view, off a quiet alleyway.

BELOW   Over an Easter holiday weekend in April 2015, the men infiltrated the safe deposit, relied on by local jewelers for being impenetrable.

During the heist, the thieves managed to drill a figure-eight-shaped hole through twenty inches of reinforced concrete.

As the Firm began the heist, they brought in tools hidden in wheeled trash cans.

Basil (*left*), a lanky figure, and Jones (*right*).

Collins, on Friday morning, surveys the street before getting into the van to pick up his fleeing accomplices.

Jones takes a break, leaning on a trash can, on Sunday, as the gang finishes the job.

05/04/2015 06:02:47:271
EVIGILO13159 - Fire Escape (640 x 480)
Camera 15 VMD - Baganza

Basil walks toward the van with a black bag obscuring his face.

Perkins and Collins met Reader at the Castle pub after the heist to boast about what they had pulled off.

A police forensics officer enters Hatton Garden following the burglary.

Paul Johnson, the soft-spoken Flying Squad officer who led the Hatton Garden investigation, proved a master of patience and perseverance.

Johnson addresses a scrum of journalists following the burglary.

Gravestone of Sidney James Hart, the father of Danny Jones's common-law wife. Jones hid some of the loot under the gravestone.

In the months after his arrest, Jones led Scotland Yard to the Victorian cemetery where he had buried some of the jewels.

Forensics officers dig up the stolen gems at Edmonton Cemetery, concealed in a plastic bag.

EJB/031115/4

Jewels found
at Edmonton
Cemetery.

EJB/031115/6

Jewels found at Edmonton Cemetery.

EJB/031115/2

RIGHT   The heist captured the imagination of London's feverish tabloid press (featured here is the *Sun*), which grew obsessed with a crime perpetrated by a group of aging men.

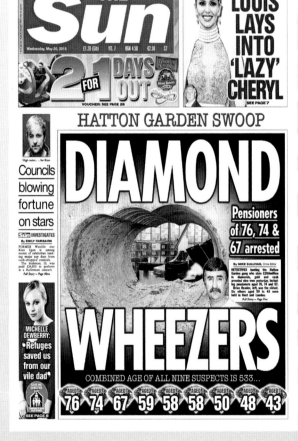

THE Sun

Wednesday, May 20, 2015

21 FOR 1 DAYS OUT
VOUCHER: SEE PAGE 26

High notes ... for Kian

Councils blowing fortune on stars

SUN INVESTIGATES
By EMILY FAIRBAIRN

FORMER Westlife star Kian Egan is among scores of celebrities landing major pay days from cash-strapped councils. The Irishman, 35, was paid £26,800 to perform at a Halloween concert.
Full Story — Page Nine

MICHELLE DEWBERRY:
• Refuges saved us from our vile dad
• SEE PAGE 8

HATTON GARDEN SWOOP

DIAMOND
Pensioners of 76, 74 & 67 arrested

By MIKE SULLIVAN, Crime Editor

DETECTIVES hunting the Hatton Garden gang who stole £200million in diamonds, gold and cash arrested nine men yesterday, including pensioners aged 76, 74 and 67. Brian Reader, left, was the oldest. Six others aged 59 to 43 were held in Kent and London.
Full Story — Page Five

WHEEZERS
COMBINED AGE OF ALL NINE SUSPECTS IS 533...

AGED 76   AGED 74   AGED 67   AGED 59   AGED 58   AGED 58   AGED 50   AGED 48   AGED 43

ELIZABETH COOK

LEFT   Court artist sketch of Michael Seed, arrested in March, whom prosecutors say is "Basil the Ghost," the mystery man who vanished after the crime.

in men. Never mind that Reader's plan had worked, minus, perhaps, Collins driving his own car to the burglary.

"I said to him the other day, you're 40 years behind, Brian. You can see what a selfish man he's been," he told Perkins, noting that Reader had become "defeated."

A sprightly sixty-seven-year-old, Perkins noted that at least he acknowledged his age and that he had fallen behind the latest in break-in technology during his long years in prison. But not Reader. "Dan, I'm out of date, I'm behind, but I know it and I admit it. He don't, does he?"[14]

He ended his assessment with one final flourish: "Fucking wanker!"

* * * *

ON FRIDAY, MAY 15, Perkins and Jones set out with Collins behind the wheel of that very same white E200 series Mercedes used in the burglary. The gang was on its way to pick up Reader, ostensibly to discuss their ongoing efforts to find someone to launder the jewels. It was about six weeks since the burglary and the men were growing more anxious. They didn't want to deal with Reader, judging by the constant verbal takedowns of their former "Master," but he was still acting as an unofficial adviser of sorts, apparently eager to get his cut.

As Jones entered the car, the Flying Squad activated the listening device and Collins's dog could be heard barking loudly. Neil Diamond's "Sweet Caroline" was blasting from the radio. The music was deafening.

Back in the car, the men turned immediately to the unfinished business of the stash and who was hoarding what. "You got any packets of diamonds in your parcel?" Perkins asked Collins nonchalantly.

"No, I haven't, no. I'm not saying no, no, I don't know," Collins replied. His ability to speak was suddenly failing him as Jones and Perkins circled him suspiciously.

Even without their nagging concern that Collins would steal part of the stash for himself, he was going deaf, slowing down, and becoming increasingly forgetful. Perkins seemed worried he might be in over his head. To make things worse, Collins's mother-in-law was in the hospital and his doting wife Millie was away. Heist or no heist, the demands of old age had not suddenly evaporated.

"Where's Millie—Clacton?" Perkins asked, referring to a seaside resort in Essex, about a two-hour drive from London.

"Her mum's in hospital in Colchester, she's gone down to visit her," Collins replied.

"So you're on your own?" Perkins asked, sounding overcome by sympathy. "You're upset about being on your own, ain't ya?" he added, ribbing his friend about his growing dependency in old age on his wife.

"No I prefer it on my own an' all, all the time," Collins replied, with more than a hint of false bravado, exerting his independence, even as his intensifying aches and pains had made him more and more in thrall to Millie. He himself had gone to the hospital that same day for a checkup.

"I told ya' I went and had a medical today. I had to count from 20 backwards, the months of the year backwards," he said.

"I couldn't do that backwards months of the year—December, November," Jones replied.

"November, October, September," Collins said slowly and stoically, seeming eager to show off that his memory was not as bad as the others thought, that he was no "wombat-thick old cunt," as Jones had described him to the others.

Collins was about to go through a red light when he suddenly noticed a car edging up behind them, perhaps one of the small army of police surveillance officers who had been tailing them for weeks. He slammed on the breaks. Was Operation Spire about to hit a snag?

"Fuck me look who's behind me!" he said, a frantic edge in his voice.

"Old Bill," Jones replied, using a Cockney expression for police, derived from the 1950s when the London County Council registered all police, fire, and ambulance vehicles with the letters *BYL*.

"I think it is, it's got the colors up," he said, referring to the sirens on the top of the car, "but I don't know if it's them or not."[15]

Considering what they had done, the men had, until now, appeared remarkably sanguine about the prospect of the police tailing them, lulled into complacency by their false confidence, fanned by the British media, that Scotland Yard believed the burglary was an inside job. Nevertheless, the question of whether they were being followed by police became a recurring leitmotif of their conversations, and the wailing sirens of passing ambulances appeared to give them heart palpitations. Jones and Perkins had even discussed whether to pay £900 ($1,350) to install a radar detector in the Citroën that could warn them if they were being followed. Little did they know they were being listened to as they spoke.

Jones told Perkins, "Oh, John, my nephew, my niece's son, said 'I got a good tool for you if you want it.' I said what is it? He said 'fit it in your car, you can hide it, hide the aerial, it's like a little black box like that and it will go bip, bip, bip, bip, bip . . . old bill 20 feet away from you, plain clothes, anything. They use Tetra radio,'" he said, referring to the digital police radio scanner that could only be monitored by other police. "It goes up to half a mile, old bill in the vicinity." He added, "900 quid to have it fitted to your motor."

"Fuck me," Perkins replied, approvingly.[16]

For now, the fear of being caught was momentarily averted as the police car sped away.

* * * *

THE GANG CONTINUED on their journey to pick up Reader, driving from the gritty environs of Enfield to his courtly home in Dartford, Kent. They kept circling back to what an old and cranky has-been he had become.

"It's old age, creeps upon everyone," Collins observed.

"He's really old now," Jones replied. "He's really old now Brian, I look at him sitting there an old man, 'cause he is an old man, ain't he?"

Reader seemed pathetic. Even he had acknowledged to the others that the heist had aged him.

"As he said to me the other day, 'I've aged five years in the last year,'" Collins recalled. "I said you have, we all keep talking about you."[17]

The car pulled up to Reader's sprawling house. Reader suddenly appeared, dressed in a moth-eaten sweater, and slowly walked toward the vehicle. When he got in, the men abruptly changed the subject and started to talk about the weather. Whatever warmth there was between Reader and the others had become as elusive as the English sun.

"They forecasted rain," said Collins.

"What tonight?" Reader replied.

"No, this afternoon."

An old Bentley passed them, and Reader, who had dabbled as a used car salesman when not breaking into safes, suddenly became animated. "Fuck me, that's an old car, ain't it. What fucking year is that?"

"About 86, ain't it," Jones replied.

"Fucking hell that's near my age," Perkins said.

Jones noted that he had recently stopped by a car showroom to check out what new car he should buy with his newfound riches and had seen an old Rolls Royce, which had logged sixty thousand miles and which its aging owner, a grand lady, hoped to sell.

"Yeah, he can give the woman five grand for it," Reader offered.

"You don't know what one it is but they are common as fuck, there are loads of 'em," Jones barked back at him. "You're way behind Brian," he said, with contempt in his voice. "You're 40 years behind Brian."

The men drove around Reader's sleepy, suburban tree-lined neighborhood for about an hour, apparently thinking it safer to discuss their next moves from inside the car. Then they dropped Reader off back at his house. He didn't dare ask about his cut from the heist, though it must have been weighing heavily on his mind.

"I'll see you next week, alright?" Reader said.

"Be careful," Jones replied.

"Yeah, alright, you've got me number," Reader said.

"You know where we are, come over our way," Jones added, sounding annoyed at the extra fifty-minute drive it took to pick Reader up when the three of them lived near one another in north London.

"Fucking come over your way?" Reader replied, his voice laced with fury.

"Well, you expect the rest of us to . . ." Perkins added. But Reader cut him off.

"I'll tell you what I don't want another poxy fucking Indian!" Reader fumed, the conversation once again eclipsed by their perennial argument over where to have lunch or dinner. "We'll have a Chinese."

"Beggars can't be choosers," Jones replied, the sarcasm and bile oozing out of his mouth. The door slammed.

Before Reader had barely made his way up the driveway toward his house, the three remaining burglars exploded with contempt.

"That cunt, he doesn't stop digging me that cunt, I'll tell ya," Jones said, sounding exasperated.

"Yeah, he does, doesn't he?" Perkins said.

"Fuck me he tells me what he's done. He tells everyone at that cafe what he done 30 years ago, 'We done this, done that,'" Jones raged. "Fuck him!"

They returned to the subject of his stinginess.

"He was saying that he paid half the bill the other night with his daughter. He never said go half with us!" Collins said, adding his voice to the Reader-bashing session.[18]

Jones, apparently emboldened, decided it was time to call Reader's loyalty into question, once and for all. He told the others that when he was in prison at Maidstone, in Kent, back in the 1990s, another prisoner, Bill Barrett, a seasoned villain who was eleven years Reader's senior and who had been Reader's mentor when he was a young thief straight out of the army, had warned Jones that Reader was not to be trusted.

"I'm gonna tell you something and that's something you don't know about him, right. Bill Barrett pulled me in the nick, I told you, didn't I?" he said, using the Cockney word for prison. "He said I don't have it with him no more because he writes statements when he got nicked on one of his things, he had written down a load of things he got nicked for, you don't know that, do you?"

The others listened in stunned silence. Reader had been reduced to a doddering old man during the heist. He was miserly and didn't buy pints at the pub. He was cranky, a know-it-all, and full of himself. But a snitch? A grass? Someone who could now sell them out, just as they were so tantalizingly close to finally getting rich from all those years of scheming and plotting?

Among the gang, Reader was the one who had been careful to avoid being detected. Now, Jones was adamant that Reader was the one they needed to worry about.

"That's what Bill Barrett told me about him. See Bill Barrett fell out with him, 'cause I was next to Bill Barrett in Maidstone, I was deep in chat with him," he said. "See Brian makes out what he is, he can come across here saying certain things. But he doesn't abide by them, does he?"

"Na," Perkins replied, finally interrupting his soliloquy.

But Collins, ever the mediator between the squabbling geriatrics, defended Reader. "You know he don't write out statements, use your fucking loaf," he said, furrowing his ample brows in Jones's direction and using the Cockney rhyming slang for loaf of bread, meaning head.

"I'm not saying that he did write some," Jones replied, sheepishly. "I'm just telling you what Bill Barrett said to me. It might be a load of bullocks."

"He's out of date," Perkins replied. Reader had fucked up every "bit of work," he repeated. "Every single thing."[19]

Jones recalled that Reader had almost cost them the job because he didn't understand that special diamond-tipped industrial drills could be used to penetrate reinforced concrete. He had initially thought that the concrete at 88–90 Hatton Garden was impenetrable!

"I said to him, 'how can you work out that the cement is upgraded from one building to the next,'" Perkins recalled.

"Fucking hell," said Collins, bragging that, from the start, he had suggested that the diamond-tipped drills could breach even the walls outside of Parliament. "I was saying that from the word go, these walls are built to put outside the houses of parliament. They're fucking more or less bomb proof, you can't have much stronger than them."

"He was saying it would be harder than that, how could it be?" Perkins added. "Common sense, that's all you got to have is common sense."

Perkins suggested it was Reader's risk aversion that had spooked them halfway through the burglary, prompting them to rush out of the vault before they had finished going through only a fraction of the 999 boxes. "We should be sitting here with half a billion pounds!" he said, "with chauffeur driven Bentleys—one for every day!"

Jones berated Reader again for abandoning the heist halfway through, for not believing in them, for succumbing to an old man's crabby defeatism.

"He's a fucking idiot by doing that," Perkins continued.

"Common sense tells ya, that he never thought we would get in," Collins said, piling on, apparently having overcome his previous instinct to defend his old friend.

"No, he didn't," said Jones.[20]

"There's only one thing that you'd give that up for, one reason ever, you must of thought that we would never get in, it's the only reason you wouldn't come back, innit?" Collins added.

"And Carl copied him," Jones said, referring to Carl Wood, their ailing, debt-ridden, bespectacled accomplice, who had also abandoned the burglary halfway through, earning the others' contempt in a measure that perhaps even surpassed their disdain for Reader.

"Carl's arsehole fell out," Jones said.

"His arsehole never went, he thought we'd never get in," Collins said, correcting him, adding, "'cause even the cunt, I said 'give it another half hour fuck we've done everything we can do, if we can't get in, we won't be able to get in, will we?'"

"And we did!" Perkins suddenly intoned with a note of triumphalism.

"Never give up, never give up," Collins said.

Giddy once again at the recollection of infiltrating the vault, Perkins mused that he wished he had taken a selfie inside the building, to commemorate their moment of triumph, and to rub it in Brian Reader's face.

"I wish I had a photo, Dan," he said to Jones. "I know you and Basil was inside. I wish I had a photo to show me sat outside on my own, right, doing what I had to do to say to him, 'that's where you left me Brian, look all on my own.' True, ain't it?"

"Yeah," said Collins.[21]

"Fucking true," Perkins repeated. Reader, he continued, had betrayed the most coveted honor among thieves by walking away from the very Firm of villains he himself had assembled. "He went home," he said, still in disbelief.

"Where it started going wrong," Collins replied, "he was quite content to let the other geezer take over," noting that Reader had only been too happy to relinquish his leadership position in the Firm to Basil, to abandon the heist before their mission had been accomplished, and to leave it to Basil and the rest of the gang to brave the risk of getting arrested.

Now that Reader had been irreparably demoted, the enigmatic Basil had supplanted him as the one who deserved admiration and respect. After all, he had duplicated the keys to the building in order to let them in, even if he had accidentally triggered the alarm.

"The only one who could get nicked was poor old Basil on the key bit, you know what I mean?" said Collins.

Reader was a foolhardy has-been, Jones and Perkins replied. He had been upstaged by Basil, a novice thief.

"Brian stopped being a thief," Perkins lamented, wielding the ultimate insult among the criminal fraternity, where having the "bottle" for a job was akin to having blood running through your veins.

"Well," Jones replied, "Basil learned in fucking two months what he had learned in forty years."

"I still don't know why Basil let that fucking alarm go off," Collins said, adding that Basil had made up some excuse and that he struggled to rebuff him since he was such a canny bullshitter.

"Well, I think he made a rip there," Perkins replied. "We were lucky."

"He ain't a liar, is he?" Jones added, defending Basil. They had apparently bonded during the burglary.

Content with their evisceration of Reader, they turned back to Wood, imaging that his decision to back out of the heist had now reduced him to violent and inconsolable rages. As it was, Wood was heavily in debt and suffered from Crohn's disease, which made him lethargic, bloated, and prone to sudden bouts of diarrhea. During the planning of the heist, he would whine constantly about his aches and pains. Now that he had foolishly abandoned them, his suffering seemed to cheer them up.

"He's had nightmares and everything, he's punched his old woman up there," Perkins said, mocking Wood, whom he noted was now reduced to working for minimum wage doing odd jobs while the rest of the Firm counted their millions.

"Yeah, yeah, fucking going to work for twenty, thirty quid a day, forty quid a day, broke his finger the other day, fell down a ladder."

Perkins and Jones imagined him coming to beg them for a loan. "Oh, can I have a bit of money for some shopping?" Perkins said, ridiculing Wood.

"Oh, I need a bit of money for a bit of puff," Jones joined in, his voice trailing off, before he quickly added, as if addressing Wood, "Fuck off!"

Jones, who had recruited his old mate Wood into the Firm, now blithely called him a "lunatic." He berated himself for failing to realize that his old and dear friend was so spineless.

"Yeah, well that's my fault with him anyway I said to him 'Stay there, if we get nicked at least we can hold our heads up that we had a last go, the last fling,' and he goes fucking right and what's he do? Blows a raspberry!"[22]

Reader and Wood, Collins said, had allowed their personal problems to overwhelm them.

"Fucking problems," Jones said, clearly exasperated.

"We all got fucking problems," Collins replied.

Little did they know that they would soon have bigger problems than they realized.

Chapter 12

The "Cut Up"

Laundering the Jewels

THE GANG FELT RESTLESS. THE ARGUMENTS OVER how to split the proceeds and launder the jewels were becoming more and more heated. The plan was to sell the haul for cash but they still hadn't figured out exactly how. Perkins was eager to melt down some of his gold. "That could be my pension," he told the others, his expressed goal all along.[1]

The men needed to be patient, but their nerves were fraying. One false move could prove their undoing. Befitting old-economy thieves, the men stashed away piles of diamond necklaces, emeralds, gold chains, and cash in an assortment of places far less secure and high tech than the safe deposit they had managed to infiltrate.

But they wanted to consolidate the stash in one place, to make sure, among other things, that it wasn't stolen by rival thieves. This led to another big mistake: Kenny Collins—forgetful and not particularly reliable—was given a key role in the logistics operation, making him the caretaker for the bulk of the loot. They were senior citizens prone to afternoon naps and apparently had forgiven him for falling asleep on the job.

Collins, who had hidden some of the gems in a casserole dish in his kitchen cupboard, arranged for the eventual transfer of the stolen jewels—or "gear"—to be handled by his friend William "Billy the Fish" Lincoln. A part-time fishmonger, Bill enjoyed going to Roman baths to expunge the smell of fish from his doughy body, and suffered from, among other things, incontinence and sleep apnea. He, in turn, hired his nephew John Harbinson, whose role would be to transport the gear in his taxi to a handover point—a parking lot outside Hugh Doyle's plumbing workshop in back of the Wheatsheaf pub in Enfield.

Even as the men contemplated their newfound riches, Perkins and Jones were feeling nervous that the circle of thieves involved in the heist had become too large. Someone could blab. As it was, Jones and Perkins had been startled to discover Lincoln had been lurking around Collins's house after the caper, with the jewels so close by. He told Jones that he had complained to Reader about it.

"I said to Brian, I said, 'ere, how does this fucking Bill know about anything,'" Perkins told Jones. "Bill, he said Bill. I said the fucking geezer round Kenny's, Bill." He added, "Bill has wound up with the fucking gear . . . I said all them big stones are already gone."[2]

Then there was Hugh Doyle, the loquacious Irishman, who had lent Collins a key to his plumbing workshop in Enfield, ostensibly so the gang could practice their drilling there. His prodigious gift of gab now seemed to be a curse. Doyle seemed to worship the older men and was impressed by their involvement in some of the most daring crimes of the century. But the respect wasn't reciprocated. Perkins and Jones thought him a bigmouth and an overfriendly dolt.

"Don't fucking leave them bags with Hughie," Perkins warned Jones. They were discussing how and when they would consolidate the jewels, believing that Doyle would inevitably steal some of it.

"He's a complete cunt. You've got to treat everyone as the enemy,"[3] Jones said.

"You wouldn't know if someone's took a stone out of these parcels."[4]

Perkins was particularly annoyed that he had managed to carry only one wheelie bin stuffed with jewels up the stairs at 88–90 Hatton Garden. But given his diabetes, he was thankful to have even come out of there standing.

"I've been thinking you know how the fuck that Bill got involved," Perkins fumed to Jones.

"Brian," said Jones, barely able to disguise his contempt as he mentioned Reader's name.[5]

The two men fretted that someone could have easily stolen part of their stash from under Collins's nose, since he was such a "thick cunt." Or Collins himself could get greedy.

"You're never going to know if anything has been taken out of there," Jones complained.

"Not in a million years, we could have lost two million pounds," Perkins said, sounding frustrated. His real estate investments aside, he lived in a simple nondescript house. But his greed seemed to have no limits. The thought that he was being ripped off irritated him. There was a twelve-carat diamond in the stash he had heard about on the telly during a news bulletin concerning the burglary. What if it was gone?

"Kenny has been fucked 24–7 all of his life," Jones said, referring to Collins. Jones, who had hidden part of his stash in the cemetery near his house, decided he was going to keep that for himself and Perkins, and not tell the others. "It's only a packet like, ain't it," he said to Perkins.

Perkins was also worried about Collins's memory lapses and reliability. "He's been fucked every day of the fucking week, every day of the week he gets fucked," he replied. "It's human nature. What if that soppy cunt gets a 12 mil stone and fucking sells it for 30 quid or something?"[6] He lamented that Collins was such a terrible thief that he had once targeted a shoe store![7] Enough was enough. They had to get the jewels back.

Meanwhile, Perkins, who had good contacts stretching back decades in London's underworld, forged ahead with finding someone to fence the jewels, gold, and diamonds. The gang seemed only too happy that Reader had jumped. But without his thieving savvy, they were fumbling badly.

* * * *

London City Metals

It was too risky to try to resell the stolen jewelry in the Garden, but to dispose of the gold, bangles, and watches in their possession, one place immediately came to mind for Perkins: London City Metals Scrap Company and his old family friend Charles "Chick" Matthews.

The scrap yard in Silvertown, on a dusty industrial strip in east London of car dealerships and warehouses, had long been a front for fencing the illegal booty of burglaries, according to Scotland Yard. Hot emeralds. Gold necklaces. Stolen Mercedes. Marble busts yanked from stately homes. What better way to spirit them out of the country than in a huge truck hauling scrap metal?

For nearly a century, the capital's gritty East End had been the stomping ground for some of London's most notorious crime families: the Krays, the Hunts, the Adams. And the borough of Newham, which hosts London City Metals, remains one of London's poorest. (Tell a Flying Squad detective you are going down to London City Metals to investigate the gang's fencing operation and they will skeptically size you up, ask if you have a death wish, and express admiration for your courage.)

The area also hosts Tate & Lyle Sugars, one of the world's largest sugar factories in the world. On the first night of the Blitz in 1940, Nazi bombs landed on the refinery, sending tens of thousands of gallons of smoking molasses flowing into the River Thames and filling the air with the smell of burned sugar. Now it is stolen goods that flow through Silvertown.

When police raided London City Metals in 2006, they uncovered a treasure trove of stolen goods from truck hijackings across the capital, including more than £1 million ($1.5 million) worth of gold and jewelry. The scrap metal outfit is owned by Charles "Chick" Matthews, fifty-three, a short and stocky man with a thick neck and sparkling blue eyes. His Irish grandfather started the business after the Second World War.

Located on the northern bank of the Thames in the shadow of Canary Wharf and across from the Millennium Dome, the area around Silvertown has hosted a teeming criminal ecosystem stretching back decades. The nearby Royal Docks, London's principal docks after World War II, received dozens of ships each day, arriving from Rotterdam, New York, and India and crammed with everything from giant crates of fruits and vegetables to cars and fine French porcelain. At the height of its success in the 1950s and 1960s, the Docks employed more than 100,000 people. They also provided a fertile thieving ground for canny young apprentice thieves growing up in the surrounding impoverished area, who would sneak in at night and steal from the ships at berth.

On Saturday, May 9, 2015, several surveillance officers from the Flying Squad's specialist crime and operations directorate team were quietly parked near Perkins's home on Heene Road in Enfield when Perkins suddenly appeared in the doorway and headed toward his car. He was wearing metal-framed glasses, a neatly ironed black sweater, and a white dress shirt as he entered the blue Citroën Saxo.[8] He had dressed up. It seems he wanted to make a good impression.

The London underworld was small, and ever since the burglary had been publicized, every crook in town wanted to get his grubby little hands on some of the booty. Guessing where the gang had stashed it had become a parlor game among the fraternity. The longer the gang waited to turn it into cash, the more they risked, not only getting caught by police but having some of it get "nicked" by the other thieves circling them.

Those apprehensions were likely milling through Terry Perkins's head as the Saxo pulled up into London City Metals at 10:25 a.m. The scrap metal yard is tucked behind a barbed wire fence mounted with CCTV cameras. Large metal containers brimmed with scrap metal, the carcasses of old and abandoned cars, pieces of bridges, the urban detritus of dozens of factories across the capital. If a black SUV with tinted windows squatted out front, its yellow license plate with the letters *CM*—or Charles Matthews—then it was likely that Chick Matthews, or "Frank," was in his office.

A large blue sign in front of the scrap metal warehouse said TODAY'S PRICES and listed the prices for, among other items, DRY BRIGHT WIRE, ELECTRIC MOTOR, and ALUMINUM WHEELS—on a recent day, respectively, £35.00, £380 and £950.

As Perkins made his way toward the scrap yard's interior, where Frank had his offices, there were large heaps of granulated cables that would be pulverized in a mill and turned into copper. There was an industrial scale outside the warehouse entrance where trucks carrying metals could be weighed. The glittering world of Hatton Garden seemed a world away.

Chick Matthews was a very respected fence in the London underworld, according to police. But Perkins knew that such a service wouldn't come cheaply, especially if he wanted to get payment in cash. Police suspect he wanted Matthews to hide some of the stolen jewels in the scrap metal yard until the frenzy surrounding the heist died down. Perkins wanted to find out what price he could get for the gold bars in the safe deposit boxes and the dozens of diamonds the gang planned to pry off from the stolen rings.

But while Perkins expressed hope that Frank could fence the gold and the diamonds, he wasn't sure about the rest of the jewels. "I ain't got a fucking clue with stones,"[9] he told Jones. He explained that while it was more straightforward to fence gold by melting it down, it was far more perilous to off-load gems, as they were easier to trace.

About a week after his visit to Frank's scrap yard, Perkins informed Jones that they couldn't afford to be tightfisted when it came to Frank. "Any shit I'll give to Frank I want to give him a bit of cream as well do you know what I mean and I know that he will take it. 'Cause he will say to me, 'What's all this shit, where's the cream?' "[10]

Jones and Perkins regretted that many of the stones would be hard to appraise and sell, but they could melt down the necklace chains for cash. But Perkins also warned Jones that getting any money for anything other than gold—including the hundreds of silver chains they had stolen—would be difficult, given that Frank had a scrap metal yard, and had an abundance of metals of every type. Marveling at an eighty-year-old antique diamond they had in the shape of a flower, he also lamented that Frank was wary of jewels that could be traced back to their owners.

"If you take it to someone like Frank, he would laugh at me," he said to Jones. "He'd say, 'oh fucking shut up. What do you want for it,' he would say, 'six grand? You are fucking mental.' "[11] As for the dozens of silver chains they now had in their possession, he added that the owner of the scrap metal yard hardly needed it: "He's got fucking 98 tons of that stuff, brass or whatever it fucking was."[12]

* * * *

Time to Move the Jewels

The gang decided that they would bring all of the stolen jewels together on the morning of Tuesday, May 19, at Terri's modest house on 24 Sterling Road in Enfield. Never mind that the area was covered with CCTV cameras.

The plan was for the exchange of the gear to take place in a parking lot outside Hugh Doyle's plumbing workshop so the thieves could
avoid being seen by passing police officers. On Sunday, May 17, Terri
would be leaving on a previously planned vacation in Portugal—paid
for by Perkins, who had a new infusion of cash following the burglary. It was a good pretext to get her out of the house and make sure
that the place was empty. But Perkins wanted to keep the gathering
small. He was house-proud and meticulous, and he was worried that
his cronies and their dogs would make a mess.

As the men put the final touches on the operation in the days leading up to an exchange fraught with the very heavy risk of getting
caught, Perkins once again fumed to Jones that their previously close-
knit fraternity had now grown into a cumbersome network. Strangers
couldn't be trusted, including Harbinson, Bill Lincoln's taxi-driving
nephew, recruited by his uncle to transfer the goods.

"I don't want the taxi driver at my daughter's den, no way!" he said.

"Bullocks!" said Jones.

"No fucking way."

Jones said they had to be more careful. To avoid detection, he said
he also planned to go to the cemetery, dig up some of his stash of jewels, and bring them to his house, the eve of the transfer, under cover
of darkness.

Perkins suggested he conceal the jewels in a jacket and dress as
a painter, and carry paint and a bucket. Mindful that he was about
to oversee the divvying up of the proceeds from the biggest burglary
in English history, he wanted to make sure that every detail was
accounted for. He even worried Jones's omnipresent pooch, Rocket,
could cause a mess while they distributed the jewels.

"Don't bring your fucking dog with you, I don't want a dog running 'round me daughter's house," he chided Jones. "Fuck that, she
ain't got a fucking mansion but you can tell it's clean, you know."[13]

On Sunday—two days before the exchange—the men rehearsed a

play-by-play of the handover operation. First, Jones and Collins would meet in the back of the Wheatsheaf pub, where they would retrieve the stashes of stolen jewels from bags in the trunk of Harbinson's taxi. Then they would transfer the bags to Collins's Mercedes and drive to Terri's house, where the diamonds, gold, watches, and jewelry could be separated and organized before it was to be sold and laundered for cash. Then Perkins would return to Frank's for an appraisal. He told Jones that he hoped that his portion could fetch at least £1 million ($1.5 million).

The logistics had to be seamless. The exchange speedy and discreet. "We can't just change over in the streets in taxis, we will lose the gear, you've only got to have Old Bill drive past," Perkins said referring to the police.

"Get the cab driver to pull up," he continued, alluding to Harbinson.

"Pretend like you're going on holiday,"[14] Jones replied.

The men even discussed what they would do if they were pulled over by the police and arrested.

"If someone comes to pull you over, say 'no comment,'" Perkins instructed. "We are arresting you for Hatton Garden, 'no comment.'" It was a rare moment of self-awareness—and paranoia—about the possible consequences of their crime. But it quickly passed. Age seemed to have emboldened their sense of invincibility, or at least a powerful sense of resignation. Or maybe they felt they had nothing to lose. Perhaps being fêted in all the newspapers and on the telly and the radio had intoxicated them. Whatever happened, they were back in the game!

But contingencies were considered. Perkins mused that if Scotland Yard nabbed them, they could use their old age and various infirmities as a cover for their crime. "I'll say, 'What you dopey cunt, I can't even fucking walk!'" Perkins boasted to Jones that, after he was arrested for the Security Express robbery three decades ago, he had used a similar technique of obfuscation and denial.

"That is what I said on the thing thirty years ago. I said, 'you're fucking joking, int'ya?' I said the only way I got my fucking money is buying and selling houses, no comment, no comment." He neglected to mention that feigning ignorance hadn't worked, and he had spent nearly twenty years behind bars. But selective memory was a form of self-protection. Or maybe he was getting a bit forgetful from all the stress?

Perkins once again confirmed the time—before 10 a.m.—and address of the "cut up." Surveillance officers watched Jones and Perkins move garbage bins from the sidewalk into the driveway in front of Jones's house, which they planned to use to store some of the loot.

"Sterling Road, I know it, number 21, ain't it?" Jones asked.

"24," Perkins replied.

"24, I know where it is."[15]

After listening in on devices planted in Perkins's car, the Flying Squad surveillance officers could barely contain their excitement. They now knew the time and the day of the transfer, and Johnson was ready.

Chapter 13

To Catch a Thief

AS THE DAY APPROACHED, JOHNSON, CRAIG TURNER, and Jamie Day gathered in a small room at the Flying Squad's headquarters in Putney to plan their strategy. Two nearly floor-to-ceiling windows in the room overlooked the Thames, and the serenity of the river below provided a tranquil counterpoint to the high-stakes operation. One false move could set the investigation back months, or, worse, send the aging thieves underground.

It was around 7 a.m. when Johnson, Turner, and their team huddled and went over the details. Four teams would tail the suspects at four addresses across the city—including the Wheatsheaf pub; Brian Reader's home in Dartford, Kent; Perkins's home in Enfield and—crucially—Terri's house at 24 Sterling Road. One team would be floating in case reinforcements were needed. Altogether, there would be some two hundred officers, who would use unmarked cars and a battering ram to knock down doors. The raids would happen simultaneously so that none of the thieves could be tipped off and flee. The police had one advantage: other than Jones, most of the gang suffered from joint pain and were poor runners, and the bags of jewels were heavy.

The Flying Squad also decided that the officers charged with nabbing the men would not be armed. In contrast to the United States, the police use of firearms in Britain is far more tightly restricted, and while Flying Squad officers have the training to carry arms, it was reasoned that the geriatric thieves hadn't physically harmed a flea during the heist, and wouldn't resist arrest. And even if they did, they were old, and wouldn't get very far. Each unit would keep a radio line open during the operation so that Turner and Johnson, back at head-quarters, could monitor every move in real time, and send reinforcements, if necessary.

"We knew that Perkins was taking his daughter to the airport and waiting for her premises to become available to transfer the goods," Turner recalled. "We overheard them saying on one of the listening devices that 'today is the day.' So, we decided to spring into action." But the police weren't exactly sure when and where the jewelry would appear and the surveillance teams assigned to Perkins and Collins had to tread carefully, to avoid being detected. One false move, and the men could escape or go underground.

"It was quite exciting," Johnson said with rare exuberance, then qualified by his usual dose of skepticism. "But if you work on these kinds of operations you get used to the intelligence saying something is happening today and then it happens a month later. Up until then, the probe had been pretty reliable every time the team said they were going to do something," he added, referring to the bugs placed in Perkins's and Collins's cars. "But it is better to not expect anything to avoid disappointment. It was like D-Day but you don't know if it is going to happen."[1]

* * * *

ON TUESDAY, MAY 19, at 8:10 a.m., with Flying Squad detectives monitoring their every move, Collins left his home in Islington in his white Mercedes to pick up Jones.

"Shut that door Ken, in case the dog jumps out," Jones warned Collins, whose dog was on the front seat.

"In the back, in the back, Pugsey, go!"[2] Jones said, trying to coax the dog toward the back seat.

If Collins and Jones were nervous, they didn't show it. It was only after nattering about the warm weather and the relative benefits of wearing shorts or trousers, that Collins warned Jones that they needed to be cautious when they moved the loot. "You don't want someone thinking we're doing a drugs changeover or something," he said.

"It looks like you've come off holiday, innit, shorts on and that," Jones replied.[3] The men were about to embark on a perilous trip, the culmination of three years of planning that would get them one step closer to the cash they so desperately craved. But it was their sartorial choices, the weather and Collins's apparent suntan that was dominating the conversation. Collins was wearing a black jacket and dark trousers. Jones was wearing beige shorts and a gray sweater.

"I love the old shorts on, don't you?" Jones asked.

"I did but it said it was going to rain all day long," Collins replied.

"Yeh, but you're so relaxed with 'em on."

"Oh ten times better, a little but when I came out this morning I thought you sure it's going to rain 'cause I'd like to put shorts on."[4]

The risk of what they were about to try and pull off didn't appear to be preoccupying them too much, at least outwardly. Perhaps the scent of money had had an anesthetizing effect. Jones seemed drunk on the gang's growing notoriety. He had conjured a fantasy that he was part of the Special Air Service, Britain's most renowned special forces unit, and this appeared to give him unwarranted confidence.

As the Mercedes slowly made its way toward the pub—Collins was a slow and meticulous driver—and the car passed by a lane, Jones suddenly recalled that he had once been pulled over there by a police officer, a "Chinese bloke."

"I got fucking pulled right here, I did," he said. When the police officer asked him why he had an army backpack in the car, Jones recalled, he told him that he was in the military, special forces. "I went, well, I teach squaddies how to survive in hostile territory. I said, 'I'm flying out actually today.'" Then, he explained, the police officer let him go.[5]

"What age can you come out of the army?" Collins asked, sounding impressed.

"You can be in it up to 50," he replied. "I mean some of them SAS officers they are in at 55, 60 as they're advisors,"[6] he added, referring to the Special Air Service. Jones appeared to idolize the elite unit, which had conducted daring covert missions during World War II against the Nazis and which was still regarded by Britons with awe. Successful SAS recruits had to pass extreme fitness tests, including marching cross-country against the clock followed by jungle training in Belize, Malaysia, or Brunei. Its motto, "Who Dares, Wins," could've been Jones's credo, and in his mind, it seems, he was an SAS man. In fact, he had never been a member of the unit—and his runs were largely limited to suburban London with his dog, Rocket, in tow.

The conversation suddenly and incongruously turned to the Christmas holidays. Collins had noticed that the Sunday papers had been full of ads for Christmas cruises, the day before.

"They are fucking relentless," Jones agreed.

With Collins's sluggish driving, the drive must have felt like an eternity. But at 9:19 a.m., on that Tuesday in May, he and Jones finally pulled up to the Wheatsheaf pub.

"That's the Old Wheatsheaf," Collins said. "You might think the car park is round there but it ain't, it's round here," he added, apparently referring to the area in the back of the pub.

There was just one problem: there was no parking space available outside the pub. A sign said DISABLED ONLY.

"Shall I park there?" Collins asked.

"Well, you're disabled, aren't you?"

"Yeah, I got a badge. It ain't a disabled special person is it?" Collins muttered. "No, it ain't, no," he answered himself.

Collins parked the car and the two walked to the back of the pub where Hugh Doyle had his workshop. Around the same time, after having bought a newspaper, Bill Lincoln arrived in his black Audi at the pub. He was wearing a bright red hooded coat. The three men moved toward the entrance of the plumbing workshop, out of view of a nearby CCTV camera.

As they strolled toward the workshop, the police surveillance team suddenly heard a disturbing sound. Collins's dog was panting, whining, and moving friskily in the back of the car.[7]

* * * *

The Trap Is Set

As the gang approached the pub, Turner and Johnson could see them on one of the three large flat computer screens arranged next to one another in the control room at Flying Squad headquarters. The screens showed footage from CCTV cameras that had been surreptitiously installed at several locations. One screen showed Perkins's house on Heene Road, and the second showed a grainy image of Terri's house on 24 Sterling Road.

The house, part of a row of attached houses on a sleepy residential street, had a brown front door, and short brick wall in the front—the kind of nondescript exterior that would not attract notice. Inside it was decorated with cheap furniture. There was a flat-screen television and children's toys in the cramped living room, which had a striped rug. Among a stack of DVDs and books were David Beckham's biography and an episode of *Friends*. Framed family photographs, including several of Terri's young daughter, were set on the fireplace mantel. One was a wedding picture of Vicky and Spencer at the beach. There was a small kitchen table at the back of the apartment, where the gang planned to sift through the gems and where they had taken out latex gloves to complete the task.

Back at the Flying Squad offices, Turner and Johnson sat next to each other. Two radios gave the commanding officers a play-by-play of what was happening in real time. One channel was turned to the officers near Sterling Road. The second was tuned to the team charged with arresting Brian Reader.

"Suspects have entered the car park," a voice on the radio suddenly blurted out, an edge of anticipation to it.

"Let them go. Stay back as much as possible," Johnson calmly replied, determined that the Flying Squad not accidentally tip off the gang when arresting them was finally within his reach.

Johnson recalled that the small group of officers gathered in the control room were excited, but also composed and very much in control. Even after nearly two decades of observing arrests in covert operations, he said his heart was racing a little. The stakes were high. The money. The intense national media scrutiny. The global headlines. The embarrassment that police had missed the alarm in the first place. The scrutiny of the top brass at Scotland Yard. The chance to bring amoral crooks to justice. Listening to the bugs had made him realize just how petty and malicious these diamond geezers were. He wanted them to pay. He wanted their retirement to take place behind bars. The operation needed to be seamless. One error and weeks of meticulous surveillance would be for nothing. It would be a disaster.

"This was the culmination of weeks of work. But you try not to get too excited in case something goes wrong," he said. The sense of suspense was heightened since the Flying Squad had expected some members of the gang to show up at the Wheatsheaf pub by 8:30 a.m. But all were late. "We were a bit annoyed," Turner said.[8]

With Flying Squad detectives monitoring their every move, Jones,

Collins, and Lincoln stood in the parking lot of the Wheatsheaf pub when Doyle suddenly emerged. Whatever he said, he quickly sped away in an Associate Response plumbing van.

At 9:41 a.m., Collins drove his Mercedes into the parking lot, its trunk visible to a nearby CCTV camera. The men loitered until Harbinson's taxi arrived, four minutes later. Harbinson, who was wearing a dark jacket with a white stripe down the arm, then exited the car and opened the passenger seat's sliding door. Jones removed a bag filled with diamonds, gold, and cash and transferred it into the trunk of Collins's Mercedes. Lincoln then removed a smaller bag from the taxi and put it in the Mercedes. He left the parking lot on foot.

Unfortunate for the crew, Noel Sainsbury, whose company, Archers Financial Services, is next to the pub and borders the parking lot, had been vandalized in the past by local youths who had sprayed graffiti on his company's window. After the incident, he had installed four CCTV cameras facing the parking lot. As the men stood there making the exchange, the cameras captured it on film. After they left, two Flying Squad detectives quickly appeared and asked if they could examine the footage. Mr. Sainsbury complied. It was yet more evidence for the Flying Squad as they closed in. It was also more evidence of the Firm's carelessnesss, given that the CCTV cameras were visible to anyone who bothered to look.

"When police came by and later watched the CCTV footage, they were shocked when they saw the tape," Sainsbury recalled. "They initially didn't tell me what it was about. But I knew it had something to do with Hatton Garden as the Wheatsheaf pub owner Phil Rice had been questioned by police. The two coppers told me, 'We are waiting for your neighbors. Those guys rent the place and there is something going on there.' One of the police was bald and excited, his name was PC Alex, and he told me that, 'So and so in the video has 20 years in jail.' He used my computer to send a still image to police headquarters. Police were here for seven or eight hours. I told my staff that this was something big, I knew it was Hatton Garden, it had been in the papers."[9]

After the exchange had taken place, Perkins and Jones then drove to Terri's house. The decision was made by the Flying Squad not to tail them to avoid attracting attention.[10]

Meanwhile, on Sterling Road, a team of unarmed Flying Squad officers was already mobilized. Jon Warren, a neighbor whose backyard overlooks the house of Terry Perkins's daughter, Terri Robinson, said an officer rang his bell and "rushed to look out the back window" at Terri's house. "We didn't know what was happening. The police were discreet. They spent about ten minutes surveying the house. There was no chopper," said Warren, a retired engineer. "I didn't know who the Perkins were—I had never heard of them. I don't know of any crime families in the neighborhood. I thought they had all moved to Essex."[11]

Back at Flying Squad headquarters in Putney, Turner and Johnson were staring intently at one of the screens in front of them when suddenly they saw Perkins and Jones arriving at Terri's house, carrying large black carrier bags filled with jewels. It was around 10 a.m. Once inside, they gathered the bags near the dining room table and looked at the glittering contents. Some of the jewel boxes were stuffed in yellow and blue supermarket bags from Lidl, the discount chain.

Johnson recalled that when he and Craig Turner saw the men with the bags, "Craig and I turned to each other and smiled. We knew we had them." Now, all that was left was to arrest them, without making any errors that could compromise the prosecution, or cause the aging gang to flee. Even if they did, they would likely not get far, given the small army of police officers who had been mobilized.

At the Flying Squad, there are three commands to officers in the field to indicate that they should close in and arrest suspects. "State green" means an investigation is ongoing, evidence and intelligence is still be gathered, and "do not arrest." "State amber" is an authorization from a commanding officer to arrest the suspects. "State red" is the actual moment when the presiding officer on the ground enforces the order to arrest the suspects.

When Johnson saw Perkins and Jones close the door, he picked up his phone to the officer on the ground, Mark Bedford, and said firmly and loudly, "State amber! State amber!"

Seconds later, an unarmed team of officers with a battering ram bashed down the door. When police breached the door, Perkins and Jones were sitting on a sofa. The element of surprise had proven effective. Johnson recalled that the gang, experienced criminals though they were, appeared shocked and ashen-faced. "They looked very disappointed," he recalled.

Jones, a one-time marathon runner, sprinted to the garden. But he didn't get far. The two, along with Collins, were arrested. At the house, police found vast quantities of sapphires and diamonds, earrings, necklaces, bangles, and brooches and a brown leather bag stuffed with Rolex, Breitling, and Omega watches. Heat-resistant porcelain pots and tongs used for smelting gold were discovered hidden in a washing machine. Police also found a set of electronic scales. There were latex gloves on the table.

After the men were arrested, Johnson and Turner shook hands. Johnson, usually self-contained, was grinning.

Meanwhile, separate teams simultaneously raided ten other addresses in north London, as well as Brian Reader's house in Kent. A visibly annoyed and surly Reader affected surprise when ten police officers broke down his door after peering through a window and spotting him sitting in a chair in his living room. His son Paul, who had allowed his father to use his cell phone during the plotting and aftermath of the burglary, was also arrested.

Sitting on a table at Reader's house was a diamond tester and a book on the diamond underworld. Police also discovered the distinctive red scarf he had worn to the burglary, picked up by surveillance cameras near Hatton Garden. Reader also had not discarded the subway pass for senior citizens he had used to get to the heist—an omission that an old associate of his said was shocking, given his risk aversion and attention to detail. Had he been reckless and forgetful in his old age?

"I think he really thought he had got away with it, the elderly hoodlum," Johnson recalled, chuckling. "He knew full well what it was about but he didn't know what we had on him. He had walked away before the job was done, and he seemed very surprised he had been caught red-handed. He didn't resist arrest, but he was very uncooperative and resentful."

Bill Lincoln, unaware that the police had finally sprung, was arrested behind the wheel of his black Audi A3 in the middle of a busy road in north London while waiting at a traffic light. As several police cars surrounded his car, he suddenly bent down, and pivoted toward the passenger seat, where he began to frantically tear up a piece of paper upon which he had written the address for the Old Wheatsheaf pub, where the jewel exchange had taken place. An unarmed officer, thinking he could be grabbing for a gun, smashed his car window and tackled him. After he was led away, police found the ripped up paper on the passenger seat floor. While in custody at the police station, Lincoln was so overcome by nerves he wet himself. Police would later put the note back together with tape.

For Johnson, just weeks away from retirement after a long career, the arrests were a particularly sweet moment. "You are only as good as your last job,"[12] he said.

* * * *

A Bungled Crime

While the plotting and planning of the Hatton Garden heist had been masterful, the execution was amateurish bordering on stupid, and the aftermath disastrous. Reader, long an able recruiter, had helped to assemble a team of elderly and grizzled cohorts who appeared to have been caught out by their age. The gang's decision to drive one of their own cars to the scene of the crime and to communicate by phone in the weeks following the heist had made them easy prey for the Flying Squad. Their inability to refrain from boasting and the eagerness with which they returned to their favorite haunts like the Castle proved to be a fatal error.

Add to that their petty jealousies and internecine rivalries, and the speed with which they incriminated themselves and were then caught—some sixty days after the door to 88–90 Hatton Garden closed behind them—was head-spinning. Whatever time Jones and the others had spent reading and rereading *Forensics for Dummies* was worthless. They had been savvy enough to wear surgical gloves and to scrub their fingerprints away but, in the end, they had been handily outwitted by a couple of surveillance bugs, a team of determined Flying Squad officers, and modern-day police forensics. Their ruse may have worked in the 1950s or 1960s, but in 2015?

"It is almost as if these guys have been locked up and then transported by a time machine to modern times to perform this crime," mused Dick Hobbs, the eminent sociologist of the capital's underworld.[13]

Ed Hall was one of the chief prosecutors, charged with building the case against the four ringleaders. Burly and rumpled, with a love of horse racing and fine wine, he liked to wear a suit jacket with his tie undone. His office at the Crown Prosecution Service in Pimlico, an area of central London known for its garden squares and regency architecture, was cramped and brimming with files.

In his two-decade career at the top of the Crown Prosecution Service, which is responsible for prosecuting all criminal cases investigated by the police in England and Wales, Hall has seen it all: Albanian human trafficking gangs; Chinese money launderers; a rapist who jumped from a five-story building and fled Britain, only to be arrested eight years later in Ghana.

But when the Hatton Garden case came across his desk, he could barely contain his glee. "I realized as soon as it happened that it was a great story. Whatever it was, it was a hugely ambitious criminal endeavor. I saw it coming. I saw that it was going to be big," he said. "The planning was brilliant. But they were sloppy and they made mistakes. It was the last great British heist. You see one of these every 30 years."

As Hall sifted through thousands of pages of evidence, including video and surveillance footage of the thieves at their favorite neighborhood bars, their statements to police, witness testimony, and their long and meandering criminal histories, he said he was struck by how close they came to getting away with the crime.

"They got 80 percent of the job right but 20 percent of the job wrong," he said.

Smiling mischievously, he quoted from the 1981 film noir *The Postman Always Rings Twice*, in which a seductive wife played by Jessica Lange and a rootless drifter played by Jack Nicholson have a steamy affair and conspire to murder her husband and steal his money. "We can't spend a dime of this for a year," the Lange character says.

"They should have slept on it for six months," Hall said, smirking. "They should have used pay-as-you-go phones. After the heist, their age kicked in."[14]

For all their professed brilliance in solving the crime, the police, too, had made mistakes. The local police had failed to respond to the alarm on Easter weekend; Scotland Yard had initially wrongly estimated that more than $200 million was missing. But in the end, the Flying Squad had swooped in and solved the crime. It was one for the history books.

* * * *

In Custody: "No Comment, No Comment"

Once in custody at the imposing redbrick Wood Green police station in north London, the gang of experienced thieves held fast. "They all had poker faces and were not looking at each other," Detective Paul Johnson recalled, smiling. "They wanted us to think that they weren't connected to each other. They still thought they could get away with it." For the first few hours they were all in same airless room, before each one was interviewed for about seventy-five minutes. Each interrogation was recorded. Befitting old-school criminals who had learned long ago to remain silent when confronted by police, each interview was an exercise in studied evasion. No matter—Scotland Yard had spent weeks gathering evidence before waiting to spring, mindful that the diamond geezers would go quiet.

The gang of four were whisked into a large custody area where they would see one another. It was a tactic calculated to unsettle them, but the men pretended not to know one another. "At various points they saw each other but as they waited to be interviewed they whistled and looked at the ceiling," Johnson recalled. He said that when Reader—who had abandoned the heist—was brought in shortly after the other three, it must have dawned on the others that they were in serious trouble, and that police had pieced together the crime. "They must've been thinking, 'What is going on here? How do they know he was there?'"[15]

Perkins entered the compact interview room at 10:37 p.m. on May 20, 2015, accompanied by a lawyer. Wearing glasses and appearing nonplussed, he sat in a chair, a blank expression on his face. After the two Flying Squad officers informed him of his legal rights, the questions began in earnest. But as he had previously vowed he would do if he was ever caught, he played the clueless and doddering old man.

"Now it is going to be a fairly lengthy interview," one of the officers began. "As you can imagine the serious nature of the offence. You've obviously been arrested for the conspiracy to commit burglary at the Hatton Garden Safe Deposit Vault over the period the 2nd of April 2015 until Saturday the 5th of April."[16]

"No comment," Perkins replied.

"Daniel Jones. Is that the person that you know?"

"No comment."

"Is he an associate of yours?"

"No comment."

"Mr. Jones drives a black Land Rover, registration HN08 UEU. Is that a vehicle that's familiar to you?"

"No comment."

"Now if you have any form of alibi or any form of defense that you may potentially rely on later, it's your opportunity really to tell us now."

"No comment."

Perkins's interview continued for more than an hour. The officers temporarily stopped the interview so he could take his insulin medication for his diabetes.

At around midnight, one of the interrogators, determined to crack Perkins, tried to play on his sense of shame. It didn't work.

"There's been various descriptions of this burglary out in the press," he began. "Some people have likened it a bit to *Ocean's Eleven*. But the bottom line is that we speak to the people that are the victims of this, and contrary to what people might have read in the paper, they are not rich people. There are some people that their family heirlooms were in there, things that are just precious to them and they wanted to keep safe. Some people had their entire pensions in there, they have all been taken. There was a guy that I was speaking to on the phone who said that his first wife died of cancer and he didn't want his current wife to know that he'd kept their wedding rings, and those are among the things that were stolen in this offense. How do you feel about that?"[17]

"No comment," Perkins replied.

"Do you feel any kind of remorse at all about it?"

"No comment."

And so it went with each of the suspects, each of whom answered "No comment," as the two detectives asked them if they knew one another. Then they slowly unspooled in forensic detail the three-day trajectory of the burglary, the precise movements of their vehicles, the heaps of stolen jewels found at their homes.

Each man was presented with the incontrovertible and detailed evidence of their involvement. Collins was informed that police had identified his distinctive white Mercedes, registered in someone else's name, and the van he had driven during the heist.

Jones was told that he has been spotted with a walkie-talkie at the scene of the crime, that police knew his role was to wield the diamond-tipped drill and to climb through the drill hole in the vault, and that CCTV video cameras had filmed him when he went with Collins to Machine Mart to buy a new pump after the first pump broke down.

Reader learned that police knew about the senior citizen's subway card he had used on his way to the burglary. In an apparent attempt to rattle him, the two officers interrogating him also played him a recording of Jones lambasting him as a "horrible man" and Perkins complaining that, among other things, he was stingy and never bought "a drink at the pub."

A visibly shaken Wood learned that the police knew that he had chickened out of the burglary after the second night, and that Perkins and the others had mercilessly mocked him for his cowardice.[18]

"Do you feel like your credibility in the underworld or criminality or being able to stand tall amongst people that could do stuff like this, do you feel this has been affected?" the interrogating officer asked him.

"No comment."

Jamie Day recalled the gang was aggressive in their contempt and resolute in their silence. Amazingly, even the incorrigibly loquacious Doyle uttered "No comment" no fewer than 222 times.

When it came to Brian Reader's turn, he was stoic and didn't even bother to utter "No comment." He remained silent, only answering a solitary "Yes" when asked whether he understood his legal rights.

"Mr. Reader we're investigating a burglary at Hatton Garden at 88–90 that took place in the basement where the vault and safety deposit boxes were kept. Do you have anything to say about that?"[19]

Silence.

"It's been in the papers, it's fairly infamous now and it was over the Easter weekend. Do you remember what you were doing over the Easter weekend?"

Silence.

"Did you put this job together; you're the head of it?"[20]

Silence.

One of the officers played a recording in which the rest of the gang referred to Reader as "the Master."

Silence.

But when police played the men snippets of their recorded conversations incriminating themselves and showed them the CCTV footage showing them at the scene of the crime, the officers watched as Perkins, Jones, and Reader grew deflated and began to sulk. Jones squirmed as the officers played the audio in which he and Perkins discussed cutting up the jewels and viciously slagged off Reader and Wood for backing out of the heist, halfway through.

"How do you think Carl Wood and Brian Reader were going to feel about you slating them?" one of the officers asked Jones.

Reader, for his part, was forced to contain his contempt and looked ahead, glassy-eyed, as the officers played an audio of a conversation in which Perkins insulted him for his ineptness as a thief. "The whole fucking 12 years I've been with him, three, four bits of work, he's fucked up every one of them," Perkins's angry voice blared out.

"Have you known Mr. Perkins for 12 years?" the detective asked him. Reader declined to answer.

Recalling the interview, Johnson said Reader was the more shell-shocked among the gang since he had backed out of the crime, and thought he was safe from prosecution, only to discover, much to his horror, that his professed involvement in the heist had been caught on tape.

But even experienced pros have their breaking points. Confronted with the audio and images of himself entering 88–90 Hatton Garden, Jones, the narcissistic showman, eventually dissolved. He had initially tried to play it cool, stating his home address as "no fixed abode" and calling himself "retired" before unleashing a steady stream of "no comments." But after listening to the barrage of evidence the Flying Squad had gathered, Jones looked up at the interviewing officer and said, "You boys have done a proper job on us here, a professional job." Referring to the evidence, he added: "It's overwhelming I suppose, init?"

"Yes," the detective interviewing him replied.

"Anyway, I ain't got nothing to say."

"If you did have some stuff to say, then we want to listen."

"I'm very stressed at the moment," Jones replied. "You appreciate that, don't you? It's almost one o'clock."[21]

But the men deflected police questions about the mysterious fifth man, "Basil," whose red hair had been captured by the CCTV camera, but who had managed to evade arrest. All insisted they didn't know who he was. It would emerge only later from Jones, never a reliable source, that Basil may have been recruited by Reader, and his identity purposely not revealed to the other members of the gang, in order to protect him, if they were caught.

Once the men were in custody, the Crown Prosecution Service, the main prosecution service for England and Wales, charged the gang with conspiracy to burgle Hatton Garden. As in the American legal system, the men had to decide whether to brave a trial in which the evidence was clearly stacked against them, or whether to plead guilty. Under the British legal system, their careful efforts to avoid violence during the burglary meant that their sentences would be circumscribed if they pleaded guilty. In any case, in Britain, prisoners are typically eligible for parole after serving only half of their sentences. So faced with the overwhelming and incontrovertible evidence Johnson and his team had meticulously gathered over several months, Reader, Jones, Collins, and Perkins pleaded guilty. The Flying Squad's methods had worked.

Johnson and Day were lauded as heroes, in a decidedly English and understated way—with pints of beer at the pub near Flying Squad headquarters, flanked by fellow officers. But the celebration was muted. The prosecution hadn't yet begun. And the aging thieves had shown themselves to be adept at wiggling out of tough situations.

As the daring antics of the Hatton Garden heist grabbed headlines, Britons of all ages and classes marveled at the old men who had managed, like the Great Train robbers before them, to buck the establishment. And while the government of Conservative prime minister David Cameron was not rocked by scandal as in the days of Harold Macmillan during the Great Train Robbery, the occupant in No. 10 Downing Street was an Old Etonian "toff," presiding over a country that remained deeply polarized by social and class divisions. That helped burnish the aging gang as working-class heroes akin to the Great Train robbers decades earlier.

For the dedicated men and women of the Flying Squad, the tendency of the media—and everyday Britons—to idolize the men was a source of deep frustration, since they had, in fact, stolen millions of dollars of valuables. Nevertheless, the crew quickly garnered fans throughout the country and across the world—including in France, where they were dubbed "Le Gang du Papys," or the Grandads' Gang.

Alan Ivens, a research scientist, and Ian Wick, an accountant, both of whom were born and raised in Enfield, have been drinking companions for the past sixty years. In the months following the burglary, the two were holding court at the Old Wheatsheaf, the century-old pub in Enfield, where the Hatton Garden gang liked to down a pint or two while they were plotting the heist and where several had gone before the ill-fated jewel exchange. The pub, with its wood paneling, warm ale, World War II memorabilia, Thursday "quiz nights," and cricket playing perpetually on the television, was a hangover from a 1950s vision of England that hadn't yet died in Enfield.

"When I heard about the heist, I thought it was just like the old times. It had a bit of style to it," said Ivens. "They had no firearms. It's like those old clever boys who tunneled under the ground to Lloyds Bank in the 1970s," he said, referring to the robbery on Baker Street, connected to Reader, in which a gang had infiltrated a safe deposit after days of digging underground. "It's amazing they are still getting to that kind of trouble at their age." It was a sentiment repeated over and over again at pubs across the capital and among people of all classes. While working-class Britons could idealize the men's success at fleecing safe deposit box holders perceived as wealthy denizens of the upper classes (in fact, many were immigrant success stories), Britons of all classes couldn't help but be impressed by men who were rappelling down elevator shafts and wielding heavy drills when most people their age were quietly enjoying their retirement.

Chapter 14

The Trial

The Plumber, the Arsehole, and Billy the Fish

Once the news broke that a group of cunning pensioners were behind an old-school heist that even defense lawyers deemed worthy of Hollywood, Britons of all ages affectionately embraced the white-haired crew. The buzz about the burglary was everywhere—on social media, on radio call-in shows, in the back seat banter of London black cabs as they whizzed across the city. In newspapers and television bulletins, the men's grizzled and wrinkly mug shots—ruddy faced, liver-spotted, and resigned—were shown over and over again.

It was part gangster film, part slapstick comedy, and the British public couldn't get enough. At a time of bloody terrorist attacks, the tortured debate over whether Britain should leave the European Union, and the economic austerity of Prime Minister David Cameron's government, the old-fashioned caper provided welcome romance, escapism, and relief.

"All I ask of the world is that elderly cat burglars be allowed to carry off enormous diamond heists in peace," mused one mesmerized fan on Twitter.

Befitting a country that had long relished elevating the underdog, the general attitude was one of appreciation and awe. How could
they . . . ? The men were portrayed as affable rogues, old-economy
criminals from a different age, with names like "the Guv'nor" and
"Billy the Fish," and ailments like leaking bladders. Forensic play-by-
plays of the heist dominated the front pages of London's tabloid press,
along with graphics of the men rappelling down elevator shafts, and
recitations of their colorful criminal backgrounds.

"BAD GRANDPAS" read the giant front-page headline in the
Daily Mail, the populist barometer of middle England. "DIAMOND
WHEEZERS" screamed Rupert Murdoch's tabloid the *Sun*, showing the astonishing photograph of the figure-eight holes bored into
the vault's concrete wall, the compromised safe deposit boxes visible
behind them.[1] "Combined ages of all nine suspects is 533," noted a
subhead on the front page, above illustrations of a row of diamonds,
each emblazoned with the ages of the men. Even the stately BBC got
in on the fun, filming its elegant home affairs correspondent Daniel
Sandford trying to wiggle his way through a hole in a makeshift concrete wall and hamming it up for the camera as he nearly got stuck.

Suddenly, Scotland Yard—and prosecutors—knew they were
fighting a war on two fronts. In total there were initially nine men
arrested in connection with the heist—the four ringleaders Reader,
Jones, Collins, and Perkins and their four accomplices Lincoln,
Wood, Doyle, and Harbinson, along with Reader's son Paul, who
was later released, apparently none the wiser what his father had
been up to.

The four ringleaders had pled guilty to the burglary, effectively
depriving the public and the frenzied media of the show trial they
craved. The result was that the prosecution of the accomplices became
a stand-in for their elder mentors. The British media was determined
to turn the trial and a bleak south London courtroom into a sensational stage upon which to reenact the burglary.

"After the main protagonists in the burglary pled guilty, the interest in the trial might've disappeared," Philip Evans, the lawyer who prosecuted the case, recalled. "But as soon as the media got wind of the case, it became an obsession, and the trial of the secondary guys became a sort of proxy for the whole gang."[2]

Prosecutors knew they had to prove the guilt of the men in court while at the same time proving their guilt in the court of public opinion, which is more difficult. The jurors in the latter are more numerous and evidence takes a back seat to a classic underdog story, made all the more difficult when the perps look like doddering grandparents. The police quickly tried to change the narrative to focus on the hard truth that the men were malicious fiends, who had heartlessly targeted the life savings of men and women their own age. It was a hard sell.

While much of the media coverage was fawning and laudatory, there were two opposing narratives in public opinion. One narrative sought to present the men as would-be members of *Dad's Army*, a wildly popular British television series in the 1970s that featured the misadventures of a group of endearing and elderly volunteer soldiers during the Second World War. The opposing narrative portrayed them as the cast of *Ocean's Eleven*, the "nasty" gang of World War II veterans from the 1960 heist film, recruited by the dapper and wily Danny Ocean (Frank Sinatra) to rob five different Las Vegas casinos.

Evans and Scotland Yard were determined that the latter narrative would prevail. They realized they faced an uphill struggle in a country with a natural inclination to thumb its nose at authority. "The real nasty blokes with the previous convictions—Brian Reader, Terry Perkins, Danny Jones—weren't in the dock," Evans recalled. "But we had to make sure the jury understood the suffering these men had caused and the callousness of their crime."[3]

* * * *

Fancy a Spot of Tea, Judge?

During their first appearance on June 4, 2015, in Southwark Crown Court via a video link from HM Prison Belmarsh, a high-security prison in southeast London, officials struggled with a patchy video link between the court and the jail where the men were being held.

Seizing on the moment, Terry Perkins put a question to the court. "Could you ask the judge and yourselves to come down to Belmarsh and we can have tea together?" he asked. Bystanders in the courtroom roared with laughter.

As court staff scrambled to overcome the technical difficulties, the gang could be heard muttering that the proceeding was a "farce" and a "joke" and "this is fucked." The judge Alistair McCreath, visibly frustrated, pressed on. But the broadcast cut out completely two minutes later. "Oh, for goodness' sake," he said, sighing.

It was not an auspicious beginning.

The prosecutor Philip Evans, who watched awkwardly as the scene unfolded, said that the men "were making a mockery of the court." He believed "they were trying to be light-humored to give the impression that they were harmless old men."[4]

The trial of the accomplices—a ragtag group of middle-aged and indebted men, including a plumber, a taxi driver, and several unemployed drifters—lasted nine weeks. Following the gang's initial appearance via video link, the trial of the accomplices took place at Woolwich Crown Court, a maximum security court in southeast London next to Belmarsh prison that is usually used for terrorism cases. The building—sprawling, modernist, and grim—provided a prosaic setting for a trial focused on a sensational and brazen heist. The venue—reserved for some of the most dangerous suspects in the country—appeared calculated to puncture the perception that the Hatton Garden heist was the work of harmless old men.

* * * *

EVANS, A FORTY-SIX-YEAR-OLD barrister, was used to big cases. He had defended serial killers and sports stars accused of corruption and he had prosecuted sensational murder cases.

He studied at Cardiff School of Law and Politics—not Oxford or Cambridge—and wears that distinction like a badge.

"I am a state school boy," he noted proudly, using the British term for a government-funded school. His wife is also a barrister, and had "taken silk" two years before, meaning she was appointed a Queen's Counsel, the highest-ranking position of a senior barrister in the British legal system. He had not yet achieved that distinction, and wanted it badly. Hatton Garden could only buttress his chances.

A former semiprofessional rugby player and an accomplished pianist, he was "head boy" at his British high school—analogous to being president of the student council in the United States. He plays the trumpet, shoots clay pigeons, and likes to bike from London to Paris for exercise when he isn't too busy prosecuting rapists, money launderers, or robbers. He speaks with the steady confidence of someone who has seldom lost a case.

The prosecution team—Evans and Philip Stott, his junior colleague—were transfixed by a section of the Flying Squad's audio recording of the gang in which Jones and Perkins boast about having undertaken the greatest jewelry heist in the history of England, blissfully unaware that they were not alone in Perkins's Citroën Saxo.

"When we heard them talking and bragging about what they had done, there was an element of humor and some relief," Evans said, recalling the moment with the pensive smile of an English prosecutor schooled to not take too much joy in the downfall of the criminals he is prosecuting, at least outwardly. "I thought, 'Well, that's a bit stupid that you are talking about what you have done so openly.' I suppose they didn't realize they were being listened to. From a prosecutor's point of view, I thought, 'that's bloody good evidence. What on earth are they going to do now?'"

As he studied the CCTV footage, Evans said he also realized they had a smoking gun. "You can see the men leaving the burglary and the moment where Wood realizes the door is locked when the rest of the gang come back to complete the job, and he decides to leave, exiting stage left," he recalled. "It was a key moment."[5]

The guilty plea of the ringleaders had deprived Evans—and the public—of the show trial they craved. It was a smart decision. Beyond the fact that a guilty plea would win them a reduced sentence, they could also get released early for good behavior. They could get as little as four years in prison. Then maybe go and recover their stolen loot. If they pled not guilty and were convicted anyway, they could die behind bars.

As the trial began, the fact that the crime was a nonviolent burglary rather than an armed robbery nagged at Evans; he knew that there were limits to the conviction he could secure. The gang had purposely decided to commit the crime over a long Easter weekend, when they likely wouldn't run into anyone—or end up in a potentially violent skirmish with a security guard. The maximum sentence for a commercial burglary was ten years, and by pleading guilty, that was automatically reduced by one-third.

"The issue that it was a burglary rather than a robbery was an important one," Evans explained. "They had made sure that there would be no one in the building over that bank holiday weekend, so that they wouldn't be placed in a position to need to threaten violence to complete the crime. I supposed that added to the romantic nature of the crime they had committed as everyone says, 'Well, they didn't hurt anyone.'"[6]

But the accomplices all pled not guilty to conspiring to steal gems and gold at Hatton Garden Safe Deposit. There was Wood, who had chickened out before the burglary; Lincoln, who had helped store the goods; Doyle, the plumber who had given the gang access to his plumbing workshop; John Harbinson, a cab driver and relative of Lincoln accused of helping to store and transfer some of the jewels in his taxi; and "Billy the Fish" Lincoln, who served as getaway driver and recruited Harbinson, his nephew, to help conceal the booty. As a result of their nonguilty pleas, the trial focused on them, even as it provided the prosecution the opportunity they desperately craved to rebrand the ringleaders in the public mind as cruel, nefarious old men.

＊ ＊ ＊ ＊

Philip Evans, the Barrister

While seemingly every young and ambitious lawyer in London had lobbied to get the case, Evans's name had come up because he had worked closely with Ed Hall, a senior prosecutor at the Crown Prosecution Service, who had been charged with the case, and admired his tireless determination. The Crown Prosecution Service, known as the CPS, is the main prosecuting authority for England and Wales, and decides what cases should be prosecuted, what charges should be filed, and, significantly for Evans, which lawyer should litigate the case in court.

"The stakes were extremely high and we needed someone who could reasonably expect to win the case," Hall noted.[7] Hall specialized in prosecutions involving unruly street protests and demonstrations and he had prosecuted dozens of people during the summer riots of 2011 when thousands of people went on a looting rampage across the capital, one of the worst cases of public disorder in Britain since the Second World War. But he had also dealt with hundreds of murders and armed robberies during his decades-long career, and he relished the prospect of prosecuting geriatric thieves in a high-profile case. A natural storyteller himself, Hall had seen Evans perform in court and had been impressed by his methodical approach, brilliant grasp of forensic evidence, diligent work ethic, and ability to construct a compelling tale, which the Hatton Garden case now offered in abundance to a lawyer with a modicum of imagination. Evans was ecstatic when the career-making (or breaking) case landed in his in-box.

In the British legal system, lawyers are divided into solicitors and barristers, the former of whom typically provide legal advice and support for a client, and the latter of whom don a wig and gown in court, where they act as advocates and plead a case in front of a judge and jury. Some barristers prefer to stick either to prosecution or to defense, for fear of coming across as ruthless opportunists. But in Evans's career, he had shown competence both as a defense lawyer and a prosecutor.

He was also no stranger to high-profile cases. In 2008 he defended the serial killer Levi Bellfield, who gained ignominy across the country after brutally killing and raping several women and girls, including Milly Dowler, a thirteen-year-old girl. He also defended Muhammad Asif, a Pakistani cricket star, who in 2010 fixed a match at Lords Cricket Ground by deliberately bowling no balls in exchange for cash. But before Hatton Garden, he had never taken a case that would get as much attention, turning him—willingly or not—into an overnight star on the ten o'clock news and making his every pronouncement in court potentially larded with Shakespearian meaning.

* * * *

EVANS WAS FEELING nervous as he arrived in court the morning of November 22, 2015, to open the prosecution's case. The scene at the blocky Woolwich Crown Court in southeast London only added to his nerves. At least half a dozen television trucks were parked outside. About fifty journalists from all the major upmarket and tabloid papers—the BBC, the *Times* of London, the *Daily Mail* among them—were already occupying all the press seats inside the court, forcing another 126 to spill over into another press room, where the trial would be transmitted live.

Presiding over the case was the unflappable sixty-four-year-old Judge Christopher Kinch QC, wearing a wig and red robe, and betraying little reaction to the frenzied scene in court number two. A judge with a long career adjudicating criminal cases, he had grown up in Bromley, Kent, not far from where Brian Reader has his imposing house. He was a circuit judge and Queen's Counsel, a designation that marked him as one of the country's best legal minds. Ruddy faced, matter-of-fact, and largely immune to irritation, he was the resident judge at Woolwich Crown Court, which hosted trials of some of the most notorious terrorists in the land, including the six men accused of the July 21, 2005, bombings on the London transport network. A gang of old-timer thieves in his courtroom was a rarity. And while he was used to high-profile cases—he had been called to the bar in 1976 and served as a judge for six years—he was acutely aware that his every word was being scrutinized.

In a gallery above the court sat the families and friends of the defendants—among them, their old prison mates, wives, girlfriends, and children. A few of them waved at the defendants, who were seated in a glass enclosure at the back of the courtroom. Several of the men had arrived earlier through an underground tunnel that connects nearby high-security Belmarsh prison with the court house, allowing suspects and defendants to be whisked in and out of court without the need to transport them and risk anyone escaping. The prison housed men considered highly dangerous—terrorists and murderers among them. The fact that the bungling elderly gang and their accomplices were being held there underscored how the Crown

Prosecution Service was determined to stress the insidiousness of their crime in the public imagination.

Doyle, out on bail and ever the charming and loquacious plumber, introduced himself and shook hands with the gaggle of assembled journalists sitting at the side of the courtroom. Sometimes he wore his plumber's uniform to court, emblazoned with the name of his company, Associated Response. Each defendant had a small team of lawyers, and the legal aid bill for the defendants would eventually breach £660,000 (about $990,000), prompting outrage. One lawyer, Philip Sinclair, who represented taxi driver John Harbinson, sported a different fresh rose on his lapel every day of the trial—an apparent tribute to his late wife.

As is the custom in British courts, the lawyers and the judge wore robes and horsehair wigs, a tradition going back to the fourteenth century. Anachronistic, itchy, and hot by all accounts, the wigs nevertheless help convey the sanctity of law and prevent juries from favoring a lawyer based on his or her dress, while also affording prosecutors some degree of anonymity from defendants out for revenge. Today, there are no strict sartorial requirements for lawyers arguing cases at the Supreme Court or in civil cases. But this being Britain, many barristers wear them, anyway.

When the moment to begin the trial finally came, the courtroom suddenly went silent and twelve members of the jury, six men and six women—including a hairdresser and a retired prison warden— shuffled in. One had taken his oath on a Koran. While the British legal system does not allow lawyers to individually vet members of the jury, Judge Kinch asked them whether they had any connection with Hatton Garden or the jewelry trade. None volunteered.

Evans, wearing glasses, his wig, and a black robe, stood in front of the jury. As he made eye contact with each member, he began to unspool the story of the heist, building a narrative that, he later recalled, he had spent more than a week honing and practicing to make sure the jury remained on the edges of their seats. The opening was typed out on several sheets of A4 paper. Evans had reread it so many times—on his way to work, while taking a bath—that he no longer needed to look at his papers.

Calling the Hatton Garden heist the "largest burglary in English history," he began by noting that the four ringleaders ranged from age sixty to seventy-six and had brought in four men—the men on trial today—to help complete the audacious raid. The old gang, he added, was responsible for some of the most brazen crimes of the century.

"These four ringleaders and organizers of this conspiracy, although senior in years, brought with them a great deal of experience in planning and executing sophisticated and serious acquisitive crime not dissimilar to this," he said. "Two of these men had been involved in some of the biggest acquisitive crimes in this country in the last century and the other two had for many years in their earlier lives been involved in serious theft."

Warming to his theme, Evans described how the oldest man on the job, Brian Reader, seventy-six, was known as "the Master" or "the Governor," and how the men had met on Friday nights at the Castle pub to plan the heist over several years. Once the Easter weekend raid was on, he told the jury, the men had maintained "radio silence" by using walkie-talkies. He meticulously recounted the evidence—how the men had disabled the elevator and then slid down into the vault; how they had wielded diamond-tipped drills to make three adjoining figure eight holes through eighteen inches of reinforced concrete; and how they had left the scene of the crime halfway through to buy a new Clarke pump and ten-ton hydraulic ram necessary to complete the job. Later during the trial the prosecution would bring in an exact replica of the holes in the drilled-through wall so the jury could visualize them.

Suppressing the desire to smirk, he added that police had discovered the book *Forensics for Dummies* at Jones's house after the men were arrested. Jones had buried some of the stolen goods at a Victorian cemetery, he told the jury, while items including face masks, a drill, and cash were found at his home. The gang, he said, had opened seventy-three safe deposit boxes, twenty-nine of which were empty. At least $12 million worth of jewels, gold, and cash hadn't been recovered.

Looking back on his opening, Evans recalled that the moment required a flawless delivery since much of the jury had likely already read about the case in the newspapers. "I dare say that in my career I have been boring on a number of occasions. But I didn't want to be boring on Hatton Garden. On the morning of the opening I was feeling pretty nervous. In hindsight this was one of the most high stakes trials of my career. The material was there for someone with a bit of flair. In that sense it was a prosecutor's dream, as you had compelling details in the narrative and a jury who really wanted to hear it. It was telling the story of this old heist, but also dispelling the myths, and making sure the jury clearly understands the evidence."[8]

Nevertheless, before the trial had barely begun, the Bad Grandpas were already providing a distracting public spectacle, even from behind bars. On the second day of the trial, it emerged that Jones had tried to dupe police about where the loot was hidden, telling them that he had hidden one bag of the missing jewels under the gravestone of his partner's father in a Victorian cemetery in Edmonton, north London.

Jones appeared to further signal his "good behavior" and cooperation by writing to a Sky News reporter from his jail cell, saying he had notified the police about the stash to "make amends to my loved ones and show I'm trying to change. I no [sic] it seems a bit late in my life, but I'm trying."

In October, Jones was given a temporary reprieve from jail and taken to the cemetery to show police where he had hidden part of the stash under a headstone. But he neglected to mention a much larger haul from the burglary buried under a different headstone at the same cemetery, which police had already discovered. Police had spent hours meticulously examining the headstones near where Jones said he had buried the loot and had excavated stashes of hidden jewels, wrapped inside of shopping bags, using small shovels.

The recounting of Jones's failed ruse, explained patiently by Evans in court, elicited sniggers among the assembled Fleet Street journalists. His gall was astounding.

The trial offered up other dramatic moments, including when Evans read out the transcript of some of the thieves' boasts about the burglary, requiring him to utter the words "fuck" and "cunt" over and over again, as the judge in his wig and red velvet cape looked on with arched brows, and a few members of the jury blanched. The defense tantalizingly tried to play up the question as to whether the heist had been an inside job, suggesting that the four ringleaders were not fully responsible.

Hesham Puri, Brian Reader's lawyer, said that the Flying Squad and the prosecution were intent on putting the elderly gang on trial through the prosecution of the accomplices, even though the senior ringleaders had already pleaded guilty to the crime. The son of Pakistani immigrants, who has become one of the capital's leading defense attorneys, Puri claimed that the degree of animus against the men and their accomplices was compounded because police were made to look like fools after failing to respond to the initial alarm during the heist. As a result, he argued, the prosecution was intent on making an example of Reader and the others, treating them like dangerous criminals when their crime had been nonviolent and they were aging men.

"They are being treated in this way because of the notoriety," he asserted. "Even our terrorist suspect clients are being better treated and these men are elderly." Far from being dangerous, he added, the case had shown that they were out of step with the times, "1980s criminals who committed a crime in the 21st century."

Moreover, he said the challenge for the defense was made all the harder by the fact that the elder ringleaders had been linked to some of the most sensational crimes of the past—Security Express, Brink's-Mat, among others—thereby making them and their hapless accomplices objects of fascination. The particular attention on Reader as the master puppeteer of the heist was deeply misplaced, he insisted, given that he had withdrawn from the burglary. "We do not accept that he was The Master. He is in the same category as Collins and the gang. If he was the Master, then why would he have pulled out?"[9]

John Luckhurst, a defense lawyer for John Harbinson, the nephew of Bill Lincoln accused of using his taxi to transport some of the stolen jewels, said that defense attorneys across the land were jockeying to participate in a case that was quickly deemed the "trial of the century." He noted palpable tension between the prosecution and the defense, with the latter regarding the former as pompous, hectoring, and patronizing, and intent on projecting the guilt of the aging gang onto the other defendants, including Harbinson, whom he said was innocent of any crime. "The prosecution was arrogant from the beginning," he said, "and seemed to look down on the defence."

Evans had reason to feel confident. The audio of the gang bragging about the crime and repeatedly mentioning Wood, Doyle, Harbinson, and Lincoln was the smoking gun the prosecution needed to secure a conviction. As a result, the admissibility of hearsay evidence became the key legal issue of the case. The defense argued that the recorded conversations should not be admissible in court since they were hearsay, or statements offered as evidence that were made outside the trial. But Evans pushed back, and argued successfully that the secretly recorded conversations were legally admissible since they were a declaration of the gang's involvement in the conspiracy—an exception to the rule banning hearsay as evidence. Moreover, he argued, the secret recordings didn't show one thief trying to persuade another of something, but, rather a group of thieves giddily reminiscing about what they had done. "If we had lost that argument, it would have very, very seriously weakened our case," he recalled.[10]

Above all, Evans had to successfully link the accomplices to the crime, which he did with great aplomb and more than a little guile, using his verbal dexterity and the poker face he had honed during his years as a prosecutor to help the defendants implicate themselves.

* * * *

Hugh Doyle: The Loquacious Tongue-Tied Plumber

Among those who fell into his trap was Hugh Doyle, the affable forty-eight-year-old Irishman, whose defense was predicated upon him being an honest and hardworking plumber whose only crime had been to let his old drinking mate John Collins have access to the courtyard outside his plumbing offices, unaware that Collins wanted to use it as an exchange for millions in stolen jewels. Doyle was accused of helping to conceal and transfer the stolen goods.

Initially charged with conspiracy to commit burglary and remanded to Belmarsh prison before his charge was reduced, Doyle had spent three and a half months in the prison, where he had lost nearly thirty pounds, whiling his days away by exercising in his cell. With a friendly streak that knows little bounds, he mingled effortlessly with convicted Islamic radicals, with whom he discussed religion, armed with a copy of Christopher Hitchens's *God Is Not Great*.

Asked under cross-examination by Evans how he knew Collins, an initially confident Doyle said he knew him from fifteen years previously when they were drinking mates at a pub called the Harlequin in Islington. He conspicuously failed to mention that he also knew Perkins, Reader, and Jones, but when pressed by an incredulous Evans, he relented.

Asked whether he knew about their criminal past in some of the most legendary robberies of the century, Doyle said he did not. He said he had no idea there was a bold heist in the works, or any crime, for that matter, and that he had given Collins a key to his office in a medieval sheep shed in Enfield, so he could "let himself in and make a coffee."

Evans arched his brows. "You say you didn't know specifically, but you knew that Mr. Reader and Mr. Perkins were two men involved, in their past, in serious crime?" he asked.

"I didn't know it was anything about serious crime," Doyle replied.

"What did you talk about on these 20 occasions, what were the general topics of conversations?" Evans asked, referring to the pub nights at the Harlequin where the men had all met.

"It was 15 years ago, so I can't remember any specifics, but they were just funny," Doyle replied, describing Collins as "a real Arthur Daley character," a reference to an iconic shifty wheeler-dealer car salesman featured in a long-running British television series called *Minder.*

Sensing that he was obfuscating, Evans hit back, insinuating that Doyle had known the men well, and that Perkins, who was on the run at the time from prison and reportedly working as a short-order cook at the Harlequin, had even made them all fish and chips. The jury smiled at the line.[11]

But Doyle's worst moment came when Evans asked him about a key he had found among Doyle's car keys that had also been found on Collins's key chain for his Mercedes, the one spotted at the scene of the crime. Evans knew from Scotland Yard that the two keys were an exact match and that Doyle had given Collins a key to the padlock of his work shed. As Evans grilled him about the key, Doyle was forced to acknowledge that he had given Collins a key to the padlock that secured the wooden doors to his small brick shed. (In the end, the transfer had been carried out in the parking lot next to the shed, in full view of CCTV cameras.)

Evans also played a secretly taped recording made by Scotland Yard. "Can you tell me what you need, 'cause we have options," Doyle can be heard saying in his distinctive Irish brogue.

Evans recalled the moment Doyle floundered with no little relish. "Doyle's problem was that he ran his case that he was the honest plumber who was going to tell the jury the whole truth and nothing but the truth. But he was caught in several lies. His whole case was based on his argument that he had only allowed them to use the area outside his workshop to transfer the bags. But now he had to explain why on earth he had given Collins the key to his premises. He became stuck."[12]

All that being said, Doyle remained outwardly upbeat throughout the trial, even using his newfound notoriety as an opportunity to drum up business for his plumbing firm. He even tweeted a message to his 197 followers saying he hoped he would go free and asking if anyone needed a new boiler.

* * * *

Carl Wood: The Grumpy Accomplice

The fifty-eight-year-old Carl Wood, wearing glasses, a beige V-neck sweater, white collared shirt, and dark trousers, appeared pensive as he sat in the back of the courtroom. He had the aura of a would-be high school civics teacher that belied his former criminal past, including his involvement in an extortion racket with two corrupt cops in the early 1990s that had landed him four years in jail after he had, among other things, been caught by police threatening to rough up the victim with a blade. During the trial, he wore a look of haggard resignation. He was often seen reading the *Daily Mail*, the conservative tabloid known for its "Little Englander" populism and lurid stories about immigrant crime. He fidgeted in his chair and looked at the assembled journalists with bemusement.

Indebted to the tune of £20,000 (about $13,300), unemployed, and suffering from Crohn's disease, Wood seemed a pathetic figure. Now, prosecutors were intent on proving that he was "Man F" in the grainy CCTV footage of the burglary that showed the men entering 88–90 Hatton Garden. Backing up their case were the surreptitiously made audio recordings of Jones and Perkins—in Perkins's blue Citroën Saxo—ruthlessly mocking Wood for chickening out halfway through the burglary after discovering that the fire escape door was closed.

After introducing Wood to the jury as a heavily indebted friend of Danny Jones for whom the burglary was to offer financial relief, Evans showed the jury a photograph of Collins's white transit van with Wood seated next to Jones in the passenger seat as the men drove home after the first night of the burglary. He also presented the surveillance images showing the men entering the building, and pointed to Wood.

"That man has glasses, lives in Chestnut, is called Carl, is white, about the right height, and he knows Danny Jones, and is in regular contact with Mr. Jones," Evans said, matter-of-factly. "It is you, isn't it?"

"I totally disagree. It is not me," Wood replied. While he acknowledged he was in debt, he said he was home at a family BBQ during the time when the heist was unfolding. He also used visits to his mother in an old people's home as an alibi, even as he stumbled over the precise dates. He was bad with numbers and couldn't remember the date of his marriage or his two daughters' birthdays, he said, by way of explanation.[13]

Evans wasn't impressed. "You are making up your evidence as you go along, aren't you?" he said, quietly chiding him. "You are lying to the jury, aren't you?"

Evans effectively rebuffed Wood, saying that his purported alibi of being at a BBQ on Saturday evening of the heist, the second night of the burglary, didn't add up, since the BBQ had ended before Wood had left to join the rest of the crew. A cell phone call between Wood's wife and one of his daughters revealed that he was not at home when the burglary was taking place. Moreover, a review of logs at the old peoples' home showed that none of the visits with his mother had taken place during the burglary.[14]

Wood had acknowledged in his defense statement that Jones had hinted to him that he was involved with something big. He said Jones told him, "That thing I was talking about—just keep watching the telly." Wood told the court that he and Jones had met thirty years before, initially united by a common love of fitness. But after he was diagnosed with Crohn's disease in his twenties, he said the two took quiet walks together and visited garden centers.

He told the court that his disease was very painful—"It feels like a mouthful of ulcers with a bottle of vinegar in your mouth," he explained. He repeatedly mentioned his aged mother Beryl, at one point bursting into tears as he described her Alzheimer's, which he said had made her bedridden for four years. He also wept as his wife described how she had been with him on the evening of the burglary.[15] It was hard to not feel sorry for him, until you remembered that he had once been accused of threatening to beat up a man and put him in a trunk. But was the jury buying it? Their faces blank, it was hard to tell.

Then, in an apparent attempt to distance himself from Jones, Wood sought to present his erstwhile best mate as an eccentric fabulist, even as prosecutors say he unleashed a torrent of lies and half truths to try to avoid a prison cell.

"Danny is a very sensitive guy, a very funny man, eccentric to extremes, everyone who knew Danny would say he was mad. He would go to bed in his mother's dressing gown with a fez on. He would read palms, tell people he could read their fortunes," he told the court. He continued: "He would sleep in a sleeping bag in his bedroom on the floor and go to the toilet in a bottle. He's got a big thing about the army. He's eccentric."

Jones, socialized from years in prison, wouldn't answer the door after 5 p.m.—a time when prisoners were locked back in their cells. "He slept on his own with his dog Rocket." He told the jury that Jones had an obsession with crime but that the two never discussed it.[16]

Reflecting back on Wood's testimony Evans said that prosecuting him was "like shooting fish in a barrel" since his testimony was undermined by so many gaping holes. "Wood's evidence was balls," he said. "He was making it all up."[17]

* * * *

"Billy the Fish" Lincoln

Prosecutors described Bill Lincoln as the "getaway driver for the stash," the man the gang asked to store the millions of pounds worth of jewels, diamonds, and cash they had stolen. Lincoln duly complied, prosecutors alleged, storing the stolen booty from Hatton Garden at his house in the gritty East End London neighborhood of Bethnal Green. He then eventually off-loaded it to his nephew, the taxi driver John Harbinson, who kept the jewels in several bags, hidden in his garage.

Accused of conspiring to commit the burglary at Hatton Garden, the sixty-year-old Lincoln sought to present himself at the trial as a simple and ailing man, a loving son, father, and grandfather, who would be more likely to be found at a market in east London buying eel or salmon for his friends or mother than involved in hiding diamonds and emeralds. But like Wood and Doyle, he, too, struggled to present a credible alibi.

The court heard how Lincoln was infirm, unable to work, and received disability allowance. Like most of his other aging cohorts, he suffered from a host of ailments including sleep apnea, bladder-control problems, and he had also had a double hip replacement.

At one point during his testimony, he broke down in tears after describing how his two-year-old grandson had been in the hospital after suffering a head injury. Lincoln had not been able to take care of him, forcing the boy to be looked after by someone else when the accident occurred.

Asked by his defense lawyer Mark Tomassi where he was during the early hours of Good Friday when the burglary began, Lincoln said he had been at Billingsgate Fish Market, a bustling and expansive fish market complex in east London whose trading hall hosts dozens of shops and a 1,500-ton freezer. Lincoln went there every Friday morning, he said, and on this occasion he said he was accompanied by "Jimmy Two Baths," a friend who he had promised to introduce to the fishmongers there so he could buy his own seafood.[18]

The jury listened in rapt and amused attention as Lincoln explained how he had met Mr. Two Baths at Porchester Spa, a majestic Edwardian art deco spa in west London that originated in the 1920s, and where the two helped bathe each other. It was the kind of place where you can imagine London gangsters discussing business through thick steam wafting in the air. Jimmy was known as "Two Baths," Lincoln explained, "because he goes down twice" in the water. He said the duo had gone to Billingsgate at 5 a.m. on April 3, and that he recalled the precise time because he had called Jimmy Two Baths on his cell phone.

When his defense lawyer asked if he was involved with the Hatton Garden burglary, Lincoln replied, "No, Sir." When his lawyer followed up by asking him if understood the charges against him, Lincoln said he did. "I am not a divvo, but I am not the sharpest knife in the drawer," he added sheepishly. The jury giggled at Lincoln, who seemed straight out of *EastEnders*, a popular British soap opera depicting the lives of the working class.

Called to the stand to vouch for his friend, Jimmy Two Baths, whose real name was James Creighton, confirmed that Lincoln was known as "Billy the Fish" and that the two hung out at the spa, where they did "quite a lot of schmeissing."[19] It was perhaps the first time the Woolwich Crown Court, known for its terrorism cases, had heard the Yiddish term used to describe someone being whipped in a hot steam room after the body is worked over with a sponge, known as a *schmeissing* besom. Since the 1920s, well-healed East Enders had made the pilgrimage to Porchester Spa for a proper *schmeissing*, a practice introduced by Jewish immigrants at the beginning of the century.

The jury appeared riveted by Lincoln's colorful testimony, but there was only one problem: his alibi didn't add up. He may well have been at the fish market at 5 a.m. on Friday morning. But his role in the heist came after the burglary when he helped store the jewels at his home, making his fishmarket alibi largely irrelevant.

The prosecution was also able to show that Lincoln's car had been caught by automatic number plate-recognition cameras on the north side of London Bridge on the first night of the burglary about five minutes before Brian Reader's subway pass had been registered going through London Street station. That strongly suggested that he had driven Reader to the station after the men abandoned the heist, midway through, on Friday evening, so that Reader could take the train back to his home in Dartford.

"It was an unfortunate twist for Mr. Lincoln," Evans said, with a wry laugh. When Lincoln's lawyer claimed Lincoln had been in the area Friday evening to shop at nearby Borough Market, that alibi also imploded, after it emerged that the market was closed at that time of day.[20]

Sympathy for Lincoln may have been buttressed when constable

Matthew Benedict described how Lincoln had wet himself after his arrest, apparently unable to control his bladder. But Lincoln's attempt to project the image of a doddering geriatric came undone after prosecutors described how he had ripped up a piece of paper with the address of the Wheatsheaf pub—the place where the jewels were exchanged—after police smashed his car window and arrested him. That piece of paper, turned into dozens of small pieces and found by police on the floor of the passenger side of Lincoln's car, would later help to seal his fate.

* * * *

Kelvin Stockwell, the Security Guard

During the trial, Kelvin Stockwell, his right hand shaking with a tremor, slowly made his way to the dock to testify. It was hard to not feel sorry for him. He appeared tired and infirm, and testified in a voice barely above a whisper.

When he arrived at the safe deposit on April 3, 2015, after the alarm was initially triggered, Stockwell said he had inspected the premises and was convinced that nothing was amiss. The doors were secure around 1:15 a.m., at which point he had called the safe deposit's owner Alok Bavishi, who was just ten minutes away from the building, but told him to go home.

"I got out of the car, went to the front of the building. I pushed through the doors, they was secure. I went round to Greville Street and I looked through the letterbox. All I could see in there, the light was on, was a metal box on the floor and a bicycle." Meanwhile, the gang was just meters away inside the vault, drilling into reinforced concrete. But that was a fact he would discover only later.

Stockwell had worked at the safe deposit for twenty years. He recalled the moment when he discovered the safe deposit had been hit after he arrived at the building on the Tuesday following the burglary. "The main front door at street level was already open. There's a lock on that wooden door and that had been popped and there was a hole and I saw we had been burgled. On the floor was tools, cutting material. I could see the lights were on. On the second door the bars were lifted up. I went into the yard to get a signal and phoned the police."

Stockwell told the jury that he was convinced that the gang must have had inside knowledge of the safe deposit, given the ease with which they had disabled the alarm and targeted boxes on the right-hand side of the vault, which held the most lucrative stashes of jewelry, cash, and gems.

Nick Corsellis, Carl Wood's lawyer, seeking to deflect guilt from his client, asked Stockwell, one of the few people who had access to the vault, the security codes, and the keys to the safe deposit and its boxes, whether he thought the burglary was an inside job. "The people who were involved in this crime must have had detailed inside information," he told the jury. "The alarm system that was in place was very sophisticated. It related to sensors in terms of a person's movement within the vaults, it related to sensors to the front door, if not other doors, it gave on a very short period of time, 60 seconds has been mentioned, to trip the alarm and then deal with it being turned off. And there had been no incidents where the alarm had been triggered since its installation in 2007. That night when you were called out to your place of work was the first time there had been an alarm activation."

Stockwell slowly nodded his head and said he agreed that the gang must have been informed by someone on the inside about the layout of the vault and how to infiltrate it. But he was adamant that that person had not been him.

"I don't know if it was a false alarm. I turned up, the building was secure and that's it,"[21] he replied.

* * * *

John Harbinson, the Clueless Taxi Driver

Lincoln's case probably wasn't helped when his nephew John Harbinson, a forty-two-year-old taxi driver, whom Lincoln had asked to store three bags of jewels in his garage, told the court that his uncle had told him that the bags containing millions of dollars' worth of stolen diamonds, emeralds, and rubies were "a load of old shit." Harbinson said he had no reason to suspect that the bags contained the jewels from the Hatton Garden heist.[22]

Asked what his reaction was when he saw the three bags stuffed with jewels in a hallway in Lincoln's terraced house, Harbinson said he didn't think twice. "I assumed it was his luggage he was taking on holiday," he said. "I asked how long he was going for because there were a couple of bags in the hallway. He said he had to put them upstairs, could I help him."

When his lawyer asked him how the stolen jewels had found their way into his taxi, a silver Mercedes, Harbinson earnestly replied, "It is a question I have been asking for the past seven months," he said, adding that his suspicions were finally aroused on the day of the transfer when the bags were taken out of his taxi and put into the trunk of Perkins's car.

"What did you think was going on?" his lawyer asked.

"I didn't have a clue to be honest, but it wasn't right."

Harbinson's professed cluelessness about the crime would soon suffer a blow after prosecutors told the jury that a copy of *Killer* by Charlie Seiga, the biography of a notorious gangster, had been found at Harbinson's house, with a bookmark on a page outlining a heist using high-powered drills that sounded eerily like the Hatton Garden burglary. But Harbinson insisted that he knew nothing about the book, nor about the raid at Hatton Garden. Police also found jewelry, including a necklace and a sovereign ring, at his home, but Harbinson testified that they had been given to him by his grandmother and parents.[23]

Looking back on the case, his defense lawyer, John Luckhurst, said Harbinson had been naïve but he was not guilty of any crime. "The only thing my client was guilty of on that occasion was of being stupid,"[24] he said.

* * * *

The Verdict

The accessories to the crime, on the whole, did not fare well, as the evidence stacked up against them. On March 9, 2016, Lincoln was sentenced to seven years in jail, and Wood to six years, while Doyle, having already served several months in prison, received a suspended sentence. Only Harbinson was not convicted of being an accessory to the crime.

Ahead of his sentence, Doyle, the irrepressible salesman who was out on bail and fitted with an electronic leg tag, had turned to Twitter to tell his followers that he hoped that he would be released. "Forget A rated prison—have you got a G rated boiler? £400 cash back for new boiler," he wrote. He also posted a photograph of one of his plumbing cars, along with a note of optimism: "On Woolwich ferry on way to court, last day of 37 days in court, hope let's hope I don't have to walk the plank!!"

The four ringleaders, meanwhile, were sentenced in March 2016 to seven years each in prison.

During the sentencing, three of the ringleaders, several using electronic hearing aids, sat in the back of the court, behind a glass enclosure. Many looked bemused. As usual, Carl Wood was reading the *Daily Mail*. Brian Reader was not present after suffering a stroke while in prison; he would be sentenced a few weeks later. Lincoln, a bulldog of a man, shuffled frequently to the bathroom. Doyle jovially chatted with reporters.

When their sentences were read out, the men listened stoically and betrayed little emotion. "Thank you, judge," said Jones. He then blew a kiss to his family in the gallery, before being led away in handcuffs.

Doyle, ever the amiable plumber, addressed reporters outside the courthouse. Not one to miss a marketing opportunity, he wore a sweatshirt emblazoned with the name of his plumbing firm, Associated Response. "I just want to spend some time with my family now and I've got boilers to fit in north London," he said. "I feel sorry for the victims for what's happened because peoples' lives have been devastated here," he continued. He added, "I'm sorry for any inconvenience."

Months after the trial, the safe deposit's website was still active. "We are currently one of London's most successful and leading safe deposit company [*sic*]," it read, promising to "protect important and irreplaceable personal belongings."

Chapter 15

Who Is Basil?

In the aftermath of the Hatton Garden heist, one pervasive mystery gnawed at the able men and women of Scotland Yard: Who is Basil?

Following the burglary, after police went through hours of CCTV footage of Hatton Garden and the surrounding area, they spotted a man with red hair wearing a cap, earmuffs, and a surgical mask, whom the other members of the Hatton Garden gang of thieves had dubbed "Basil." It was an apparent reference to the children's television glove puppet Basil Brush. Or was it? The red hair might have been a wig.

Before they were caught, the ringleaders were secretly recorded by police expressing their concerns that they could be found if police traced the crime to Basil. "The only one who could get nicked was poor old Basil on the key but, you know what I mean,"[1] Collins said, while driving around in his bugged car.

Daniel Jones suggested Basil was a novice, albeit a quick study, who had rapidly learned the criminal trade under the tutelage of Brian Reader: "Well Basil learnt in two months what he had to learn in 40 years." But Collins wasn't quite as taken with Basil's skills as Jones was. "I still don't know why Basil let that fucking alarm go off," he remarked.[2]

Skilled or clumsy, Basil eluded capture, long after the other members of the gang were arrested. The British tabloid media dubbed him "the Ghost." Toward the end of 2015, Detective Superintendent Craig Turner of the Flying Squad said Scotland Yard knew nothing about Basil, and police professed ignorance of who he is. None of the other men divulged a single detail about the mystery villain, apparently either in the dark about his true identity, or trying to protect him.

"The investigation will be still ongoing. We will seek to identify the individual known as Basil. I refresh our appeal and offer a £20,000 [$28,400] reward," Turner said. "We don't know anything about Basil, that is why we are putting out the appeal." Police feared he had fled with as much as £10 million worth of jewelry, gems, and gold. Asked about him two years after the burglary, Turner sported his best poker face. "We don't know. There is an ongoing investigation. The Hatton Garden investigation has not been shut."[3]

There was no sign of forced entry during the heist and police say that Basil may have been the "inside man" in the operation. But who is he? While the gang disabled several CCTV systems at the safe deposit box, they missed one near the fire exit: Basil can be seen from Greville Street walking toward 88–90 Hatton Garden, his face purposely covered by a bag he was holding. In another frame, he is seen walking toward the white escape van, a phantom of a man, again holding a bag over his shoulder to cover his face. The fact that he covered his face suggests that he had staked out the building and knew its layout.

After entering the building on the evening of April 2, apparently with a key, he likely made his way upstairs to survey the building and make sure no one else was there. The jeweler Lionel Wiffen, whose office shared a courtyard with the safe deposit box at the back of the building near the fire escape, told police that in the months leading up to the heist, he had an eerie and distinct feeling he was being watched. Was the person watching him Basil?

After confirming that Wiffen was not in his office, Basil can be seen on the CCTV cameras in the courtyard of 88–90 Hatton Garden. It seems that he walked into the front of the building while it was still open during office hours, hid for a few hours, before going down a staircase from the main lobby of the building through a door that is not locked. Basil then opened the fire escape door and let the others in.

In the video footage, Basil appears to tower over some of the others, suggesting he is at least six feet tall. But the images are murky. He is wearing a cap, earmuffs, a surgeon's mask, white forensic gloves, a dark blue jacket, dark trousers, and shoes. His face is obscured.

After the men loaded the escape van with the plastic wheelie containers stuffed with gold and jewels on April 5, Basil is seen coming out of the main entrance, the last to leave the building, before their getaway.

Basil's share of the booty was later alluded to by the rest of the gang. Jones said, "Tell you what, I wonder what he would do now, Basil." Perkins replied, "Think of what he's got at the moment, right he's got that gold, some of that gold." He then appears to suggest that while he took the cheapest jewelry, he got the largest stash of cash— £82,000, or about $123,000. "That will last him right through," Jones said. But maybe that wasn't all the cash he made off with, because Perkins added, "That foreign money he fucking won will probably last him ten years."[4] The two men then also suggested that he lived abroad and would have to come back to England to discuss how to divvy up the goods.

The British media speculated that Basil, who disabled the safe deposit company's alarm system, is a computer expert who was talent hunted by Reader and the older members of the gang who were out of touch with modern alarm system technology. While Jones and Perkins appeared to suggest in the surveillance recording that he may have absconded with heaps of foreign cash, the other theory was that he only got a measly

£180,000 ($270,000) in total from the heist, was double crossed by his greedy coconspirators, and would come back to wreak revenge. Or was it he who duped them and escaped with the bulk of the booty?

The British tabloid press, drunk on rumors, reported that the gang, except for Reader, did not know Basil's identity. The *Mirror*, a tabloid newspaper known for its blaring headlines and reports on lurid crimes, reported that the Ghost was a single man from the southeast of London in his mid-fifties and appeared to be much taller than Jones, who was five feet nine inches. CCTV footage suggested that he had hidden his real hair under a ginger wig. The British media claimed that he lived around the Hatton Garden area, and had been involved in several high-profile burglaries over the past two decades, always disappearing without a trace. While his father had passed away, the Ghost's mother was still alive and he had brothers and sisters living in Britain.[5] But Scotland Yard had not confirmed any of these details, at least publicly.

Citing an unnamed source from the criminal underworld, the *Mirror* reported that Basil was canny and intelligent. "He's a clever kid and the police won't have much on him, he's too good for that. He will have hidden his whack somewhere secure in the UK and gone on his toes. I don't know where he is now. On every job you need a good alarm man and The Ghost is the best."[6]

The mystery of Basil's identity took a new twist in February 2016. Jones wrote another letter to Sky News—apparently his favorite way of communicating with the world—saying that Basil was a former police officer who was involved in private security. "Basil was the brains, as I was recruited by him," Jones wrote in the letter, published from Belmarsh prison in southeast London ahead of his sentencing. "He let me in on the night of the burglary, he hid keys and codes throughout the building." The confession—viewed by police as a ruse—contradicted the evidence and police surveillance that Reader had been the chief recruiter and brains behind the operation.

Jones said he had come to Basil's attention through a fellow police officer after being arrested in connection with a similar theft on Bond Street in central London in 2010. He did not know Basil's true identity, and he would not reveal it if he did. "It's not a done thing where I come from as fear for family members," he wrote in his letter.[7] Whatever his identity, police were skeptical of the claims made by Jones, who has a history of burglaries and has not always proven to be the most reliable narrator.

Jones told Sky News that he had seen Basil about four times. "He came and went," he wrote. "I don't know nothing about him, where he lives." He added, "I wasn't interested."

Another theory was that Basil is a cleaner who worked at the safe deposit, is Eastern European, and had absconded to Bulgaria or Romania with $10 million in stolen gold and gems.

As the conspiracy theories continued to swirl, the mystery of Basil's identity appeared to have finally been solved in late March 2018, when police arrested a fifty-seven-year-old jeweler called Michael Seed, bringing a three-year manhunt to an end. Or so it seemed.

A taciturn man with gray hair, Seed was arrested at a run-down and boxy housing estate in Islington, about two miles from where the Hatton Garden theft took place, after police raided his home. Scotland Yard refused to confirm whether Seed was, in fact, Basil. But investigators familiar with the case said Seed was the shadowy and enigmatic figure known as "Basil the Ghost." Police said he had been arrested following a search warrant and after several items were seized from the premises, including jewelry, precious gems, and gold ingots.

When Seed appeared at Woolwich Crown Court in May 2018, to enter a plea via a video link from prison ahead of his trial on September 24, he appeared pensive. Wearing a red T-shirt and glasses and hunched over an orange folder, he pleaded not guilty to conspiring to commit burglary at Hatton Garden or conspiring to convert or conceal stolen property. He said he was a jeweler and confirmed his name, date of birth, and nationality. He spoke in a British accent that hinted at a background more refined than the rest of the gang. The British media reported that in contrast to the working-class credentials of the other members of the firm, Seed is the son of a renowned University of Cambridge scientist, John Seed, who was self-taught until he studied for a doctorate in biophysics. John Seed died several years ago but Seed has a ninety-year-old mother who lives in Cambridge, as well as three siblings.

Seed's aunt Kathleen Seed told the *Times* of London that the notion of her nephew participating in the Hatton Garden heist was absurd. "The idea of him being a safebreaker is outlandish," she said.[8]

A person close to the gang believes that the Flying Squad, despite their protestations, knew who Basil was all along and have had him under surveillance, in London, where he has been the entire time. As he was so careful at avoiding police surveillance and was so discreet during the planning and aftermath of the heist, it took years to gather enough evidence in order to prosecute him. He appears to have been adept at remaining under the radar and neighbors said he was friendly but quiet and seldom spoke to them. He wore the same clothes every day so they assumed he was impoverished.

Chapter 16

The Chatila Heist

Hatton Garden Redux?

IN THE AFTERMATH OF THE HATTON GARDEN HEIST, Scotland Yard once again focused on the Chatila caper of late August 2010, when four men wearing high-visibility jackets and masks targeted the jewelry store to the stars on Bond Street in Mayfair, stealing £1 million ($1.5 million) in jewelry and precious stones from a showroom.

As in Hatton Garden, they had chosen a holiday weekend, targeted a jeweler in the heart of London, traveled to the crime in a white van, wielded a diamond-tipped drill, disabled and climbed down an elevator shaft, and then badly bungled by being unable to get into the vault. Eventually, they gave up on penetrating the vault's wall and instead ransacked the showroom, spiriting away the booty in white containers and bags, before finally vanishing.

Sound familiar?

Scotland Yard thought so, too, and the Flying Squad decided to reexamine the earlier burglary. The similarities with the raid at 88–90 Hatton Garden were eerily familiar. Could it be that the Bad Grandpas had struck before?

In the summer of 2016, Scotland Yard raided London City Metals, the east London scrap metal yard where Perkins had indicated to

Jones he hoped to fence the Hatton Garden gold and gems. He had told Jones of his plans while driving in his blue Citroën Saxo, and Scotland Yard, which had overheard the conversation from the bug in Perkins's car, had every reason to believe that some of the booty from the heist could still be there. After an exhaustive search of the vast warehouse, they discovered two large emerald stones, a gold bangle, and a £90,000 ($117,000) watch hidden in a false ceiling in Matthews's office.

Initially police thought the items were stolen during the Hatton Garden break-in. But further investigation revealed that the goods had come from the 2010 raid on Chatila.

In July 2016, with the evidence pointing squarely at Reader, Jones, and Perkins, police questioned the trio at Belmarsh prison about the Chatila burglary. Most damningly, DNA found on a glove at the Chatila boutique in April 2015 was linked to Danny Jones. He claimed that the DNA was there prior to the 2010 heist and initially denied any wrongdoing. But Jones had a habit of sagging under aggressive questioning and incontrovertible evidence and he eventually admitted the crime and pleaded guilty to conspiring to raid the flagship store. Perkins and Reader, meanwhile, strenuously denied any involvement.

Matthews, who has been charged with receiving stolen goods, told prosecutors he was tricked into storing the purloined gems, while police suspect that Basil may have played a role in disabling the alarm during the Chatila break-in.

The parallels between the Hatton Garden and Chatila raids are uncanny. In the 2010 burglary in Mayfair, the thieves used scaffolding outside the store to climb to the roof. From there, they broke into the building and deactivated the alarm. As in Hatton Garden, staff discovered the break-in on the Tuesday after a holiday weekend. As in Hatton Garden, the thieves also stole gems, watches, and cash.

"All the evidence suggests that at least some of the same men were involved," said Jamie Day, when the Chatila trial began in late 2016.

In early February of 2017, a pretrial hearing for the Chatila case was convened at Southwark Crown Court, the same south London court where the Bad Grandpas had initially appeared after being arrested. Seated behind a glass enclosure in the back of the court, Jones craned his head and pressed his ear to the glass. "I can't hear a word you're saying," he said, interrupting as the clerk read out the charges. Finally, after the charges were read out again, Jones was asked how he would plead. "Guilty," he replied. Both Perkins and Chick Matthews have denied any involvement in the crime.

The judge, Joanna Korner, appeared to not have been briefed on who was being prosecuted. "Is there anything particularly interesting about this burglary?" she asked the prosecutor, adding, "It was a straightforward burglary on a jewelry store." When the prosecutor Philip Stott informed her that Jones had been one of the burglars in the Hatton Garden heist—by now, the most publicized burglary in the land of the past several decades—she looked stunned.

Matthews, for his part, told the court that he had no idea that the jewels that he had stored in the ceiling of his office were stolen, and he rejected suggestions that he had been hoarding jewelry or that he had any commercial dealings with Terry Perkins. Matthews said that the jewels found at London City Metals had been given to him at Christmastime 2014 by a friend called James Tibbs, who had asked him to put them in a secure place. He said the gems had been in a locked box, and that he hadn't opened it. After Tibbs had returned in January 2015 to take some of the jewels, Matthews said Tibbs left the remaining valuables in a thin white garbage bag, which he had put in a safe. But after Matthews observed that the safe's bolts had been damaged, he said he had come up with the idea of stashing the large emerald stones and gold bangle watch in his office ceiling. The jury looked on incredulously.

Whatever the veracity of Matthews's testimony, Jones and Perkins's case may have been buttressed after it emerged that police had destroyed more than two hundred hours of CCTV footage from neighboring jewelers next to Chatila on Bond Street, which could have been used to implicate the men. Only five hours of video footage remains. The rest was destroyed by police during the routine process of discarding old evidence. The remaining stills show the white van the men used, but not the men themselves, potentially undermining the prosecution's case.[1]

Even without that evidence, in March 2017, the judge ordered a retrial in March after she became aware that members of the jury had been secretly reading the lurid headlines of the Hatton Garden case. Given all the attention the Hatton Garden burglary generated, prosecutors face a difficult challenge in finding a jury oblivious of Jones and Perkins's most celebrated heist.

Chapter 17

Life Behind Bars

DETERMINED TO SHOW THE BRITISH PUBLIC THAT
the pill-popping grandpas they had embraced were, in fact, dangerous, malevolent, and deserving of harsh punishment, the British state
confined the men to Belmarsh, known among the criminal fraternity
as "hellmarsh."

The prison houses some of the most dangerous criminals in the
country, among them Abu Hamza, the hook-handed Egyptian
Islamic hate preacher who was found guilty in 2014 of, among other
things, plotting to set up a terror camp in rural Oregon and support-
ing terrorists in Afghanistan. It has also been home to Ian Huntley,
a school caretaker who murdered two ten-years-olds, and Charles
Bronson (born Michael Gordon Peterson), an armed robber dubbed
Britain's "Hannibal Lecter," who has spent thirty-seven years in solitary confinement after repeatedly attacking prison staff. In 1998 he
took two Iraqi airplane hijackers and another inmate hostage at Belmarsh, demanded that they address him as "General," and threatened
to eat one of his victims unless he received a helicopter to take him to
Cuba, along with two Uzi submachine guns and an ax. The episode
added another seven years to his sentence.

In 2001, Belmarsh was used to detain suspected terrorists who hadn't yet been charged, leading to accusations that it had become Britain's Gitmo. Today, it hosts so many convicted Islamic terrorists that guards and prisoners complain it is becoming a "jihadi training camp," where non-Muslim prisoners are pressured to convert to Islam and then become radicalized.[1]

While the prison was built in the 1990s to house men deemed a serious threat to public or national security—something perhaps hard to square with the Bad Grandpas—the notoriety of a crime trumps considerations of age. Prior to the imprisonment of the gang in 2016, perhaps its most notorious elderly inmate was Ronnie Biggs, the ringleader of the Great Train Robbery, who turned himself in in 2001 at the tender age of seventy-one.

After escaping from HM Prison Wandsworth in southwest England in 1965 by scaling down the prison's imposing walls with a rope, Biggs spent thirty-six years on the road in, among other places, Rio and Sydney. In 1981 he was kidnapped by former-British-soldiers-turned-bounty-hunters hoping to get a handsome reward. But when their speedboat broke down off the coast of Barbados, Biggs was sent back to Brazil since Barbados had no extradition treaty with Britain. His sense of humor intact, he went on to sing vocals for the German punk band Die Toten Hosen. The name of the song? "Police on My Back."

Buffeted by a debilitating stroke, he finally turned himself in, saying that all he wanted was to "walk into a Margate pub as an Englishman and buy a pint of bitter." While in prison, he married a former Brazilian samba dancer in a private ceremony attended by several prison guards and guests who were carefully frisked. Biggs lived in the prison's hospital wing, and was eventually transferred to Margate prison, in the seaside town where he craved a pint of beer, on humanitarian grounds. Toward the end of his life, he was forced to use a spelling board to communicate after a series of strokes had rendered him partially paralyzed. He died in 2013 at the age of eighty-four.

The high-profile nature of the Hatton Garden heist destined the gang for incarceration in Belmarsh, even if the only weapon they had wielded was a diamond-tipped drill. The men were nevertheless initially classed as Category A prisoners, which meant being placed in HM Prison Belmarsh's High-Security Unit, a special prison within a prison reserved for the nation's worst offenders. The unit, a windowless gray concrete structure has two floors, split into four wings, each with twelve single-occupancy cells. Initially built to house IRA prisoners, it is separate from the main Belmarsh prison quarters and its security is so tight that no two doors can be opened at the same time. Visitors and guards alike must undergo forensic body searches before entering—including examinations of the inside of their mouths and the soles of their feet.[2]

Since the gang entered prison, family members and their lawyers say they have been suffering from the harsh conditions, the deep sense of isolation, and the challenge of getting medical care for their various ailments. During the first part of their imprisonment, the men were put in cells for two about six-feet wide by ten-feet long, each with a small window. Cells in the unit have a small television in one corner on a plastic desk and a metal toilet. Even Category A prisoners are allowed a kettle, no small thing for the diamond wheezers, who love their English breakfast tea. But Belmarsh guards have long tried to ban the luxury for prisoners in the ward for fear that the more menacing among them could throw boiling water in their faces. The Hatton Garden gang, a docile bunch, pose no such threat.

Hesham Puri, Brian Reader's lawyer, whose appeal to get his client's seven-year sentence reduced was rejected, contended that Scotland Yard had pressed for the harshest punishment possible since the Yard was still smarting over its hapless and bungled failure to prevent the heist. Puri said Belmarsh was unduly draconian for men in their sixties and seventies, many of whom were susceptible to illness and whose natural habitat should be a retirement home. "The British legal system is widely seen as a fair one," he maintains. "But that is not the case in its treatment of elderly prisoners. The Flying Squad is flexing its muscles. They are old men."[3]

But Philip Evans, the chief prosecutor on the case and Paul Johnson, the Flying Squad detective inspector, countered that the punishment befits the gravity of the crime and that the men—in rude enough health to wield power tools and spend a long weekend boring holes through reinforced concrete—are a flight risk and a threat to public security. They deserve no pity or special treatment, Evans said, underlining that they had brought misery to dozens of pensioners their own age. Moreover, the bulk of the stolen gems they spirited away have never been recovered.

"They are hardened criminals, nasty men who would steal the shirt off your back, and the punishment fits the crime,"[4] he said.

Despite his protestations, Puri conceded that keeping the elderly gang away from the general prison population had at least sheltered them from the skirmishes and sudden bursts of violence that Belmarsh was notorious for. He said the men had been able to converse with one another, but had been moved to the main, less secure part of the prison. Their mail is scrutinized by prison staff and they are allowed two visitors a month.

Puri said that Reader, the oldest among the seven men imprisoned for the burglary, was gravely ill and suffering from a litany of illnesses, including blindness in one eye, deafness, Bell's palsy, and a stroke he suffered in prison in the spring of 2016, about a year after his arrest. He complained that when Reader was hospitalized after his stroke, he had been handcuffed to a prison officer while in bed and guarded by nine officers, including six armed with machine guns.[5]

"I don't want him to come out of there in a box," his daughter Joanne told the *Guardian*.[6]

Nick Corsellis, Carl Wood's lawyer, said that Wood was despondent in prison since he would likely never see his ailing and bedridden parents again. He complained that the gang typically only got half an hour of exercise a day at Belmarsh and only half an hour of daylight, and that it was having a detrimental psychological effect on Wood.

Perkins—the most stoic among the gang after having spent so many years in prison—had to take twenty-nine different tablets a day, in addition to insulin shots for his diabetes, and in prison, his health quickly deteriorated. In June 2017 he collapsed in Belmarsh with a heart attack and was rushed to St Thomas' Hospital in central London, where he was fitted with a pacemaker to help control abnormal heart rhythms. He was then sent back to Belmarsh to convalesce in the prison's hospital wing.

Collins, the second eldest in the gang after Reader, suffers from diabetes, high blood pressure, arthritis, rheumatism, and memory loss, but friends say he is tenacious and resigned to his current life behind bars. Kevin Lane, an old pal of Collins's, spent eighteen years in prison for a murder conviction, including several in the high-security unit at Belmarsh where he endured weeks in solitary confinement "on a slab of concrete." Lane said that he had visited Collins in prison and that he was not the type to complain. "It is outrageous that a bunch of old men are in Belmarsh, a maximum security prison," Lane argued, noting that his friend was tough as nails. "You don't get bleeding sentimental. These guys are old school criminals. They will do their time, and they will not complain."

Some of the younger members of the gang, however, have managed to cope quite well. Perhaps the most upbeat among the prisoners was the loquacious plumber Hugh Doyle. During his short stint in prison, he lost nearly thirty pounds, whiling his days away by exercising in his cell. "He is a fundamentally honest man who has made one big mistake and he is here to pay for that today," his lawyer told the judge during his sentencing in March 2016.

As for sixty-three-year-old Danny Jones, whose lithe physique allowed him to slither through the figure-eight holes during the heist, friends say he has made use of his time in prison to exercise, doing sit-ups and push-ups in his cramped cell. Ever the vain showman, he is also writing his memoirs with a view toward burnishing his legacy. After pleading guilty to the Chatila burglary and admitting that he stole £1 million ($1.5 million) in jewelry and precious stones, he will likely be a very old man before he gets out.

Yet for all the hardships of life behind bars, the men continue to bask in their fame, which prison has done little to dull, and in fact has been enhanced by a movie about the heist, *King of Thieves*, starring Michael Caine as Brian Reader and Ray Winstone as Danny Jones. Fact is rather harsher than fiction, however, and at the beginning of 2018 the gang faced confiscation hearings aimed at assessing how much of their personal assets should be seized by the state, given that three-quarters of the estimated £14 million ($21 million) in gems, gold, and cash they stole had still not been recovered, a value that has fluctuated in the years following the burglary. In June 2016, following the massive media attention focused on the trial, a woman told Scotland Yard that she had lost £7 million ($10.5 million) worth of gold bars during the heist, but had only remembered she had them in the safe deposit after the case came under the spotlight. Investigators on the case said the woman's claim was credible; she came from a billionaire family "for whom £1 million was the equivalent of a tenner," or £10. That brought the total value of stolen gems to £21 million ($31.5 million), though some estimates have valued the haul at £25 million ($37.5 million), of which only £4 million ($6 million) has been recovered. Friends of the gang suspect some of them are still sitting on their stashes while doing their time, hoping to enjoy the spoils of the heist in their advanced old age. "What's the point of doing it, if you bloody give it back?" asked one longtime associate.

In late January 2018 at Woolwich Crown Court, judge Christopher Kinch said that the men had jointly benefited from an estimated £14 million ($21 million) worth of cash, gold, and stolen gems from the heist, and he ruled that together they owed £27.5 million ($41 million). If they failed to pay back that amount, each would have about another seven years in prison added to their sentences.

Mindful of their advanced age, the judge nevertheless argued that the men did not merit special treatment. "A number of these defendants are not only of a certain age, but have in some cases serious health problems," he told the court. "But as a matter of principle and policy it is very difficult to endorse any approach that there is a particular treatment for someone who chooses to go out and commit offences at the advanced stage of their lives that some of these defendants were."

Among the Firm, Collins was ordered to pay the highest share: £7,686,039 (about $10.4 million). The others had mocked him as a "wombat-thick old cunt" but it seems he was the most successful among them and his smuggled cigarette and fireworks businesses had yielded stacks of cash, along with expensive properties in north London and abroad.

During the confiscation hearings, Brian Reader's legal team tried to argue that he didn't owe anything since he didn't profit from the crime. "They call him 'The Master' but how can he be the 'Master' when he walked away," his lawyer, Puri, protested.[7]

Weakened by a stroke and prostate cancer, and suffering from partial blindness and diminishing hearing, Reader struggled to hear during the part of the proceedings he attended, repeatedly craning his head in the dock at the back of the courtroom, encased in glass.

James Scobie QC, one of his lawyers, told the court that Reader had abandoned the heist after the first night once the men had been unable to access the safe deposit boxes, depriving himself of any of the looted gems. Referring to the Flying Squad's secretly recorded audio of the men discussing how to divvy up the loot following the heist, he said there was no evidence to suggest that he got a single diamond, gold bar, or pence.

But Judge Christopher Kinch, decked in his velvety robes and armed with the same skepticism he had worn throughout the gang's legal proceedings, was unconvinced, and ordered Reader to pay back about £6.5 million (about $9.2 million) more, or face additional prison time. His home in Dartford, along with some land, was valued at about £1.2 million ($1.6 million), and his lawyer told the court that he would likely die in prison. However, Reader got a reprieve, and in July 2018, he was released from prison after serving a little more than three years, about half of his orginal six-year and three-month sentence, even though millions of pounds in jewels remains missing. He was seventy-nine years old as he walked out of Belmarsh's doors. The oldest member of the gang, Reader had been given a sentence seven months shorter than the other ringleaders because of his very poor health.

The *Sun* commemorated the moment with the headline: "GET OUT OF JEWEL FREE CARD." The newspaper reported that Reader, frail and walking with two sticks, was seen basking in the sunshine in the garden in front of his large home and being ferried around town by his son in a red Porsche. Prosecutors and the good men of the Flying Squad were understandably peeved that he walked free while his victims, some of them ailing and aged themselves, continue to suffer from their losses. But with an order by the court to pay about £6.5 million (about $9.2 million) or face another seven years of jail time, Reader's freedom could prove short-lived. Nevertheless, he is challenging the order and the Court of Appeal has decided to allow him to remain free while his case is decided.[8]

Jones and Perkins were ordered to pay back the same amount as Reader. Perkins's lawyer told the court his client would have to sell his apartment in Portugal, but even that would nowhere near cover the £6.5 million ($9.2 million) he now owed. He added that Perkins "had no prospect of any further funds." The shock appeared to be too much, even for the unflappable Perkins, who suffered from diabetes and heart failure. On February 4, 2018, just days after learning of his additional punishment, Perkins died in his prison cell from natural causes, possibly taking the secret of where the missing loot has been hidden to his grave. Two prison guards tried to revive his slumped body. He was 69 years old.

As for Jones, he will serve the default time after he claimed he only had a little cash in the bank and no assets. The sprightly "youngster" among the Hatton Garden ringleaders will be an old man by the time he finishes serving his long sentence.

In July 2018, Jones was sentenced to an additional three years for his role in the Chatila burglary. During his sentencing, he gave a letter to the judge, Joanna Korner, lamenting his life of crime. "I would urge any young lad who is thinking of being a thief, it doesn't work, it leaves a trail of destruction on both sides—the victims of crime and your family," the letter said. "Your conscience will eat you away. I feel sorrow and regret for all the trouble I have put my family through."

Graham Trembath, Jones's lawyer, told the court that Jones had been profoundly shaken by Perkins's death, and had observed the prison guards trying to resuscitate him. "He realizes that this is a futile way of life—the impact of Terry Perkins's death at such a relatively young age caused him to reflect and to realize that," he said. He added that Jones's 16-year-old son had cut him off, viewing him as "utterly selfish, thinking only of himself and no one else—including his mother."

The judge appeared sympathetic. "I am satisfied," she said, "that finally, though you were clearly a professional criminal, you do not intend to return to a life of crime after you leave prison."

Until recently, the families of the Bad Grandpas were living affluent lives in homes that were likely the product of past thefts, a reasonable conclusion given that none of the men have permanently held down well-paying day jobs. Danny Jones's former partner Valerie Hart resided in the couple's sprawling Swiss-style house in Enfield.

Brian Reader's son Paul lived for a time in his father's country manor in Dartford, Kent.

Collins's elderly wife Millie spends her days in their handsome home in Islington, visiting Collins at Belmarsh whenever she can, according to friends. The Perkins clan still live in their modest homes in Enfield, their presence confirmed by the vigor with which they slammed their front doors when approached on a recent day. "What do you want?" sneered Terri Robinson, his daughter. When asked about the Hatton Garden case, she said, "Read the papers!" Her mood was perhaps sour as she and her brother-in-law Bren Walters, had pleaded guilty to concealing, converting, or transferring criminal property. After a judge held them liable for some of the millions of pounds in jewels stolen at Hatton Garden, Robinson told the court she had available funds of £139.54—about $190. Walters declared that he had £1—about $1.35.[9] The families' days of leisure, however, could be numbered. In addition to the seizure of bank accounts and real estate investments, prosecutors said that other more sentimental objects could also be confiscated, including diamond earrings, gold bands, and wedding rings.

"They deserve no pity," insisted Evans.[10]

* * * *

THE POLICE, MEANWHILE, have struggled to identify thousands of identical-looking chains and gems that have been recovered from the burglary. Among the many millions of pounds' worth of loot that have still not been found, at least some has probably been melted down, laundered, or stashed away.

As for Hatton Garden Safe Deposit, it was forced into liquidation, and the safe deposit's new owner David Pearl, a property mogul, said he was considering relocating the vault—including the now iconic drilled-through wall and the ransacked safe deposit boxes—

to the Museum of London so visitors could see firsthand what the safe deposit looked like when the hapless security guards arrived at the scene on the morning of April 7, 2015. Pearl predicted it could become among the capital's most popular tourist attractions.[11]

"People don't seem to look at it as a robbery," he told the *Telegraph*. "They don't look at it in the same way as other crimes, where their reaction is 'Hang 'em, whip 'em!' Here they say 'Ok, they were just some old men chancing their luck.' It's strange, but there you go. I can't explain it, but I'm no psychiatrist."

The Hatton Garden neighborhood has enjoyed something of a renaissance since the headline-grabbing caper put it on the map. On Bond Street, Hatton Garden's more upmarket jewelry rival, shopkeepers complain that the Garden gets all the attention. Locals refer to "the last job" as "the world's best advertising campaign" and estimate that revenues have jumped by nearly a quarter. "Thanks to the heist," said Jacob Meghnagi, a resident jeweler, "the whole world knows Hatton Garden."

Acknowledgments

In the spring of 2015, I had barely arrived in London as a new correspondent for the *New York Times*. I woke up one morning to find a page from the *Sun* spread out over my desk, with the headline "Diamond Wheezers" announcing that the thieves behind the audacious Hatton Garden heist were, in fact, a group of grumpy and aging men. An editor had stuck a yellow Post-it Note on the article: "One for you?"

It was. Hatton Garden was about a ten-minute bike ride from my house. The Castle pub where the men plotted the biggest burglary in English history over warm beer was my local pub. Within days of my story on the caper being published, it was optioned by Hollywood. I had stumbled on the true crime tale of a lifetime—and a dream subject for a book. I am grateful to my editor Kyle Crichton for helping to plant the seed.

The cat-and-mouse game at the center of this book has been hugely enriched by the willingness of the leading Scotland Yard officers and prosecutors on the case—Paul Johnson, Craig Turner, Jamie Day, Philip Evans, and Ed Hall—to share their detailed recollections. For law enforcement officials trained to be invisible, braving my never-ending barrage of questions over many months was not always comfortable, and I am very grateful for their generosity.

Roy Ramm, a former chief of the Flying Squad, was instrumental in sharing his first-hand knowledge of the workings of the Flying Squad, and his investigations of some of London's most memorable heists. Tony Connell, a twenty-year veteran of Britain's Crown Prosecution Service, shared his memories of meeting Perkins as a young lawyer. Tony Lundy, a former Scotland Yard detective, provided invaluable insights about old-school criminals like Reader and the gang, whom he had spent years hunting.

Here, too, I am indebted to Freddie Foreman, the self-described "Godfather of British Crime," who opened his door when I came knocking and regaled me with tales of English criminal outlaws over glasses of wine. Kevin Lane, a former inmate of Belmarsh prison, also patiently explained some of the ins and outs of the London criminal ecosystem and the challenges of prison life for men in their seventies.

Also essential to this book were Paul Lashmar, one of Britain's most storied crime reporters, who shared his recollections of Hatton Garden and the old-school criminals who lingered there, and Dick Hobbs, Britain's leading sociologist of crime, who grew up himself on the mean streets of east London and helped me to bring them to life. Daniel Sandford, the BBC's debonair and knowledgeable Home Affairs correspondent, was endlessly generous and collegial when I arrived at a foreboding criminal court in southeast London to cover the case.

Working for the *New York Times* is a blessing for any reporter and aspiring book writer and here I must thank my beloved friend and colleague Danny Hakim, who has been a tireless cheerleader, and gave me wise counsel whenever my reporting hit a wall. My colleague and dear friend Catherine Porter has provided much-needed commiseration. I would also like to raise a glass to Jim Yardley, the Europe editor of the *Times*, for being a kind and generous mentor when I most needed it.

So many countless friends and loved ones put up with my book obsessing, and I'd like to thank Navtej Dhillon, Kurt van der Basch, and Amita Joshi for their love, support, and feedback on drafts.

A big hats off to my literary agent Todd Shushter for his expert shepherding; to Michael Moore, my film agent, for seeing the story's potential; and to Elias Altman, for his deft editing of my book proposal.

I would also like to thank Helen Thomaides at Norton for her tireless work on the book and Jasmin Lavoie for pitching in with fact-checking.

Finally, I am especially grateful to John Glusman, the editor in chief of Norton, whom I was lucky enough to have edit this book, and who did so with flair, a keen eye, and enviable humor and equanimity.

Dan Bilefsky
July 24, 2018

Notes

Chapter 1

The Inspiration of a Botched Crime

1. Hatton Garden trial, Woolwich Crown Court, London, December 14, 2017.
2. Chatila trial, Southwark Crown Court, London, February 28, 2017.

Chapter 2

The Making of a Master Thief

1. Metropolitan Police Service, Operation Spire, transcripts relating to audio recordings of Citroën Saxo EN51EUD.
2. Interview with Tony Lundy, August 1, 2016.
3. Tom Pettifor and Nick Sommerlad, "Incredible Story of How Hatton Garden Mastermind Brian Reader Became Britain's Most Prolific Thief," *Daily Mirror*, September 2, 2016.
4. Interview with Dick Hobbs, London, January 30, 2017.
5. Brian Reader testimony during Brink's-Mat gold-laundering trial, 1987.
6. Duncan Campbell, "One Last Job: The Inside Story of the Hatton Garden Heist," *Guardian*, January 23, 2016.
7. Interview with Paul Lashmar, London, June 16, 2016.
8. Interview with Dick Hobbs, London, January 30, 2017.
9. Dick Hobbs, obituary of "Charlie Richardson: Shrewd and Ruthless Leading Figure of London's 1960s Criminal Scene," *Independent*, September 21, 2012.
10. Interview with Dick Hobbs, London, January 30, 2017.
11. Interview with Paul Lashmar, London, June 16, 2016.

12. Brian Reader testimony during Brink's-Mat gold-laundering trial, 1987.

13. Interview with Tony Lundy, London, August 1, 2016.

14. Brian Reader testimony during Brink's-Mat gold-laundering trial, 1987.

15. Interview with Roy Ramm, London, March 8, 2016.

16. Wensley Clarkson, *Public Enemy Number 1* (London: John Blake, 2006), 115–126.

17. Duncan Campbell, "One Last Job: The Inside Story of the Hatton Garden Heist," *Guardian*, January 23, 2016.

Chapter 3
The Making of the Firm

1. Metropolitan Police Service, Operation Spire, transcripts relating to audio recordings of Citroën Saxo EN51EUD, 380.

2. Metropolitan Police Service, Operation Spire, transcripts relating to audio recordings of Citroën Saxo EN51EUD, 430.

3. Metropolitan Police Service, Operation Spire, transcripts relating to audio recordings of Citroën Saxo EN51EUD, 433.

4. Metropolitan Police Service, Operation Spire, statement of Kelvin Stockwell, April 20, 2015.

5. Sentencing Council for England and Wales; Sentencing Myths website, https://www.sentencingcouncil.org.uk/about-sentencing/sentencing-myths/.

6. Interview with Freddie Foreman, London, March 29, 2017.

7. Interview with Philip Evans, prosecutor of Hatton Garden case, London, May 3, 2017.

8. Interview with Freddie Foreman, London, March 29, 2017.

9. Metropolitan Police Service, Operantion Spire, transcripts relating to audio recordings of Mercedes E200 CP13BGY, 481.

10. Metropolitan Police Service, Operation Spire, transcripts relating to audio recordings of Citroën Saxo EN51EUD, 402.

11. Interview with Tony Connell, London, May 2, 2017.

12. Interview with Valerie Hart, London, January 17, 2017.

13. Metropolitan Police Service, Operation Spire, crime scene images.

14. Interview with Kevin Lane, London, January 16, 2017.

15. Metropolitan Police Service, Operation Spire, transcripts relating to audio recordings of Citroën Saxo EN51EUD, 397.

16. "Hotel Room Sting That Nailed Two Corrupt Detectives in Torture Plot," *Guardian*, June 7, 2002.

17. Hatton Garden trial, Woolwich Crown Court, London, January 2016.

18. Metropolitan Police Service, Operation Spire, transcripts relating to audio recordings of Citroën Saxo EN51EUD, 395.

19. Interview with Freddie Foreman, London, March 29, 2017.

20. Bruce Weber, "Bruce Reynolds, Audacious Mastermind of Great Train Robbery, Is Dead at 81," *New York Times*, February 28, 2013.

21. Interview with Freddie Foreman, London, March 29, 2017.

22. "Bruce Reynolds, Mastermind Behind Great Train Robbery Dies at 81," *Independent*, February 28, 2013.

23. Steven Morris, "Great Train Robber Back at the Scene for Charity," *Guardian*, August 9, 2003.

24. Nick Russell-Pavier and Stewart Richards, *The Great Train Robbery* (London: Wiedenfeld & Nicolson, 2012), 9–10.

25. Nick Russell-Pavier and Stewart Richards, *The Great Train Robbery* (London: Wiedenfeld & Nicolson, 2012), 27.

26. "Great Train Robbery Memorabilia Sold at Auction," BBC, February 19, 2015.

27. Nick Russell-Pavier and Stewart Richards, *The Great Train Robbery* (London: Wiedenfeld & Nicolson, 2012), 297.

Chapter 4
The Target

1. Nicolas Harris, *Memoirs of the Life and Times of Sir Christopher Hatton* (London: Richard Bentley, 1847).

2. Paul Lashmar, "Jewellery and Junk," *Independent*, August 11, 1998.

3. Rachel Lichtenstein, *Diamond Street: The Hidden World of Hatton Garden* (London: Penguin Books, 2013), 227.

4. Rachel Lichtenstein, *Diamond Street: The Hidden World of Hatton Garden* (London: Penguin Books, 2013), 62.

5. Rachel Lichtenstein, *Diamond Street: The Hidden World of Hatton Garden* (London: Penguin Books, 2013), 61.

6. Rachel Lichtenstein, *Diamond Street: The Hidden World of Hatton Garden* (London: Penguin Books, 2013), xvi.

7. "History of the London Diamond Bourse," London Diamond Bourse.

8. Interview with George Katz, London, November 1, 2016.

9. Interview with Jacob Meghnagi, London, November 1, 2016.

10. Tom Pettifor and Nick Sommerlad, *One Last Job* (London: Mirror Books, 2016), 199.

11. Interview with George Katz, London, November 1, 2016.

12. Geoffrey Howse, *Murder and Mayhem in North London* (Barnsley, UK: Pen and Sword Books, 2010), 182.

13. Metropolitan Police Service, Operation Spire, witness statement of Manish Bavishi, May 21, 2015, 350.

14. Metropolitan Police Service, Operation Spire, witness statement of Kelvin Stockwell, April 20, 2015, 27–29.

15. Interview with Roy Ramm, London, March 8, 2016.

16. Rachel Lichtenstein, *Diamond Street: The Hidden World of Hatton Garden* (London: Penguin Books, 2013), 112–13.

17. Paul Lashmar, "Jewellery and Junk," *Independent,* August 11, 1998.

18. Paul Lashmar and Richard Hobbs, "The Garden of British Crime: How London's Jewellery District Became a Nursery for Villains," *Conversation*, March 9, 2016.

19. Will Bennett, "£7m Diamond Raiders Beat Combination Locks," *Independent*, July 16, 1993.

20. Oliver Burkeman, "If He Could Get Away with It Here, No Lock in the World Is Safe," *Guardian*, July 17, 2003.

21. Interview with Jacob Meghnagi, London, November 1, 2016.

Chapter 5

The Firm Plots

1. "World's First ATM Machine Turns to Gold," Reuters, June 27, 2017.

2. Letter from Teikoku Bank Limited to Mosler Safe Company, May 22, 1950.

3. Elizabeth Rosenthal, "Near Arctic, Seed Vault Is a Fort Knox of Food," *New York Times*, February 29, 2008.

4. Metropolitan Police Service, Operation Spire, transcripts relating to audio recordings of Mercedes E200 CP13BGY, 483.

5. Interview with Freddie Foreman, London, March 29, 2017.

6. Interview with Kevin Lane, London, January 16, 2017.

7. Paul Lashmar, "Hatton Garden Ringleader Brian Reader Also Master-minded Lloyds Baker Street Heist 45 Years Ago," *Independent*, January 15, 2016.

8. Interview with Craig Turner, London, February 3, 2017.

9. Metropolitan Police Service, Operation Spire, witness statement of Lionel Wiffen, May 29, 2015, 78–80.

10. Stuart McGurk, "Hatton Garden: The Biggest Jewel Heist in British History," *GQ*, May 19, 2016.

11. Metropolitan Police Service, Operation Spire, witness statement of Lionel Wiffen, May 29, 2015, 79.

12. Metropolitan Police Service, Operation Spire, witness statement of Lionel Wiffen, May 29, 2015, 80.

13. Metropolitan Police Service, Operation Spire, witness statement of Katya Lewis, June 1, 2015, 99–100.

14. Metropolitan Police Service, Operation Spire, witness statement of Katya Lewis, June 1, 2015, 99–100.

Chapter 6
The Heist

1. Metropolitan Police Service, Operation Spire, transcripts relating to audio recordings of Citroën Saxo EN51EUD, 392.

2. Jonathan Levy, "The Keystone Crooks," *Daily Mail*, November 18, 2017.

3. Opening note, Hatton Garden trial, Woolwich Crown Court, 21.

4. Metropolitan Police Service, Operation Spire, transcripts relating to audio recordings of Citroën Saxo EN51EUD, 401.

5. Metropolitan Police Service, Operation Spire, transcripts relating to audio recordings of Mercedes E200 CP13BGY, 482.

6. Opening note, Hatton Garden trial, Woolwich Crown Court, 25.

7. Metropolitan Police Service, Operation Spire, transcripts relating to audio recordings of Citroën Saxo EN51EUD, 401.

8. Opening note, Hatton Garden trial, Woolwich Crown Court, 26.

Chapter 7
Paul Johnson

1. Kelvin Stockwell testimony, Hatton Garden trial, Woolwich Crown Court, London, December 2, 2015.
2. Interview with Paul Johnson, London, March 1, 2017.
3. Interview with Roy Ramm, London, March 8, 2016.
4. Andrew Walker, "The Sweeney's Proud History," BBC, May 17, 2004.
5. Interview with Craig Turner, London, February 3, 2017.
6. Interview with Paul Johnson, London, March 1, 2017.
7. Katrin Bennhold and Alan Cowell, "Ex-Tabloid Executive Acquitted in British Phone Hacking Case," *New York Times*, June 24, 2014.
8. "Met Police Commissioner Sir Paul Stephenson Quits," BBC, July 18, 2011.
9. Interview with Craig Turner and Paul Johnson, New Scotland Yard Headquarters, London, March 17, 2016.
10. "Hatton Garden Raid Has Ruined Lives and Livelihoods," BBC, May 7, 2015.
11. "Hatton Garden Gem Raid Was an Inside Job Says Heist Firm Boss," *Daily Mail*, April 18, 2015.
12. "Hatton Garden Gem Raid Was an Inside Job Says Heist Firm Boss," *Daily Mail*, April 18, 2015.
13. "Jewelry Heist Likely an Inside Job," Sky News, April 9, 2015.
14. Doreen Carvajal, "Arrest of 2 Pink Panthers May Shed Light on Heists," *New York Times*, May 15, 2009.
15. Doreen Carvajal, "The Heist at Harry's," *New York Times*, December 12, 2008.
16. Interview with Ed Hall, London, September 22, 2016.

Chapter 8
An Investigation Takes Shape

1. Interview with Jamie Day, London, March 17, 2016.
2. Interview with Jamie Day, London, March 17, 2016.
3. Metropolitan Police Service, Operation Spire, witness statement of Kelvin Stockwell, April 20, 2015.

4. Interview with Jamie Day, London, March 17, 2016.

5. Interview with Jamie Day, London, March 17, 2016.

6. Ryan Gallagher and Rajeev Syal, "Police Forces Come Together to Create New Regional Surveillance Units," *Guardian*, July 25, 2011.

7. Jason Lewis, "Met Police Spends Millions of Pounds on Secret Aircraft," *Telegraph*, October 29, 2011.

8. Regulation of Investigatory Powers Act 2000, Chapter 1, Section 5, https://www.legislation.gov.uk/ukpga/2000/23/section/5.

9. Wensley Clarkson, *Public Enemy Number 1* (London: John Blake, 2006), 115–26.

10. Wensley Clarkson, *Public Enemy Number 1* (London: John Blake, 2006), 174–75.

Chapter 9
A Game of Cat and Mouse

1. Interview with Craig Turner and Paul Johnson, New Scotland Yard Headquarters, London, March 17, 2016.

2. Metropolitan Police Service, Operation Spire, transcripts relating to audio recordings of Citroën Saxo EN51EUD, 391.

3. Julian Franklyn, *A Dictionary of Rhyming Slang* (London: Routledge, 1992), 9.

4. "OMG! Cockney Rhyming Slang Is Brown Bread," Reuters, March 29, 2012.

5. James Orr, "Londoners Baffled by Cockney Rhyming Slang," *Daily Telegraph*, March 29, 2012.

6. Opening note, Hatton Garden trial, Woolwich Crown Court, 30.

7. Metropolitan Police Service, Operation Spire, statements relating to surveillance, 376–79.

8. Interview with Paul Johnson, London, March 1, 2017.

9. Interview with Craig Turner and Jamie Day, London, February 3, 2017.

10. Metropolitan Police Service, Operation Spire, statements relating to surveillance.

11. Metropolitan Police Service, Operation Spire, transcripts relating to audio recordings of Citroën Saxo EN51EUD, 401.

12. Metropolitan Police Service, Operation Spire, transcripts relating to audio recordings of Citroën Saxo EN51EUD, 392.

13. Metropolitan Police Service, Operation Spire, transcripts relating to audio recordings of Citroën Saxo EN51EUD, 401.

14. Metropolitan Police Service, Operation Spire, transcripts relating to audio recordings of Citroën Saxo EN51EUD, 385.

Chapter 10
The Art of Snooping and Waiting

1. Interview with Paul Johnson, London, March 1, 2017.

2. Interview with Philip Evans, London, March 5, 2017.

3. Interview with Philip Evans, London, March 5, 2017.

Chapter 11
The Flying Squad Is Listening

1. Metropolitan Police Service, Operation Spire, transcripts relating to audio recordings of Citroën Saxo EN51EUD, 352.

2. Metropolitan Police Service, Operation Spire, audio recordings related to Citroën Saxo EN51EUD, May 7, 2015.

3. Metropolitan Police Service, Operation Spire, transcripts relating to audio recordings of Citroën Saxo EN51EUD, 330.

4. Metropolitan Police Service, Operation Spire, audio recordings relating to Citroën Saxo EN51EUD, May 7, 2015.

5. Enfield Council, Enfield Borough Profile 2017.

6. Metropolitan Police Service, Operation Spire, transcripts relating to audio recordings of Citroën Saxo EN51EUD, 331–33.

7. Metropolitan Police Service, Operation Spire, transcripts relating to audio recordings of Citroën Saxo EN51EUD, 345.

8. Metropolitan Police Service, Operation Spire, transcripts relating to audio recordings of Citroën Saxo EN51EUD, 347.

9. Metropolitan Police Service, Operation Spire, transcripts relating to audio recordings of Citroën Saxo EN51EUD, 364.

10. Metropolitan Police Service, Operation Spire, transcripts relating to audio recordings of Citroën Saxo EN51EUD, 365.

11. Metropolitan Police Service, Operation Spire, transcripts relating to audio recordings of Citroën Saxo EN51EUD, 377.

12. Transcript of Brink's-Mat gold-laundering trial, 1987.

13. Metropolitan Police Service, Operation Spire, transcripts relating to audio recordings of Citroën Saxo EN51EUD, 386.

14. Metropolitan Police Service, Operation Spire, transcripts relating to audio recordings of Citroën Saxo EN51EUD, 422.

15. Metropolitan Police Service, Operation Spire, transcripts relating to audio recordings of Mercedes E200 CP13BGY, 473.

16. Metropolitan Police Service, Operation Spire, transcripts relating to audio recordings of Mercedes E200 CP13BGY, 391.

17. Metropolitan Police Service, Operation Spire, transcripts relating to audio recordings of Mercedes E200 CP13BGY, 477.

18. Metropolitan Police Service, Operation Spire, transcripts relating to audio recordings of Mercedes E200 CP13BGY, 479.

19. Metropolitan Police Service, Operation Spire, transcripts relating to audio recordings of Mercedes E200 CP13BGY, 480–81.

20. Metropolitan Police Service, Operation Spire, transcripts relating to audio recordings of Mercedes E200 CP13BGY, 481.

21. Metropolitan Police Service, Operation Spire, transcripts relating to audio recordings of Mercedes E200 CP13BGY, 482.

22. Metropolitan Police Service, Operation Spire, transcripts relating to audio recordings of Mercedes E200 CP13BGY, 485.

Chapter 12
The "Cut Up"

1. Metropolitan Police Service, Operation Spire, transcripts relating to audio recordings of Citroën Saxo EN51EUD, 380.

2. Opening note, Hatton Garden trial, Woolwich Crown Court, 22.

3. Opening note, Hatton Garden trial, Woolwich Crown Court, 433–37.

4. Opening note, Hatton Garden trial, Woolwich Crown Court, 438.

5. Opening note, Hatton Garden trial, Woolwich Crown Court, 378.

6. Opening note, Hatton Garden trial, Woolwich Crown Court, 383.

7. Opening note, Hatton Garden trial, Woolwich Crown Court, 397.

8. Metropolitan Police Service, Operation Spire, statements relating to surveillance, 385.

9. Metropolitan Police Service, Operation Spire, transcripts relating to audio recordings of Citroën Saxo EN51EUD, 413.

10. Metropolitan Police Service, Operation Spire, transcripts relating to audio recordings of Citroën Saxo EN51EUD, 395.

11. Metropolitan Police Service, Operation Spire, transcripts relating to audio recordings of Citroën Saxo EN51EUD, 415.

12. Metropolitan Police Service, Operation Spire, transcripts relating to audio recordings of Citroën Saxo EN51EUD, 416.

13. Metropolitan Police Service, Operation Spire, transcripts relating to audio recordings of Citroën Saxo EN51EUD, 416.

14. Opening note, Hatton Garden trial, Woolwich Crown Court, 32.

15. Metropolitan Police Service, Operation Spire, transcripts relating to audio recordings of Citroën Saxo EN51EUD, 457.

Chapter 13
To Catch a Thief

1. Interview with Craig Turner and Paul Johnson, London, February 3, 2017.

2. Interview with Craig Turner and Paul Johnson, London, February 3, 2017.

3. Metropolitan Police Service, Operation Spire, transcripts relating to audio recordings of Mercedes E200 CP13BGY, 463.

4. Metropolitan Police Service, Operation Spire, transcripts relating to audio recordings of Mercedes E200 CP13BGY, 462.

5. Metropolitan Police Service, Operation Spire, transcripts relating to audio recordings of Mercedes E200 CP13BGY, 464.

6. Metropolitan Police Service, Operation Spire, transcripts relating to audio recordings of Mercedes E200 CP13BGY.

7. Metropolitan Police Service, Operation Spire, transcripts relating to audio recordings of Mercedes E200 CP13BGY, 465.

8. Interview with Craig Turner and Paul Johnson, London, February 3, 2017.

9. Interview with Noel Sainsbury, London, March 12, 2016.

10. Interview with Craig Turner and Paul Johnson, London, February 3, 2017.

11. Interview with Jon Warren, London, March 12, 2016.

12. Interview with Craig Turner and Paul Johnson, London, February 3, 2017.

13. Interview with Dick Hobbs, London, January 30, 2017.

14. Interview with Ed Hall, London, September 22, 2016.

15. Interview with Paul Johnson, London, March 1, 2017.

16. Metropolitan Police Service, Operation Spire, interview transcripts, 556.

17. Metropolitan Police Service, Operation Spire, interview transcripts, 556–80.

18. Metropolitan Police Service, Operation Spire, interview transcripts, 488–784.

19. Metropolitan Police Service, Operation Spire, interview transcripts, 597.

20. Metropolitan Police Service, Operation Spire, interview transcripts, 617.

21. Metropolitan Police Service, Operation Spire, interview transcripts, 553.

Chapter 14
The Trial

1. "Diamond Wheezers," *Sun*, May 19, 2015.

2. Interview with Philip Evans, London, May 3, 2017.

3. Interview with Philip Evans, London, May 3, 2017.

4. Interview with Philip Evans, London, May 3, 2017.

5. Interview with Philip Evans, London, May 3, 2017.

6. Interview with Philip Evans, London, May 3, 2017.

7. Interview with Ed Hall, London, September 22, 2016.

8. Interview with Philip Evans, London, May 3, 2017.

9. Interview with Hesham Puri, London, September 9, 2016.

10. Interview with Philip Evans, London, May 3, 2017.

11. Hatton Garden trial, Woolwich Crown Court, London, January 5, 2016.

12. Interview with Philip Evans, London, May 3, 2017.
13. Hatton Garden trial, Woolwich Crown Court, London, December 16, 2016.
14. Interview with Philip Evans, London, May 3, 2017.
15. Hatton Garden trial, Woolwich Crown Court, London, December 16, 2015
16. Hatton Garden trial, Woolwich Crown Court, London, December 14, 2015.
17. Interview with Philip Evans, London, May 3, 2017.
18. Hatton Garden trial, Woolwich Crown Court, London, December 16, 2015.
19. Hatton Garden trial, Woolwich Crown Court, London, December 21, 2015.
20. Interview with Philip Evans, London, May 3, 2017.
21. Hatton Garden trial, Woolwich Crown Court, London, December 2, 2015.
22. Hatton Garden trial, Woolwich Crown Court, London, December 21, 2015.
23. Hatton Garden trial, Woolwich Crown Court, London, December 22, 2015.
24. Interview with John Luckhurst, London, November 15, 2016.

Chapter 15
Who Is Basil?

1. Metropolitan Police Service, Operation Spire, transcripts relating to audio recordings of Mercedes E200 CP13BGY, 483.
2. Metropolitan Police Service, Operation Spire, transcripts relating to audio recordings of Mercedes E200 CP13BGY, 483–84.
3. Interview with Craig Turner and Jamie Day, London, February 3, 2017.
4. Metropolitan Police Service, Operation Spire, transcripts relating to audio recordings of Citroën Saxo EN51EUD, 389.
5. "The Hatton Garden Trial: Who Is Basil?" *Daily Mirror*, January 14, 2016.
6. "Hatton Garden Gang Member Dubbed the Ghost," *Daily Mirror*, January 14, 2016.

7. "Escaped Hatton Garden Raider Is Ex-Cop," Sky News, February 8, 2016.

8. John Simpson and Georgie Keate, "Hatton Heist Suspect Is Son of Biology Pioneer," *London Times*, March 30, 2018.

Chapter 16
The Chatila Heist

1. "CCTV of Hatton Garden-Linked Burglary Destroyed," BBC, March 2, 2017.

Chapter 17
Life Behind Bars

1. Interview with Kevin Lane, London, June 29, 2016.

2. Mark Hughes, "A Tour of the Jail within a Jail That Houses Britain's Most Dangerous Convicts," *Independent*, July 30, 2010.

3. Interview with Hesham Puri, London, September 9, 2016.

4. Interview with Philip Evans, London, May 3, 2017.

5. Interview with Hesham Puri, London, September 9, 2016.

6. Duncan Campbell, "Family of Hatton Garden Heist Leader Complain about His Treatment," *Guardian*, July 4, 2016.

7. Interview with Hesham Puri, London, September 9, 2016.

8. Mike Sullivan, "Get Out of Jewel Free Card," *Sun*, July 16, 2018.

9. Crown Prosecution Service press release, "Hatton Garden Burglars Ordered to Pay £8.2m or Face Extra Prison Time," January 30, 2018.

10. Interview with Philip Evans, London, May 3, 2017.

11. Patrick Sawer, "Hatton Garden Vault: From Daring Heist to Fascinating Museum Piece," *Daily Telegraph*, April 23, 2016.

Illustration Credits

The Firm plotted the crime at the Castle pub in Islington (Andrew Testa).

Brian Reader, known as "The Master" (Metropolitan Police).

Mugshots (Metropolitan Police via AP).

The thieves entered 88–90 Hatton Garden from the fire escape (Andrew Testa).

Freddie Foreman, a former hitman for the Kray twins (Dan Bilefsky).

The men infiltrated the safe deposit (David Parry / Press Association via AP Images).

The thieves managed to drill a figure-eight-shaped hole (Metropolitan Police via Getty Images).

They brought in tools hidden in wheeled trash cans (Metropolitan Police).

Basil and Jones (Metropolitan Police).

Collins surveys the street before getting into the van (Metropolitan Police).

Jones takes a break (Metropolitan Police).

Basil walks toward the van with a black bag obscuring his face (Metropolitan Police).

Perkins and Collins met Reader at the Castle pub (Metropolitan Police).

Forensics officer enters Hatton Garden (Dominic Lipinksi / Press Association via AP Images).

Paul Johnson (Andrew Testa).

Johnson addresses a scrum of journalists (JUSTIN TALLIS / AFP / Getty Images).

Gravestone of Sidney James Hart (Andrew Testa).

Jones led Scotland Yard to the Victorian cemetery (Metropolitan Police).

Forensics officers dig up the stolen gems at Edmonton Cemetery (Metropolitan Police).

Jewels found at Edmonton Cemetery (Metropolitan Police).

The heist captured the imagination of London's feverish tabloid press (The Sun, News Licensing, 20.5.2015).

Court artist sketch of Michael Seed (Elizabeth Cook / Press Association via AP Images).

Index